THE SPIRIT OF SHAMANISM

"Easily readable, this book will be enlightening for anyone wanting more information on this ancient art."

ALA Booklist

"A well-considered guide to the history of shamanism. Walsh offers solid guidance to mental-health professionals and laypeople interested in these ancient shortcuts to altered consciousness."

Kirkus Reviews

"Unquestionably the most rounded, compact introduction to shamanism available today. This book will open important doors for numerous people."

Georg Feuerstein, M.Litt, editor, *Spectrum Review*

"I know of no other work that brings this important but bewildering phenomenon into as clear a focus."

Huston Smith, author of *The Religions of Man*

"Rarely does a book impact mainstream thinking and multiple academic disciplines at the same time . . . [this] is such a book!"

Angeles Arrien, Ph.D., anthropologist

"An interesting and comprehensive review of knowledge about shamanism from ancient times to the present."

Donald F. Sandner, M.D., author of *Navaho Symbols of Healing*

"I know of no other work that brings together the full range of anthropological, psychological, and psychiatric literature on this vital subject. *The Spirit of Shamanism* does so with openness and sensitivity, and is still scholarly and clear."

Christie W. Kiefer, Ph.D., Associate Professor of Anthropology, University of California at San Francisco

THE SPIRIT OF SHAMANISM

Also by Roger Walsh:

Staying Alive: The Psychology of Human Survival

With Deane Shapiro:

Beyond Health and Normality: Explorations of Exceptional Psychological Well-Being

Meditation: Classic and Contemporary Perspectives

With Frances Vaughan, as coeditor:

Beyond Ego: Transpersonal Dimensions in Psychology

Accept This Gift

A Gift of Peace

A Gift of Healing

THE SPIRIT OF SHAMANISM

ROGER N. WALSH, M.D., Ph.D.

JEREMY P. TARCHER, INC.
Los Angeles

The author would like to thank the following people and institutions for permission to reprint artworks or quotations:

National Museum of Denmark, Department of Ethnography:
Aua. Taken by Peter Freuchen, 1922.
Igjugarjuk. Taken by Knud Rasmussen, 1922.

Gyldendalske Boghandel, Nordisk Forlag:
Knud Rasmussen, 1929. *Intellectual Culture of the Iglulik Eskimos.* Report of the Fifth Thule Expedition, 1921–24, Vol. 7, No. 1.

Hunter House:
Grof, S., 1980. *LSD Psychotherapy.*

National Museum of Natural History, courtesy Department of Library Services:
Neg. #4131—A Buryat shaman wearing a tunic appliqued with ribs and sternum.

Harriette Frances, for her drawings of the death-rebirth experience.

Library of Congress Cataloging in Publication Data

Walsh, Roger N.
The spirit of shamanism / Roger Walsh.
p. cm.
Includes bibliographical references.
ISBN 0-87477-562-0
ISBN 0-87477-580-9 (pbk)
1. Shamanism—Psychology. I. Title.
BL2370.S5W35 1990
291'.01—dc20 89-48642
CIP

Jeremy P. Tarcher, Inc.
5858 Wilshire Blvd., Suite 200
Los Angeles, CA 90036

Distributed by St. Martin's Press, New York

Design by Tanya Maiboroda
Jacket illustration: Jan Salerno. Limited edition hand-pulled etchings available. Contact Jan Salerno 213/546-6138

Manufactured in the United States of America
10 9 8 7 6 5 4 3 2 1

First Edition

This book is dedicated to

Ken Wilber

scholar, practitioner, inspiration, friend

and to

the welfare, healing, and awakening

of all

Contents

CONTENTS

PART III
THE SHAMAN'S UNIVERSE

PART IV
SHAMANIC TECHNIQUES

PART V
SHAMANIC STATES OF MIND

CONTENTS

PART VI
ANCIENT TRADITION IN A MODERN WORLD

Acknowledgments

I would like to express my deep appreciation to the many people who offered assistance with the writing of *The Spirit of Shamanism*. These contributors include William Andrew, Allyn Brodsky, Etzel Cardena, Marlene Dobkin de Rios, Steve Donovan, Betty Sue Flowers, Gordon and Maria Globus, Tom Hurley, Stan Krippner, John Levy, Michael Murphy, Patrick Ophals, Don Sandner, Bruce Scotton, Deane Shapiro, Huston and Kendra Smith, John White, and Michael Winkelman. Members of a Psychiatry Residents Seminar at the University of California at Irvine who gave valuable feedback include Gary Bravo, Melissa Derfler, Charles Grob, Diane Harris, Barbara Kaston, Mitch Liester, Jim McQuade, Pat Poyourow, Susan Seitz, Ken Steinhoff, and Nathan Thuma. In addition I would like to extend special thanks to several people who were exceptionally generous with their time, feedback, and assistance. These include Angeles Arrien, Michael Harner, Arthur Hastings, Chris Kiefer, Charles Tart, and, as always, Frances Vaughan, whose support was invaluable. Bonnie L'Allier provided her usual excellent administrative and secretarial assistance.

PART I

What and Why Is Shamanism?

CHAPTER 1

Why Shamanism and Why Now?

The old gods are dead or dying and people everywhere are searching, asking; What is the new mythology to be?
JOSEPH CAMPBELL

How could interest in shamanism, the most ancient of humankind's religious, medical, and psychological disciplines, revive in an age of spaceships and superconductors? How could healing and spiritual practices that preceded the Bible, Buddha, and Lao Tsu by tens of thousands of years become popular in our Western scientific culture?

Yet shamanism is definitely "in." Numerous articles and workshops now offer introduction to these "archaic techniques of ecstasy," as they have been called. Yet only a few years ago there was serious concern that these ancient practices might be lost forever. Now housewives, businesspeople, and psychologists are learning them. What has happened, and why?

This surge in popular and professional interest reflects many factors, including recent changes in Western culture. These changes include a growing interest in non-Western cultures, particularly their healing and meditative practices. Some of these practices, such as yoga and meditation, have become so popular that literally millions of Westerners now use them.

The speed and effectiveness of some shamanic techniques have also contributed to this interest. Disciplines such as meditation or yoga may be powerful but may require weeks or months of practice to induce significant effects. This is not so for shamanism.

Though true mastery may require years, some people with no prior training may walk into a workshop and, within minutes of listening to shamanic drumming, attain meaningful insights.

The books of Carlos Casteneda have also had an enormous, though highly controversial, impact. They claim to report Castaneda's years of intensive training under a Yaqui Indian "man of knowledge." Casteneda's early books were based on his Ph.D. thesis and received considerable acclaim. His subsequent books, however, though extremely popular, have met with increasing suspicion and their authenticity is hotly debated. But whether or not they are genuine, they have proved to be valuable teaching stories for many people. Although the techniques and experiences they describe are only partly those of shamanism, they have certainly fueled interest in it.

More firsthand information about shamanism has become available recently. Although researchers have studied the tradition for decades, most of them observed and reported on it without any personal experience of its practices. This situation has begun to change. A number of Western researchers have undergone shamanic training and have reported that their own personal experiences have deepened and changed their understanding of the tradition.

To date almost all scientific studies of shamanism have been by anthropologists. This is hardly surprising, for it is the anthropologists who have braved everything from Arctic winters to tropical jungles to observe native shamans at work. However, the time has come to complement and enrich anthropological contributions with psychological ones.

Unfortunately, psychology's past contributions to the study of shamanism have been a mixed blessing. Many studies are now outdated. Others have been flawed by insufficient anthropological data, superficial interpretations, and lack of personal experience of shamanic practices. So while psychology has produced valuable insights it has also produced notable misunderstandings, some of which have distorted our view of shamanism for decades.

One source of these misunderstandings has been psychoanalysis. Long the dominant school of Western psychiatry, it fostered a distinctly negative view of shamanism. This occurred because Freud and the psychoanalysts who followed him took a dim view of religious experiences, regarding them as expressions of defense mechanisms at best or severe psychopathology at worst. Transcendent experiences—even the most profound and ecstatic—have often been regarded as pathological regressions of near-psychotic proportions. Mystical experiences have been diagnosed as "neurotic regressions to union with the breast," and enlightenment has been dismissed as a regression to intrauterine stages.[194] Yogis, saints, shamans, and sages have thus all been chopped down to neurotic size.

It is therefore not surprising that shamanism has often fared badly at the hands of Western psychiatrists, psychologists, and psychoanalytically minded anthropologists. Since shamans may exhibit periods of bizarre behavior, enter altered states of consciousness, have visions, and claim to commune with spirits, they have often been dismissed as psychologically disturbed. Schizophrenia, hysteria, and epilepsy have been the most common diagnoses in spite of considerable evidence to the contrary. The unfortunate result has often been a tragic insensitivity to the deeper, positive aspects of the shamanic tradition.

If psychological explanations have been distorted in the past, is there any reason to think that they might be better now? Yes, indeed. Western psychology has advanced significantly. The field is no longer so tightly wedded to psychoanalysis, and several schools have emerged that are more sympathetic to religious experience—humanistic, transpersonal, and Jungian psychologies, for example. New research fields have emerged and considerable work has been done on topics directly relevant to shamanism, such as psychosomatic healing, states of consciousness, dreaming, meditation, psychedelic drugs, mystical experiences, and placebo effects. This research throws new light on shamanic practices. Finally, a small but growing number of psychologists and psychiatrists have under-

taken shamanic training themselves. The net result is that Western psychology is now better positioned to understand and appreciate, rather than to pathologize and denigrate, religious practices in general and shamanism in particular.

The time is therefore ripe for new psychological explorations of shamanism, and this book aims to begin them. *The Spirit of Shamanism* is intended to do several things. The first is to provide a broad introduction and overview of shamanism, its practices, techniques, beliefs, and effects. The second is to examine these in the light of modern psychology to assess if, how, and why these practices work. What will become apparent is that though shamanic techniques may at first seem superstitious and nonsensical, some of them are based on sound psychological principles. Indeed, some predate by thousands of years similar Western therapeutic techniques.

The third goal is to evaluate the extremist claims that have been made about shamans. On one hand, many researchers have diagnosed and dismissed them as merely neurotic or psychotic, charlatans or con men. On the other hand, popular writers often portray them as superhuman saints or sages. This book attempts to steer a middle course between these wild extremes.

The Spirit of Shamanism also aims to examine shamanism from a larger cross-cultural and historical perspective. For the first time in human history we have access to most of the world's religious, healing, and consciousness-altering disciplines. Consciousness-altering disciplines are traditions or practices, such as yoga or meditation, that teach practitioners how to induce beneficial states of consciousness. Examples include states of deep concentration or calm that enhance physical, psychological, or spiritual well-being. As we will see, shamanism is one—indeed the first—of these traditions. Now that we have information about several such traditions from around the world, it is possible to compare shamanic practices, initiation, training, beliefs, and states of consciousness with those of other traditions.

Such comparisons allow us to recognize important similarities between shamanism and other traditions as well as equally important differences. For example, they make clear the similarities between the shaman's life and training and "the hero's journey"—the archetypal life pattern displayed by great heroes from many times and cultures. They also allow us to recognize crucial differences, such as differences in the type of information or the states of consciousness sought by shamanism and yoga.

These differences will be made clear by describing and mapping shamanic states of consciousness much more precisely than has previously been done. This will allow us to better appreciate the nature of shamanic states and to distinguish them from others with which they have often been confused, such as schizophrenia and yoga.

Comparisons such as these also make possible another goal of *The Spirit of Shamanism*: to examine ways in which consciousness-altering techniques have evolved across the centuries, and how this evolution has both reflected and fostered the evolution of human consciousness and religion. We can then see where shamanism fits within this vast evolutionary panorama.

The Spirit of Shamanism is a beginning, not an end. We have only recently begun the psychological exploration of these topics, and there is much yet to be learned. But we can begin by investigating and understanding the spirit of shamanism in a new and very different way.

CHAPTER 2

What Is a Shaman?

The spirit is the master, imagination the tool, and the body the plastic material.
PARACELSUS

What is a shaman? On this crucial point there has been remarkably little agreement. Indeed, "practically every scholar forms his own opinion of what constitutes shamanism."[87]

DEFINITIONS

The term itself comes from the word *saman* of the Tungus people of Siberia, meaning "one who is excited, moved, raised." It may be derived from an ancient Indian word meaning "to heat oneself or practice austerities"[18] or from a Tungus verb meaning "to know."[87] Whatever its derivation, the term *shaman* has been widely adopted by anthropologists to refer to specific groups of healers in diverse cultures who have sometimes been called medicine men, witch doctors, sorcerers, wizards, magicians, or seers. However, these terms are far too vague to adequately define the specific group of healers who fit the more stringent definition of shaman to be used in this book. The meaning and significance of this definition, and of shamanism itself, will become clearer if we examine the way in which our definitions and understanding of shamanism have evolved over time.

Early anthropologists were particularly struck by the shamans' unique interactions with "spirits." Many in the tribe might claim to revere spirits, to see or even be possessed by them. However, only the shamans claimed to have some degree of control over spirits and to be able to command, commune, and intercede with

them for the benefit of the tribe. Thus Shirokogoroff, one of the earliest explorers of the Siberian Tungus people, stated that:

> In all Tungus languages this term (saman) refers to persons of both sexes who have mastered spirits, who at their will can introduce these spirits into themselves and use their power over the spirits in their own interests, particularly helping other people, who suffer from the spirits.[165]

The use of the term *spirits* in this book is not meant to necessarily imply that there exist separate entities that control or communicate with people. Rather the term is simply used to describe the way in which shamans and mediums interpret their experience. The possible nature of these "spirits" will be examined in a later chapter.

Whereas early explorers were most impressed by the shamans' interactions with spirits, later researchers have been most impressed by shamans' control of their own states of consciousness in which these interactions occur. As Western culture has become more interested in altered states of consciousness (ASC), so too researchers have become interested in the widespread use of altered states in religious practices. It appears that the first tradition to use such states was shamanism, and contemporary definitions of shamanism have therefore focused on them.

As we will see, there are many possible states of consciousness, and therefore the question naturally arises as to which ones are peculiar to, and defining of, shamanism. There are broad and narrow definitions. In the broad definition the "only defining attribute is that the specialist enter into a controlled ASC on behalf of his community."[140] Such specialists would include, for example, mediums who enter a trance and then claim to speak for spirits. So a broad definition of shamanism would include any practitioners who enter controlled alternate states of consciousness, no matter which particular alternate states these may be.

Narrow definitions, on the other hand, specify the alternate state(s) precisely as ecstatic states. Indeed, for Mircea Eliade, one of the greatest religious scholars of the twentieth century, "A first definition of this complex phenomenon, and perhaps the least hazardous, will be: shamanism = technique of ecstasy."[41] Here ecstasy infers not so much bliss but more a sense, as the Random House dictionary defines it, "of being taken or moved out of one's self or one's normal state and entering a state of intensified or heightened feeling." This definition of ecstasy is particularly appropriate for shamanism.

The distinctive feature of the shamanic ecstasy is the experience of "soul flight" or "journeying" or "out-of-body experience." That is, in their ecstatic state shamans experience themselves, or their soul or spirit, flying through space and traveling either to other worlds or to distant parts of this world. In Eliade's words, "The shaman specializes in a trance during which his soul is believed to leave his body and ascend to the sky or descend to the underworld."[41]

These flights reflect the shamanic view of the cosmos. This comprises a three-tiered universe of upper, middle, and lower worlds, the middle one corresponding to our earth. The shaman ranges throughout this threefold world system in order to learn, obtain power, or to diagnose and treat those who come for help and healing. During these journeys shamans may experience themselves exploring other worlds and meeting the people, animals, or spirits who inhabit them, seeing the cause and cure of a patient's illness, or interceding with friendly or demonic forces.

So far, then, we have three key features of shamanism to include in any definition. The first is that shamans can voluntarily enter altered states of consciousness. The second is that in these states they experience themselves "journeying" to other realms. Third, they use these journeys as a means for acquiring knowledge or power and helping people in their community.

Two other features also need to be considered. One is the

shaman's interaction with spirits. In addition, Michael Harner, an anthropologist who may have more personal experience of shamanic practices than any other Westerner, suggests that a key element of shamanic practices may be "contact with an ordinarily hidden reality." Thus he defines a shaman as "a man or woman who enters an altered state of consciousness—at will—to contact and utilize an ordinarily hidden reality in order to acquire knowledge, power, and to help other persons."[73]

Should these two additional elements, contacting a hidden reality and interaction with spirits, be included as essential elements of a definition of shamanism? Here we are on tricky philosophical ground. Certainly these elements describe what shamans experience and believe they are doing. However, it is an enormous philosophical leap to assume that this is what they are actually doing. The fundamental nature (or, in philosophical terms, the ontological status) of both the realms that shamans experience themselves traversing and the entities they meet is an open question. To the shaman they are usually interpreted as independently and fully "real"; to a Westerner with no belief in other realms or entities, they would be interpreted as subjective mind creations. These philosophical questions will be examined in a later chapter. Suffice it to say for now that the interpretation of the nature of these phenomena depends on one's own philosophical leanings or world view. We will be on safer ground in defining shamanism if we skirt these questions of philosophical interpretation as much as possible.

Putting all this together, what do we get? Shamanism can be defined as a family of traditions whose practitioners focus on voluntarily entering altered states of consciousness in which they experience themselves or their spirit(s), traveling to other realms at will, and interacting with other entities in order to serve their community.

This definition seems to cover the major features of shamanism. The reference to "a family of traditions" acknowledges that

there are variations among shamanic practitioners. At the same time the definition is precise enough to clearly distinguish shamanism from other traditions and practices as well as from various psychopathologies with which it has been confused. For example, priests may lead rituals and medicine men may heal, but they rarely enter altered states; mediums may enter altered states but do not usually journey; Tibetan Buddhists may sometimes journey, but this is not a major focus of their practice; those suffering mental illness may enter altered states and meet "spirits," but as involuntary victims rather than as voluntary creators of these states.

Of course, this definition will not satisfy everyone or include every conceivable shaman. Judging from the enormous number and range of definitions, no single one can. Nevertheless this definition is useful for our purposes since it is reasonably narrow and precise. This will allow us to focus our investigation on a clearly distinguished group of practices and practitioners that almost all researchers would agree are indeed shamanic.

It is interesting to note that this definition focuses on practices and experiences rather than on beliefs and dogma. This is consistent with Michael Harner's claim that "shamanism ultimately is only a method, not a religion with a fixed set of dogmas."[76]

Of course, it is hard to deny that shamans hold a body of relatively fixed beliefs; probably no tradition can survive without some consistent shared belief system. For example, shamans tend to believe that the entities they meet on their travels are indeed spirits, that the universe consists of three major worlds, and that they can roam these worlds at will. On the other hand, it is also true that there is greater emphasis on personal experience in shamanism than in many other religious traditions.

There is debate over whether shamanism can properly be called a religion. Rather than becoming embroiled in this argument—and of necessity also the debate over what exactly defines a religion—here I will sidestep the issue. I will refer to shamanism not as a religion but as a religious tradition, implying that it has

definite religious elements but may not always meet sociologists' technical definition of religion.

Origins

Shamanism is one of humankind's most ancient traditions. Archaeologists have found indications of it spanning tens of thousands of years, and there is no way of assessing just how remote its origins may be. Indeed, Eliade claims that "nothing justifies the supposition that during the hundreds of thousands of years that preceded the earliest Stone Age, humanity did not have a religious life as intense and as various as in the succeeding periods."[41]

But no matter when or where it first arose, shamanism subsequently spread around the world. It is found today in areas as widespread as Siberia, North and South America, and Australia and is believed to have existed in most parts of the world at one time or another. The remarkable similarities among shamans from widely dispersed areas of the world raise the question of how these similarities developed. One possibility is that they emerged spontaneously in different locations, perhaps because of a common innate human tendency or recurrent social need. Another possibility is that similarities resulted from migration and diffusion from common ancestors.

If migration is the answer, that migration must have begun long, long ago. Shamanism occurs among tribes with so many different languages that diffusion from a common ancestor must have begun at least 20,000 years ago.[207] It is difficult to explain why shamanic practices would remain so stable for so long in so many cultures while language and social practices changed so drastically. This makes it seem unlikely that migration alone can account for the long history and far-flung distribution of shamanism.

It follows that if the worldwide, history-long distribution of shamanism cannot be attributed solely to diffusion from a single

invention in prehistoric times, then it must have been discovered and rediscovered in diverse times and cultures. This suggests that some recurring combination of social forces and innate abilities must have repeatedly elicited and maintained shamanic roles, rituals, and states of consciousness.

There does seem to be evidence of an innate human tendency to access certain specific altered states. For example, for 2500 years Buddhists have described accessing eight highly specific and distinct states of extreme concentration. These concentrated states, the so-called *jhanas,* are extremely subtle, stable, and blissful and have been precisely described for millennia.[27, 62] Today a few Western meditators are beginning to access these states. I have been fortunate to interview three of these people. In each case their experiences tallied remarkably well with ancient accounts. Clearly, then, there seems to be some innate tendency in the human mind to settle into certain specific states of consciousness if given the right conditions or practices.

The same principle may hold for shamanic states. Observations of Westerners in shamanic workshops suggest that most people are able to enter shamanic states to some degree.[75] These states can be induced by a wide variety of conditions, suggesting that there may be some inherent tendency for the mind to adopt them. The conditions that induce these states will be discussed in detail later; they include such common experiences as isolation, fatigue, hunger, and rhythmic sound, and thus they are likely to be rediscovered by different generations and cultures. Since these states may be pleasurable, meaningful, and healing, they are likely to be actively sought and the methods for inducing them remembered and transmitted across generations.

Thus shamanism and its widespread distribution may reflect an innate human tendency to enter certain pleasurable and valuable states of consciousness. Once discovered, rituals and beliefs that support the induction and expression of these states would also arise and shamanism would emerge once again.[207]

This natural tendency might be supported and amplified by communication between cultures. For example, shamanism in Northern Asia may have been modified by the importation of yogic practices from India.[41] Thus the global distribution of shamanism may be due to both innate tendency and diffusion of information. The end result is that this ancient tradition has spread across the earth and may have survived for tens of thousands of years, a significant portion of the time that fully developed human beings (modern Homo sapiens) have been on the planet.

Distribution of Shamanism in Different Societies

Given that shamanism has endured so long and spread so widely, the question naturally arises as to why it occurs in some cultures and not in others. Answers are beginning to emerge from cross-cultural research.

One notable study examined 47 societies spanning almost 4000 years from 1750 B.C. (the Babylonians) to the present century.[208] It is striking to note that, prior to Western influence, all of these 47 cultures used altered states of consciousness for religious and healing practices. However, although shamanic practices were found in most regions of the world, they occur only in particular types of societies, primarily simple nomadic hunting and gathering societies. These peoples rely very little on agriculture and have almost no social classes or political organization. Within these tribes the shaman plays many roles, both sacred and mundane: medicine man, healer, ritualist, keeper of the cultural myths, medium, and master of spirits. With their many roles and the power vacuum offered by a classless society, shamans exert a major influence on their tribe and people.

As societies evolve and become more complex, it appears that this situation changes dramatically. As societies become fixed rather than nomadic, agricultural rather than foraging, and so-

cially and politically stratified rather than classless, shamanism as such seems to disappear. In its place appear a variety of specialists, each of whom focuses on one of the shaman's many roles. Thus, instead of shamans we find healers, priests, mediums, and sorcerers/witches. These specialize respectively in medical, ritual, spirit possession, and malevolent magic practices. A contemporary Western parallel is the disappearance of the old medical general practitioner, or G.P., and the appearance of diverse specialists.

It is interesting to compare some of these ancient specialists with the shamanic "G.P." who preceded them. Priests emerge as representatives of organized religion and are often religious, moral, and even political leaders. They are the leaders of social rites and rituals; they pray to and propitiate the spiritual forces on behalf of their society. Unlike their shamanic ancestors, however, they usually have little training or experience in altered states.[83]

Whereas the priests inherit the socially beneficial religious and magical roles of the shaman, the malevolent roles are usually inherited by people known as sorcerers and witches. As we will see, shamans are often ambivalent figures for their people, revered for their healing and helping powers and at the same time feared for their malevolent magic. Sorcerers and witches are the specialists in malevolent (black) magic and as such may be feared, hated, and persecuted. Of course, most contemporary witches would disagree strongly with this traditional definition, since they claim to use only beneficial (white) magic.

Mediums are the specialists in spirit possession. While they do not journey, they do enter altered states in which they experience themselves as receiving messages from the spirit world. It will be remembered that some researchers advocate a broad definition of shamanism that includes anyone using altered states to serve the community. Such a definition fails to distinguish between shamans and mediums, both of whom use altered states, though of different types. Cross-cultural studies suggest that mediums and shamans tend to be found in different types of societies, and this provides

further evidence for distinguishing them.[21, 208] This is not to deny that some shamans are capable of spirit possession; it is to say that they are also capable of more than this.

It seems, therefore, that as cultures evolve so do their religious practitioners. Although shamans as such largely disappear from complex societies, most of their roles and skills are retained by various specialists. There is one exception, however—journeying, the practice that is one of the defining characteristics of shamanism. None of the shaman's successors journey.

Why this practice should largely disappear is a mystery. Michael Harner attributes it to suppression of shamanic practices by organized religion. Indeed, during the last century it was even a criminal offense in parts of Europe to own a drum. Another factor may have been the discovery of other consciousness-altering techniques, such as those associated with yogic and meditative practices. However, it is unclear whether these factors alone could account for the virtual disappearance from complex societies of a practice that was powerful enough to spread around the world, survive for thousands of years, and form the basis for humankind's most ancient and durable religious tradition: shamanism.

PART II

The Life of the Shaman

CHAPTER 3

The Hero's Journey

The decisive question for man is: Is he related to the infinite or not? That is the telling question of his life. Only if we know that the thing which truly matters is the infinite can we avoid fixing our interests upon futilities and upon all kinds of goals which are not of real importance.

CARL JUNG

To the people of their tribe, shamans are figures of awesome power whose help can mean the difference between health and sickness, life and death. They therefore stand at the head of a long lineage of individuals who have excelled, fought, triumphed, or loved so well that ordinary mortals have regarded them with awe or jealousy or both. These are humankind's heroes, the people who have triumphed over human limitations. These are the warriors, rulers, healers, saints, and sages who have inspired and protected, served and enlightened, and whose lives stand as monuments to the untapped potentials within each of us. Their lives have been immortalized in myth, legend, and biography. Ordinary mortals have wondered and puzzled about them, venerated and even worshipped them, and often believed that they must be more than merely human, even when the heroes themselves made no such claims.

"Are you a God?" they asked the Buddha. "No," he replied.
"Are you an angel, then?" "No."
"A saint?" "No."
"Then what are you?"
Replied the Buddha, "I am awake."[173]

Now for the first time in history, we have access to accounts of the heroes of different cultures and times. It is possible to compare and integrate these accounts and to discern the common contours of the lives of these extraordinary people. Joseph Campbell, one of the great mythologists of the twentieth century, did just this in his book *The Hero with a Thousand Faces.*[29] Campbell was able to identify and map out certain common themes and life stages in "the hero's journey." While there are variations according to the culture, historical period, and type of hero, the common contours and crises are clear enough to enable us to recognize the universal themes underlying the individual variations.

What I want to suggest is that shamans may be heroes of their cultures, and that their lives can mirror the general pattern Campbell has identified. As we will see in later chapters, the stages of the shaman's quest—the challenges, crises, training, and eventual triumph—can parallel those of countless heroes of other times and places. Therefore, before we examine the details of the shaman's life, let us look at the common characteristics of the lives of humankind's great heroes from different centuries and cultures. Then, in the following chapters, we will place the shaman within this species-wide, history-long, hero-tall framework. Doing this allows us to examine shamans from a panoramic perspective and to compare and contrast them with the heroes of other times. Thereby we can recognize the goals, challenges, training, and traps common to shamans and other heroes as well as the unique features of the shaman's path.

TYPES OF HEROES

At this stage it is necessary to supplement Joseph Campbell's scheme. Campbell's map, brilliant as it is, does not distinguish well between different types of heroes. What Campbell did was to collect diverse accounts (myths, fairy tales, biographies) of all types of heroes (rulers, warriors, healers, saints, and gods). From these

diverse sources he distilled the common stages of life and adventure that heroes pass through. Campbell's genius lay in recognizing the unity behind diversity, the common thread that runs through these many lives, and in being able to unify them into a single grand story.

But this grand unification comes at the price of obscuring the differences between different types of heroes. For while it is true that there are similarities between the life journey of a saint on one hand and a ruler or warrior on the other, there are also major differences. Campbell tends to elevate them all to the same transcendent status.[160, 202]

What Campbell has given us, therefore, is a brilliant *horizontal* map that traces the development or life stages of the composite hero. To this we can now add a *vertical* map of the different levels on which life's aims, games, and journeys can be played. The vertical map enables us to distinguish among different types of heroes, to distinguish saints from warriors, sages from power seekers. What we have then is a scheme that allows us to recognize the universal, the stages common to all heroes—while at the same time acknowledging the particular, the different types and levels of life goals, games, and heroes. Different types of heroes reflect different types of games. We therefore need to examine the types of games that people in general, and heroes in particular, play in order to decide just what type of hero the shaman is.

The word *game* is a little tricky since it is often used to imply something trivial or frivolous. However, it can also be used to refer to something much more significant, namely the choice to confront meaningful challenges that test and hone our abilities as we strive for cherished goals. It is in this sense that the word is used here.

Without meaningful games we languish in boredom and meaninglessness. "What people really need and demand from life is not wealth, comfort or esteem, but *games worth playing*." Thus we are advised to "seek, above all, for a game worth playing. . . . Having found the game, play it with intensity—play as if your life and sanity depended on it. (They do depend on it.)"[34]

But there are games and there are games. Some are ultimately destructive to both the individual and society no matter how satisfying they may seem initially. Others are constructive and valuable to both the player and society. In his book *The Master Game,* Robert De Ropp makes incisive analyses of various games. He points out that

> life games reflect life aims and the games men choose to play indicate not only their type, but also their level of inner development. . . . We can divide life games into "object" games and "meta" games. Object games can be thought of as games for the attainment of material things, primarily money and the objects which money can buy. Meta-games are played for intangibles such as knowledge or the "salvation of the soul."[34]

In other words, object games aim for the concrete things of the world, especially for "the physical foursome" of money, power, sex, and status. Meta-games, on the other hand, are more subtle. They aim for intangibles such as truth, beauty, and knowledge.

At the summit of these meta-games De Ropp places the Master Game: the quest for enlightenment, liberation, salvation, or awakening. This is the game played by the great saints and sages across cultures and centuries. It is the game of exploring and mastering, not the things of the outer world, but the things of the inner world, one's own mind and consciousness. Ultimately its goal is to recognize and dissolve into one's most profound and true nature and to know, from one's own direct experience, that this nature is divine. Different traditions express this in different ways but the message is clearly the same. Christianity tells us that "the Kingdom of Heaven is within you" or, in the words of Saint Clement, "He who knows himself knows God"; Buddhism says "Look within. Thou art the Buddha"; in Siddha Yoga the message is, "God dwells within you as you"; and in Islam, "He who knows himself knows his Lord." De Ropp writes:

> The basic idea underlying all the great religions is that man is asleep, that he lives amid dreams and delusions, that he cuts himself off from the universal consciousness . . . to crawl into the narrow shell of a personal ego. To emerge from this narrow shell, to regain union with the universal consciousness, to pass from the darkness of the ego-centered illusion into the light of the non-ego, this was the real aim of the Religion Game as defined by the great teachers, Jesus, Gautama, Krishna, Mahavira, Lao-tze and the Platonic Socrates.[34]

This emergence, reunion, and enlightenment is the aim of the Master Game. Although it has been taught for centuries by sages of all traditions, it remains much misunderstood, and as De Ropp points out:

> It still remains the most demanding and difficult of games and, in our society, there are few who play. Contemporary man, hypnotized by the glitter of his own gadgets, has little contact with his inner world, concerns himself with outer, not inner space. But the Master Game is played entirely in the inner world, a vast and complex territory about which men know very little. The aim of the game is true awakening, full development of the powers latent in man. The game can be played only by people whose observations of themselves and others have led them to a certain conclusion, namely, *that man's ordinary state of consciousness, his so-called waking state, is not the highest level of consciousness of which he is capable.* In fact this state is so far from real awakening that it could appropriately be called a form of somnambulism, a condition of waking sleep.[34]

This then is the Master Game, perhaps the most profound and misunderstood of all games. How does this relate to shamanism? What I want to suggest is that shamans, at their best, may have been the earliest forerunners of the Master Game player. Alternately, we could say that shamans played the Master Game to the extent and depth they could, given their cultures and times.

They were the first to systematically explore and cultivate their inner world and to use their insights, images, and dreams for the benefit of their people.

To say that some shamans were the original Master Game players, or at least their forerunners, is not to make them out as unblemished saints. In fact, from what we know of their activities, they probably mixed genuine insights and abilities with liberal trickery and deceit. Nor is it to claim, as some people do, that the techniques, experiences, and states of consciousness of early shamans were identical to those of the saints and sages who followed them thousands of years later. No, the Master Game seems to have evolved over millennia, both reflecting and molding the evolution of human consciousness. Early shamans may have been humankind's first Master Game players and explorers of consciousness, but their explorations were limited by their times since the techniques and understandings for such exploration have evolved over centuries.

Later we will compare shamans with later players and try to identify the ways in which the Master Game has evolved. For now it is enough to suggest that some of the early shamans may have been, as Ken Wilber puts it, "the true Heroes of the . . . times, and their individual and daring explorations in transcendence could only have had a truly evolutionary impact on consciousness at large."[201]

Having considered the type of game played by shamans at their best, let us turn to the general contours of the lives of this game's great players. Let us examine the hero's journey, particularly the journey of those heroes who play the Master Game.

Stages of the Journey

Campbell's book *The Hero with a Thousand Faces* traces the development of the composite hero—the warrior, ruler, and lover as much as the Master Game–playing shaman, saint, and sage. Since

we are concerned here only with the latter group, this account draws deeply and gratefully on Campbell but also differs from it in several ways. What follows is not a definitive description; rather it is an initial outline of one of the more common forms of the Master Game player's life and journey.

We can divide the journey into five major stages: the hero's early life as a more or less conventional citizen, the call to adventure and awakening, the period of discipline and training, the completion of the quest, and the final phase of return and contribution to society.

Conventional Slumber

In the first stage the hero is born into and slumbers within the conventions of society much as do the rest of us. Society's beliefs are accepted as real, its morals regarded as appropriate, its limits seen as natural. This is the stage of conventionality, where most of us remain unquestioningly throughout our lives. This conventionality is traditionally said to be associated with an impaired, clouded state of mind. In Asia this impairment has been called *maya*, or illusion; in the West it has been described as a shared hypnosis, consensus trance, or collective psychosis.[180, 192] This impairment or clouding of mind tends to go unnoticed because we all share in it.

The hero's task is to recognize and go beyond these conventional limitations. This task involves more than simply reacting against social norms in blind countercultural defiance. Rather it involves recognizing these limits and distortions, their illusory and arbitrary nature, and hence escaping from them and from one's limited tribal world view. This is the process of "detribalization" by which a person matures from a tribal to a more universal perspective.[12] Such a person no longer looks at life through limiting and distorting cultural biases but rather begins to examine these biases and correct them. In fact, this correction of cultural biases is

the final task of the hero. Before this final task can succeed, however, many other tasks must be accomplished. The first of these is to emerge from conventional slumber by responding to the call to adventure and awakening.

The Call to Adventure and Awakening

At some stage the hero's conventional slumber is challenged by a crisis of life-shattering proportions, an existential confrontation that calls all previously held beliefs into question. It may be personal sickness, as with the shaman; it may be a confrontation with sickness in others, as with the Buddha. It may be a sudden confrontation with death.

The call to adventure and awakening may also come as a pull from within. It may take the form of a powerful dream or vision, as with some shamans, or of a deep heartfelt response to a new teacher or teaching. It may emerge more subtly as "divine discontent," a growing dissatisfaction with the pleasures of the world or a gnawing question about the meaning of life. In our culture this may take the form of an existential or mid-life crisis, although the deeper causes and questions of the crisis are rarely fully recognized. But however this challenge arises, it reveals the limits of conventional thinking and living and urges the hero beyond them.

The recipient of the call now faces a terrible dilemma. He or she must choose whether to answer the call and move into the new and unknown realms of life that it demands, or to deny the call and retreat into the familiar. Those who deny the call have little choice but to attempt to repress the message and its far-reaching implications. Only by such repression can the nonhero return to the seductive but anesthetic comforts of conventional unawareness and entrancement; to sink into what has been called "tranquilization by the trivial." Such a refusal is no small matter. It is the basis for what existentialists call inauthentic living and alienation. The shaman who refuses the call is said to be at risk for sickness,

insanity, even death. Abraham Maslow put the dilemma succinctly: "If you deliberately plan to be less than you are capable of being, then I warn you that you will be deeply unhappy for the rest of your life."[118]

If the call is unanswered, it may lead next to a process of renunciation. For if the purpose of life has changed, then much that previously seemed valuable may no longer appear so and it may be appropriate to let it go. If one is leaving family and home in order to find a teacher, then positions and possessions may now seem more impediments than valuables. (Indeed the Latin term for baggage was *impedimenta*, from which we derive our word *impediment*.) Many of the great spiritual heroes—Jesus, Buddha, Mahavira, Shankara—have been penniless wanderers who relinquished home, possessions, status, and even family in their single-minded quest for awakening. Others, including shamans, may relinquish their positions and possessions temporarily, reclaiming them at the completion of their quest.

Discipline and Training

Next begins the phase of discipline and training. For this a teacher is usually essential, and so the phase of renunciation may be followed by the search for a teacher. Sometimes the teacher is an internal one—an inner guide, guru, or spirit. This is particularly common among shamans. More often an outer teacher is essential and then, as De Ropp points out,

> the would-be player of the Master Game encounters at the outset one of the most difficult tests in his career. He must find a teacher who is neither a fool nor fraud and convince that teacher that he, the would-be pupil, is worth teaching. His future development depends largely on the skill with which he performs this task.[34]

Once the teacher has been found, the phase of discipline and training begins. This may take many forms and may involve physi-

cal, psychological, contemplative, and social disciplines, some of them of extraordinary severity.

Physical disciplines may involve such things as dietary modification or fasting, sleep deprivation, physical exertion, and exposure to extremes of heat or cold. Contemplative practices may involve meditation, yoga, ritual, or prayer, often combined with periods of quiet and solitude. Social disciplines may include compassionate service to all who cross one's path or the performance of menial tasks in order to instill humility.

Whatever the method, the aim is always the same: to train and cultivate the mind so as to reduce compulsions such as greed, hatred, and fear; to strengthen capacities such as will, concentration, and wisdom; and to cultivate emotions such as love, compassion, and joy.

The intensity with which some students have practiced these disciplines is mind-boggling. Prolonged starvation, exposure to arctic conditions, and days without sleep have been common fare for the more ascetic Master Game players. Indeed, extreme but unsuccessful players have sometimes starved or frozen themselves to death.

The Culmination of the Quest

For successful players, years of discipline culminate in breakthroughs of life-changing proportions. These may be visions, insights, and understandings or experiences of death and rebirth. They may be enlightenment, satori, and liberation or they may be a sense of union with God, the All, or the Tao.

Any name given to these experiences is clearly inadequate. Inasmuch as they can be described at all, they are usually said to be ineffable, sublime, beyond the world, beyond words, beyond description, and even beyond thought. For Master Game players such experiences are both the goal and highest good of existence.

This is not to say that all realizations are the same. Rather, while there is some so-called "transcendental unity of religions," there are also significant differences between religions in the type and depth of realization.[200] We will explore some of these differences in a later chapter.

Return and Contribution

With the great quest now complete, the seeker has become a knower, the pupil a teacher, the student a sage. But there is one more phase before the journey is complete: the return and contribution to society. With one's own questions answered, the world's confusion begs to be cleared; with one's own suffering relieved, the pain and sorrow of the world cry for healing; and with one's own egocentric motives reduced, the desire to contribute becomes central and compelling. The direction of the journey now reverses. Whereas the hero had formerly turned away from society and into his or her self, now the hero turns back to society and out into the world.

There are numerous metaphors for this return. In Plato's parable, after escaping from the cave the hero reenters it to help others make their escape. In Zen the enlightened one "enters the marketplace with help-bestowing hands." In shamanism the novices first tame their spirits and then use them for the benefit of the tribe. For Christian mystics this return is the final stage of "the spiritual marriage" with God—the stage of "fruitfulness of the soul." After the mystic has united with God in divine love, this spiritual marriage bears fruit for all humankind as the mystic reenters the world to heal and help. In her classic book on Christian mysticism, Evelyn Underhill describes how the accomplished mystic now

> accepts the pains and duties in the place of the raptures of love; and becomes a source, a "parent" of fresh spiritual life. . . . This forms

> that rare and final stage in the evolution of the great mystics, in which they return to the world which they forsook; and there live, as it were, as centers of transcendental energy. . . . Hence something equivalent to the solitude of the wilderness is an essential part of mystical education. But, having established that communion, re-ordered their inner lives upon transcendent levels—being united with their Source not merely in temporary ecstasies, but in virtue of a permanent condition of the soul, they were impelled to abandon their solitude; and resumed, in some way, their contact with the world in order to become the medium whereby that Life flowed out to other men. To go up alone into the mountain and come back as an ambassador to the world, has ever been the method of humanity's best friends.[186]

This return to the cave or fruitfulness of the soul is the final stage of a life cycle that historian Arnold Toynbee called "withdrawal and return."[184] Toynbee found that this cycle was common to those people who have had the most beneficial impact on human history. Such people live in both worlds, inner and outer, transcendental and mundane. They have access to the transcendent depths within but work to translate and express them in the world outside.

This, then, is a brief outline of one form of the hero's journey. It is a journey that has been played out with countless variations over countless years and countless cultures. Its greatest players, the great saints and sages, have been said to represent the highest development and fullest flowering of human potential and to have had the greatest impact on human history. So at least have said the historian Toynbee, the philosophers Bergson, Schopenhauer, and Nietzsche, as well as the psychologists James, Maslow, and Wilber.

Of course, the spiritual hero's journey can also be played out less fully and dramatically. Many set out on the path but few attain the greatest heights. Nor is the journey always a single great circle of withdrawal and return. Rather it may consist of a series of circles like a spiral in which one returns again and again but each

time to a higher vantage point with greater perspective. The hero's journey is therefore not limited solely to great saints and sages; rather, it is available to all of us to greater or lesser degrees depending on the sincerity with which we undertake it.

Let us turn now to the earliest heroes, the shamans, and see to what extent their lives correspond to this universal template.

C H A P T E R 4

The Initial Call and Initiation Crisis

If you bring forth what is within you
What you bring forth will save you.
If you do not bring forth what is within you,
What you do not bring forth will destroy you.
THE GOSPEL OF THOMAS

The hero's journey begins with the call to adventure, a call that may take many forms. In shamanism this call occurs most often in adolescence or early adulthood. The shaman-to-be is usually recognized by unusual experiences or behavior that are interpreted as signs from the spirits of the person's calling. Sometimes individuals select themselves for the profession. Occasionally a shaman's child is chosen at birth to carry on the family tradition.

When selection occurs at birth it may place an enormous responsibility on the future shaman, the family, and, indeed, on the whole community. The appropriate rituals and taboos must be followed in minute detail and can be painfully restrictive.

Knud Rasmussen, whose description of both American and Iglulik Eskimo shamans remains a classic, noted that: "So seriously are all preparations considered, that some parents, even before the birth of the shaman-to-be, set all things in order for him beforehand by laying upon themselves a specially strict and onerous taboo. Such a child was Aua, and here is his own story. . . .

"'Mother was put on very strict diet, and had to observe difficult rules of taboo. If she had eaten part of a walrus, for instance, then that walrus was taboo to all others; the same with seal and caribou. She had to have special pots, from which no one

else was allowed to eat. No woman was allowed to visit her, but men might do so. My clothes were made after a particular fashion; the hair of the skins must never lie pointing upwards or down, but fall athwart the body. Thus I lived in the birth-hut, unconscious of all the care that was being taken with me.

"'For a whole year my mother and I had to live entirely alone, only visited now and again by my father. He was a great hunter, and always out after game, but in spite of this he was never allowed to sharpen his own knives; as soon as he did so, his hand began to swell and I fell ill. A year after my birth, we were allowed to have another person in the house with us; it was a woman, and she had to be very careful herself; whenever she went out she must throw her hood over her head, wear boots without stockings, and hold the tail of her fur coat lifted high in one hand. . . .

"'At last I was big enough to go out with the grown up men to the blowholes after seal. The day I harpooned my first seal, my father had to lie down on the ice with the upper part of his body naked, and the seal I had caught was dragged across his back while it was still alive. Only men were allowed to eat of my first catch, and nothing must be left. The skin and the head were set out on the ice, in order that I might be able later on to catch the same seal again. For three days and nights, none of the men who had eaten of it might go out hunting or do any kind of work. . . . Even after I had been married a long time, my catch was still subject to strict taboo.'"[147]

Such a life, hemmed in by countless taboos and circumscribed by self-chosen restrictions, is hard to imagine. Yet for tribal peoples these taboos are as essential to life as eating. To flout them means offending the spirits and thereby risking death and disaster. Thus the taboos may be kept for generation after generation even though, as Rasmussen found, "Everyone knew precisely what had to be done in any given situation, but whenever I put in my query: Why?, they could give no answer."[147]

From a Western scientific perspective these are examples, plain and simple, of superstitious behavior based on false beliefs. Since shamanic traditions seem to comprise a mixture of both effective techniques and superstitious rituals, it is worth examining how superstitions are learned and maintained.

The major explanations center around faulty learning and stem from experiments originally conducted by behavioral psychologist B. F. Skinner. Skinner placed a pigeon in a box and gave it grains of food every 15 seconds, no matter what it was doing. The bird didn't have to lift a feather to get these free meals, but nevertheless it soon started turning in circles. Other birds engaged in even more bizarre rituals—bobbing the head up and down, stretching the neck toward a corner, making brushing movements over the floor—apparently believing that their behavior caused the arrival of the food.

It seemed that whatever behavior the bird was engaged in when it was initially fed was reinforced since the animal, understandably but falsely, assumed that its behavior had caused the arrival of the food. Naturally enough, it therefore repeated the behavior—and sure enough, the food arrived again. Though there was actually no causal relationship between behavior and food—the food invariably arrived every 15 seconds—the bird soon assumed there was. The coincidental reward first led the animal to believe there was a relationship, and then maintained both the behavior and the belief.[9]

Similar mechanisms may underlie much superstitious behavior in humans. Coincidental rewards or punishments can lead individuals and tribes to assume causal relationships where none exist. They then engage in unnecessary, ineffective behavior. In time this behavior can harden into socially enforced rituals and taboos, and those who violate them may be ostracized, punished, or even executed.

In humans, coincidental learning may be enhanced by additional factors. The human desires for understanding and control

tend to make people uncomfortable with ambiguous situations. They therefore tend to postulate causal relationships even where none exist. This may reduce feelings of helplessness; when one has a belief about how something is caused, one also has at least some sense of how to influence it.

In addition, superstitions are easily learned from other people, a process called social contagion. Thus Aua, the Eskimo shaman whose parents' taboos were described above, told Rasmussen that "our fathers have inherited from their fathers all the old rules of life which are based on the experience and wisdom of generations. We do not know how, we cannot say why, but we keep those rules in order that we may live untroubled."[147]

The net effect of all these factors—coincidental reward and punishment, desire for understanding and control, learning from one another—may largely account for the extent and severity of tribal superstitions, rituals, and taboos and the willingness to endure the severe life restrictions demanded by them. In the face of a dangerous, mysterious, and unpredictable world, the pressure to adopt any behavior and institute any ritual that promises some degree of control must be strong indeed. Thus it is not surprising that large numbers of rituals and taboos are found among tribal peoples and particularly among the shamans who are the mediators with the spiritual world. Indeed, one of the major tasks in a psychological examination of shamanism is to attempt to distinguish between effective psychological techniques on one hand and ineffective superstitions on the other.

One further point about the nature of superstitions is important: superstitions do not necessarily imply a lack of logic or rationality. Superstitions may be inaccurate beliefs about causal relationships and may result in unnecessary, ineffective behavior. However, these beliefs may be quite logical from the perspective of a particular culture and world view. Some tribal and shamanic behavior may seem superstitious from our Western scientific perspective, but this does not necessarily mean, as is sometimes im-

plied, that theirs is a primitive or irrational logic. If one believes in malevolent spirits, then rituals designed to appease them make perfect sense. It may also seem perfectly logical to assume that an adolescent who is bothered by the spirits may have special connections with them and may therefore make an effective shaman.

The Initial Call

Aua, whose life and taboos we examined above, was selected on the basis of heredity. Others, men or women but more often men, may be chosen because of some striking feature or experience—an unusual physical appearance, an illness such as epilepsy, unexpected recovery from severe illness, or a variety of other omens. Alternately, they may experience curious symptoms, feelings, and behaviors. These may be so dramatic that they have been called the shamanic initiation crisis.

The call may also come during a vision quest or dream. A vision quest is a period spent in solitude and fasting devoted to receiving a guiding vision for one's life. Dreams about spirits may constitute a shamanic call in the Inuit Eskimo tribes, while in California tribes it may be dreams about deceased relatives. The significance of these dreams may require confirmation by mature shamans—who were probably the world's first professional dream interpreters.[105]

This election by dreams occurs in a number of religious traditions. Recall, for example, the Old Testament: "Hear my words: If there is a prophet among you, I the Lord make myself known to him in a vision, I speak with him in a dream."[16]

The call to shamanism may be received with considerable ambivalence, and those who receive it may be regarded as "doomed to inspiration."[19] Many of the elect attempt to decline the invitation at first. This is what Joseph Campbell termed "refusal of the call." However, the spirits, symptoms, or dreams may be distressingly

persistent and eventually win out. Indeed, many shamanic traditions, like many hero traditions, hold that refusal of the call can result in sickness, insanity, or death. One of the earliest shamanic researchers, Bogoras, claimed that "the rejection of the 'spirits' is much more dangerous even than the acceptance of their call. A young man thwarted in his call to inspiration will either sicken and shortly die, or else the 'spirits' will induce him to renounce his home and go far away, where he may follow his vocation without hindrance."[19] Of course, there are some who do reject the call or accept it reluctantly and then practice their art very little.

In a few tribes individuals may also select themselves. However, such people are often regarded as less potent masters than those whose selection is ordained by outside forces. One notable exception is the Jivaro Indian tribe of South America. Here would-be shamans select themselves and established practitioners sell them their knowledge (a practice enthusiastically followed by today's Western shamans in their weekend workshops).

The Jivaro payment is neither cheap nor benign. It usually consists of such spiritual necessities as one or two shotguns together with gunpowder, a blowgun, and a machete. Since up to a quarter of Jivaro men may be shamans, this obviously leads to a major arms trade.[74]

Elsewhere, shamans are chosen because of unusual events, the most dramatic and mysterious of which is the initiation crisis.

The Initiation Crisis

While the call to adventure in dreams can sometimes be ignored and suppressed, the shamanic initiation crisis certainly cannot. It explodes through the shaman-elect with life-shattering force, disintegrating the old equilibrium and identity and demanding birth of the new.

It usually announces itself shortly after adolescence with an

onslaught of unusual psychological experiences. These sometimes include talents such as heightened sensitivity and perception. More often the shaman-to-be starts to exhibit unusual—even bizarre, dangerous, and life-threatening—behavior. The result may be weeks, months, or even years of unpredictable chaos that disrupts the lives of the shaman, his family, and his tribe.

The onset may be abrupt or gradual. Eliade notes that there are "'sicknesses,' attacks, dreams, and hallucinations that determine a shaman's career in a very short time." On the other hand, "sometimes there is not exactly an illness but rather a progressive change in behavior. The candidate becomes meditative, seeks solitude, sleeps a great deal, seems absent-minded, has prophetic dreams and sometimes seizures. All these symptoms are only the prelude to the new life that awaits the unwitting candidate. His behavior, we may add, suggests the first signs of a mystical vocation, which are the same in all religions and too well known to dwell upon."[41]

Among the Chukchee Indians:

> For men the preparatory stage of shamanistic inspiration is in most cases very painful, and extends over a long time. The call comes in an abrupt and obscure manner, leaving the young novice in much uncertainty regarding it. . . . He feels "bashful" and frightened; he doubts his own disposition and strength, as has been the case with all seers, from Moses down. Half unconsciously and half against his own will, his whole soul undergoes a strange and painful transformation. This period may last months, and sometimes even years. The young novice, the "newly inspired" (tur-ene'nitvillin), loses all interest in the ordinary affairs of life. He ceases to work, eats but little and without relishing the food, ceases to talk to people, and does not even answer their questions. The greater part of his time he spends in sleep.
>
> Some keep to the inner room and go out but rarely. Others wander about in the wilderness, under the pretext of hunting or of keeping watch over the herd, but often without taking along any

> arms or the lasso of the herdsman. A wanderer like this, however, must be closely watched otherwise he might lie down on the open tundra and sleep for three or four days, incurring the danger, in winter, of being buried in drifting snow.[19]

A Nepalese shaman described his own initial crisis as follows:

> When I was thirteen, I became possessed. I later learned that the spirit was my dead grandfather, but at the time I did not know what was happening. I began to shake violently and was unable to sit still even for a minute, even when I was not trembling. . . .
>
> Finally, all the people in the village came looking for me. When they caught up with me, I stopped shivering and woke up. I was taken home and given food. My family was very concerned. I had no appetite and that night began shaking again.[139]

In the West such behavior would of course be regarded as evidence of severe psychopathology. However, in shamanic cultures this crisis is interpreted as proof that the victim is destined to be a shaman. Such widely divergent interpretations raise fascinating questions about the effects of different cultural expectations, diagnoses, and treatments, and these will be discussed in a later chapter. What is significant to note for now is that the "newly inspired" is understood by the tribe to be undergoing a difficult but potentially valuable developmental process. If handled appropriately this process is expected to resolve in ways that will benefit the whole tribe and provide them with new access to spiritual realms and powers. Such, apparently, is usually the case.

CHAPTER 5

A Life of Learning: Shamanic Training and Discipline

The greatest of all wonders is not the conqueror of the world but the subduer of himself.

WILL DURANT,
The Story of Philosophy

When the hero has answered the call to adventure and found a teacher, the period of training and discipline begins. In this period the mind is trained, the body toughened, cravings are reduced, fears faced, and strengths such as endurance and concentration are cultivated. This is usually a slow and lengthy process where success may be measured in months and years and patience is not only a virtue but a necessity. The goal is to hone both body and mind so as to awaken to, and be an effective instrument of, spirit. The process has been pithily summarized by Chuang Tzu, one of the greatest of the Taoist sages:

First gain control of the body
and all its organs. Then
control the mind. Attain
one-pointedness. Then
the harmony of heaven
will come down and dwell in you.
You will be radiant with Life.
You will rest in Tao.[120]

The shaman's instructions come from both inner and outer worlds. In the outer world it consists of apprenticeship to a master shaman. From the teacher the apprentice learns both theory and practice: the myths and cosmology, rituals and techniques of the shamanic culture. These provide the means by which the apprentice shaman's experiences are cultivated, interpreted, and made meaningful within the tribal and shamanic traditions.

In the inner world the apprentice learns to cultivate and interpret dreams, fantasies, visions, and spirits. Ideally, both inner and outer worlds align to mold the novice into a mature shaman who can mediate effectively between these worlds, between the sacred and profane, the spiritual and mundane.

The length of apprenticeship may vary from as little as days to months or years. After the novice has been accepted, his first task may be a ritual purification in which he must confess any breaches of taboo or other offenses.[147] After this the actual instruction by the teacher, aided of course by the teacher's spirits, begins.

Much must be learned. On the theoretical side the apprentice must become a mythologist and cosmologist. To become an effective "cosmic traveler" he must learn the terrain of this multilayered, interconnected universe in which he will quest for power and knowledge. He must also become familiar with its spiritual inhabitants—their names, habitats, powers, likes and dislikes, how they can be called, and how they can be controlled. For it is these spirits whom he will battle or befriend, who will help or hinder him as he does his work. It is they who represent and embody the power at work in the cosmos, and it is his relationship with them that will determine his success. So the cosmology the would-be shaman learns is no dry mapping of inanimate worlds but a guide to a living, conscious, willful universe.

Much of this cosmic terrain and the guidelines for relating to it are contained in the culture's myths. Indeed, throughout most of human history myths have provided the major cultural guidelines

for the conduct of life. It is only in our own time that major cultures have lacked a common, coherent myth—a grand, unifying picture, story, and explanation of the cosmos. Indeed this lack of a common myth may be a major factor in the fragmentation and alienation that haunts so much of the contemporary world. Much may depend on our ability to create a new myth appropriate to our time and needs.

Joseph Campbell suggests that myths serve four major functions: developmental, social, cosmological, and religious. Their developmental function is to provide guidelines for individuals as they mature through life's stages. Their social function is to support the social structure and provide a shared understanding of life and relationship. Their cosmological and religious roles are to provide an image and understanding of the cosmos and of humankind's role and responsibility in it.[30]

Myths serve the shaman in all four ways. This is not surprising since many myths may have originated in shamanic journeys and reflect the terrain discovered there.[41] They guide the shaman's development, give him his place in society and cosmos and indicate how he is to relate to them. In addition, myths provide the belief system he and his patients will share. This may be crucial since contemporary research suggests that a shared belief system may be a vital part of an effective therapeutic relationship.

In addition to learning myths, the would-be shaman must learn diagnostic and healing practices, master the arts of entering altered states and of journeying, and acquire his own helping spirits.

These helping spirits constitute the shaman's inner teachers. They may appear to him in dreams, daydreams, images, journeys, or visions. Consequently, much of the shaman's training concerns learning how to cultivate the circumstances and states of consciousness that will coax the spirits to reveal themselves and their messages. The most dramatic of these circumstances include ascetic practices and periods of isolation.

Ascetic practices are the atom bombs of religious discipline. These powerful tools are said to strengthen and purify practitioners by forcing them to confront their limits, fears, and self-deceptions. They are tools of high risk and high gain, for although they can be beneficial, they can also be misused.

Traditionally, ascetic practices are said to strengthen and purify. They may strengthen warrior qualities such as will, courage, and endurance; remove both physical and mental impurities; and foster clarity and concentration of mind.[18] The sum total of these benefits is power—power of body, mind, and spirit. It is power to control one's faculties and responses, power to overcome temptations and obstacles, power over spirits, and power to serve and benefit others.

Like any spiritual path, asceticism has its traps. Feelings of righteousness are common, as is puritanical denial of the beauty and joy of life.[188] Another trap is extremism, since asceticism can be carried to dubious and dangerous extremes, even to the point of self-torture, mutilation, and death. But assuming that ascetic practices can also confer benefits, the logical question is, how do they do this?

Several possible mechanisms exist. Those who succeed in meeting challenges have been found to enchance their sense of self-esteem and effectiveness.[11] Thus the ascetic who masters extreme challenges might well be expected to develop an exceptional sense of personal power.

Holding fast to their goals despite the pull of conflicting desires and fears means that ascetics give little reinforcement to these motives. Unreinforced motives tend to diminish and even disappear. This weakening of conflicting drives, which is a goal of most religions, is traditionally called "purification." Some traditions claim that, in the higher reaches of spiritual mastery, competing desires can become so stilled that the mind rests in peace, free of all conflict. This claim has recently received support from studies of advanced Buddhist meditators whose unique and remarkable

Rorschach test patterns showed "no evidence of sexual or aggressive drive conflicts."[24] While there is little evidence that shamans strive for this remarkable degree of purification, they may confront and overcome diverse fears and desires, thus attaining unusual degrees of concentration and power.

Assuaging guilt may also play a role in the effectiveness of asceticism. If practitioners believe they are sinful and must pay for their sins, then asceticism may seem a logical way to do so. While such logic and practices may work to some extent, they are also very tricky. Self-punishment may assuage guilt temporarily but may also strengthen the belief in the necessity and appropriateness of both guilt and punishment.

Ascetic practices occur in varying degrees in different parts of the world. Almost absent in some places, they take extreme forms in parts of India and Japan. For centuries Japanese ascetics have undertaken practices of almost incomprehensible, life-threatening proportions.

Many of these Japanese ascetics have been described as shamans.[18] If we look closely, however, relatively few of them seem to meet our definition of shamanism. No distinction is made between shamans and mediums; beyond that, contemporary shamanism in Japan seems to have degenerated significantly from former times. Few contemporary Japanese shamans enter altered states and actually journey. It appears that most simply act out the classic trance and journey in symbolic rituals.

> Today this trance occurs only rarely. The capacity for this kind of dissociation, and for the visionary journey which goes with it, seems to have diminished in recent centuries, and today the magic journey is most commonly accomplished by symbolic action in fully waking consciousness.[18]

This is an example of what might be called the ritualization of religion: the process in which transcendence-inducing practices degen-

erate into ineffective rituals, direct experience gives way to symbols of experience, and the understanding and appreciation of effective altered states are lost.

Whatever its current limitations, Japanese shamanism has historically been highly ascetic, and some ascetic practices persist even today. The three major types include dietary restriction, cold, and solitude.

In its mildest form dietary restriction involves the avoidance of certain foods, such as meat, salt, or cooked substances, that are believed to inhibit the acquisition of power. In its most extreme form it involves fasting to the point of death. One such extreme is the mind-boggling discipline of "tree eating."

Though its practitioners were not really shamans, the discipline is valuable in showing the extremes to which some ascetic practices have been carried. Practitioners would vow to follow the discipline for one thousand, two thousand, or even three thousand days.

> During the first part of the discipline their diet consisted of nuts, bark, fruit, berries, grass and sometimes soy in fair abundance. The quantity of these things was then reduced, until by the end of their allotted period they had undergone a total fast of many days. Ideally, if the discipline were properly calculated, the man should die from starvation, upright in the lotus posture, on the last day of his avowed fast. His body should have been reduced to skin and bone.[18]

Such a practice was obviously not for the faint of heart.

A second major austerity is exposure to cold. Common in both Arctic areas and Japan, this technique is considered very effective in developing power. Once again the severity of the practices can reach almost incomprehensible extremes.

"To stand under a waterfall, preferably between the hours of two and three in the morning and preferably during the period of the great cold in midwinter, is believed to be an infallible method of gaining power."[18] Indeed, one female ascetic reported that such a

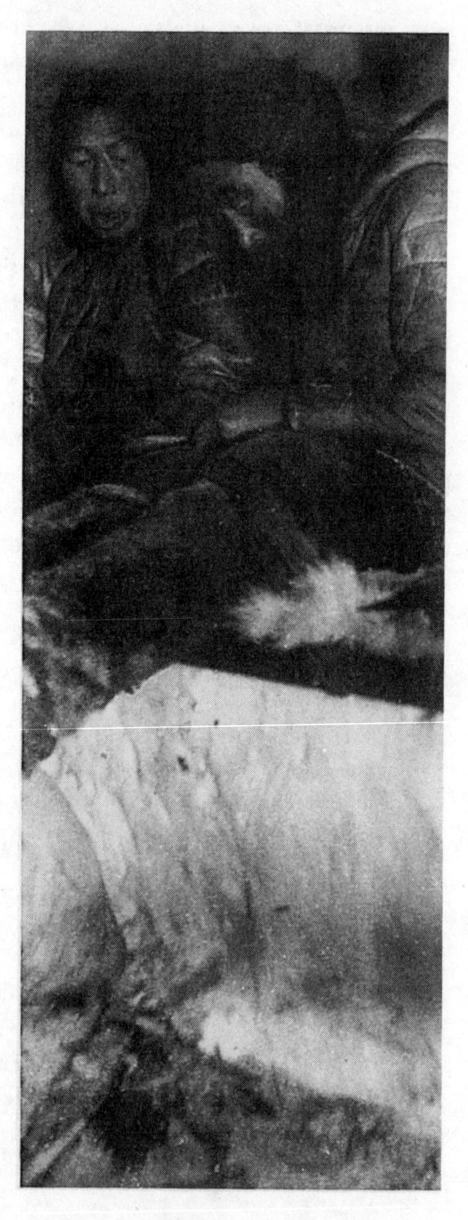

FIGURE 1. Aua with his wife Orula.

practice "no longer felt in the least cold to her. It rather promoted an unrivalled concentration of mind . . . which formed the very basis of her ascetic power."[18]

The third major ascetic practice, periods of solitary withdrawal from society, is common to diverse religious traditions. Such periods mark the lives of many great saints and religious founders. Witness Jesus' 40 days of fasting in the wilderness, Buddha's solitary meditation, and Mohammed's isolation in a cave. Such practices have been part of the training of Eskimo shamans, the Christian desert fathers, Hindu yogis, and Tibetan monks who may be walled away in caves for up to 13 years.

The reason for seeking solitude is essentially to allow attention to be redirected away from the distractions of the world and toward the spiritual. This spiritual realm is ultimately found to reside within the seeker—for example, "The Kingdom of Heaven is within you"; "Look within, Thou art the Buddha"—but to find it requires intense contemplation and introspection. Concentration must be cultivated, sensitivity to one's inner world deepened, the mind quietened, and the clamor of competing desires stilled.

"Know thyself" is the motto of these practices. The demands and distractions of society usually hinder profound inner searching and self-knowledge. Consequently, periodic withdrawal and solitude may be essential. As Wordsworth explained so poetically:

The world is too much with us; late and soon,
Getting and spending, we lay waste our powers;
Little we see in Nature that is ours;
We have given our hearts away. . . .

(Overleaf) FIGURE 2. The rock engravings of Les Trois Frères cave in France are among the most dramatic examples of early human art. Tens of thousands of years ago unknown artists crawled deep underground to draw a tangle of literally hundreds of animals. These animals surround a lone bison-headed human figure, thought to represent one of humankind's earliest shamans. (Tracing by Henri Breuil of rock engravings in Les Trois Frères cave.)

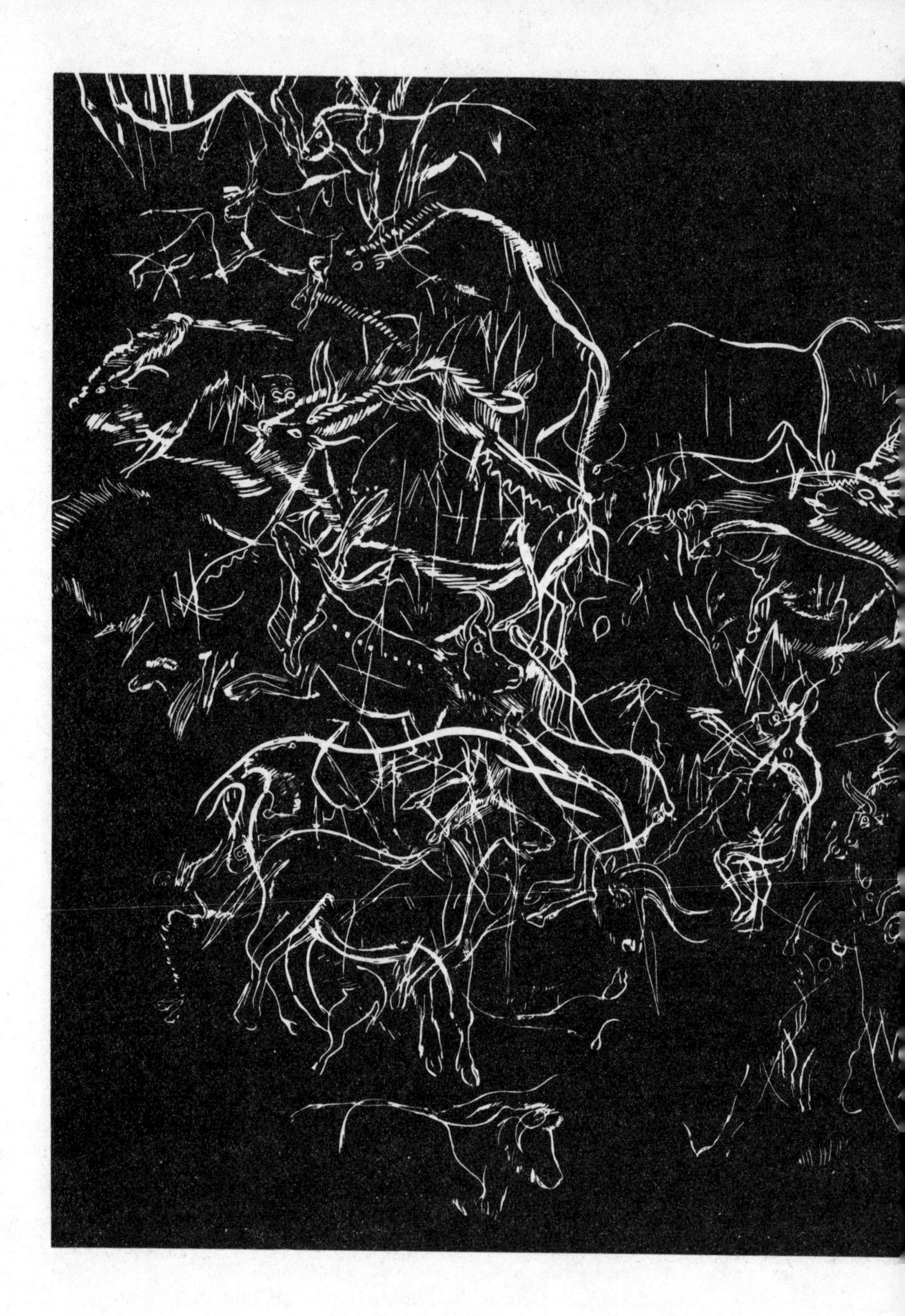

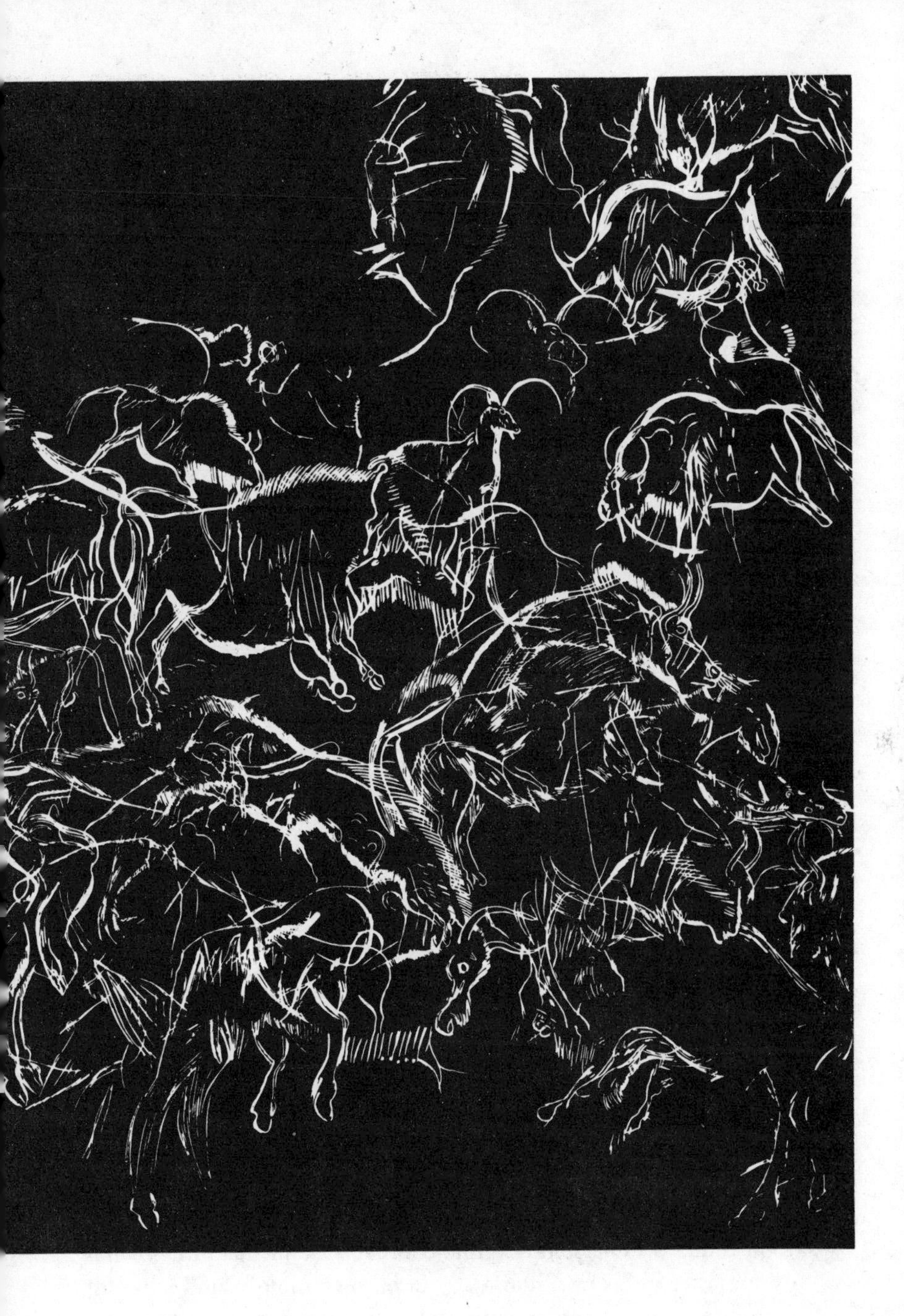

Shamans were the first to appreciate the far-reaching benefits of solitude for psychological and spiritual development. They were the first to learn from direct experience that, to use their own words, "The power of solitude is great and beyond understanding."[147]

The numerous trials faced by those willing to confront isolation and themselves in this way have been the subject of countless spiritual biographies. The Eskimo shaman Aua, whose parents' rituals and taboos were outlined earlier, described his period of solitude as follows.

> Then I sought solitude, and here I soon became very melancholy. I would sometimes fall to weeping, and feel unhappy without knowing why. Then, for no reason, all would suddenly be changed, and I felt a great, inexplicable joy, a joy so powerful that I could not restrain it, but had to break into song, a mighty song, with only room for the one word: joy, joy! And I had to use the full strength of my voice. And then in the midst of such a fit of mysterious and overwhelming delight I became a shaman, not knowing myself how it came about. But I was a shaman. I could see and hear in a totally different way.[147]

Note the extreme mood swings and lack of control. These are common initial reactions to solitude and can be surprisingly powerful. After my own first retreat I wrote of experiencing "sudden apparently unprecipitated wide mood swings to completely polar emotions. Shorn of all my props and distractions there was just no way to pretend that I had more than the faintest inkling of self-control over either thoughts or feelings."[189]

Those who face themselves in solitude soon come to appreciate just how restless and out of control the untrained mind is. They soon come to understand Sigmund Freud's claim that "man is not even master in his own house . . . in his own mind"[52] and why "all scriptures without any exception proclaim that for attaining salva-

tion mind should be subdued."[145] Solitude and fasting are traditional ways of subduing the mind.

Not content with the rigors of solitude, fasting, or cold alone, shamans sometimes combine all these, as in the following account by an Eskimo shaman, Igjugarjuk. While still young he received his call to adventure in the form of mysterious dreams. "Strange unknown beings came and spoke to him, and when he awoke, he saw all the visions of his dream so distinctly that he could tell his fellows all about them. Soon it became evident to all that he was destined to become an angakoq [a shaman] and an old man named Perqanaoq was appointed his instructor. In the depth of winter, when the cold was most severe, Igjugarjuk was placed on a small sled just large enough for him to sit on, and carried far away from his home to the other side of Hikoligjuaq. On reaching the appointed spot, he remained seated on the sled while his instructor built a tiny snow hut, with barely room for him to sit cross-legged. He was not allowed to set foot on the snow, but was lifted from the sled and carried into the hut where a piece of skin just large enough for him to sit on served as a carpet. No food or drink was given him; he was exhorted to think only of the Great Spirit and of the helping spirit that should presently appear—and so he was left to himself and his meditations.

"After five days had elapsed, the instructor brought him a drink of lukewarm water, and with similar exhortations, left him as before. He fasted now for fifteen days, when he was given another drink of water and a very small piece of meat, which had to last him a further ten days. At the end of this period, his instructor came for him and fetched him home. Igjugarjuk declared that the strain of those thirty days of cold and fasting was so severe that he 'sometimes died a little.' During all that time he thought only of the Great Spirit, and endeavored to keep his mind free from all memory of human beings and everyday things. Toward the end of the thirty days there came to him a helping spirit in the shape of a woman. She came while he was asleep and

FIGURE 3. Igjugarjuk (photographed by Knud Rasmussen in 1922).

seemed to hover in the air above him. After that he dreamed no more of her, but she became his helping spirit. For five months following this period of trial, he was kept on the strictest diet, and required to abstain from all intercourse with women. The fasting was then repeated; for such fasts at frequent intervals are the best means of attaining to knowledge of hidden things."[146]

Igjugarjuk's conclusion from all this was that "the only true wisdom lives far from mankind, out in the great loneliness, and it can be reached only through suffering. Privation and suffering alone can open the mind of a man to all that is hidden to others."[134]

Igjugarjuk would therefore probably have agreed with the French existentialist Albert Camus that "when a man has learned—and not on paper—how to remain alone with his suffering, how to overcome his longing to flee, then he has little left to learn."[209]

So practices such as solitude and fasting enhance access to the inner world and its images, visions, dreams, and spirits. The range

of these inner experiences is vast, but commonalities emerge across cultures. For the successful candidate these practices climax in certain experiences which indicate that a degree of shamanic mastery has been attained. Two of the most frequent shamanic culmination experiences—those of being immersed in light and of death-rebirth—are examined in the next chapter.

CHAPTER 6

The Culmination of the Quest: Light and Death-Rebirth

In order that the mind should see light instead of darkness, so the entire soul must be turned away from this changing world, until its eye can learn to contemplate reality and that supreme splendor which we have called the good. Hence there may well be an art whose aim would be to effect this very thing.

SOCRATES

Some experiences are unique to certain paths while others occur so widely across different traditions as to be almost universal. Two such widely occurring experiences are those of light and death-rebirth, often regarded as major milestones on the spiritual path, and in shamanism these experiences may even be regarded as signs that the quest is complete.

LIGHT

It is no accident that one of the terms most often used to describe the goal of the spiritual quest is *enlightenment.* The word has both literal and metaphorical meanings. Metaphorically it refers to a dramatic sense of insight and understanding; literally it refers to an experience of being filled, illuminated, or suffused with light. In the West the best-known example is probably Saint Paul, who was literally blinded by the brilliance of his vision. Likewise the great

church father Saint Augustine "beheld with the mysterious eye of my soul the Light that never changes."[186] The famous mystic shoemaker Jacob Boehme, while wrestling with his "corrupted nature," discovered that "a wonderful light arose within my soul. It was a light entirely foreign to my unruly nature, but in it I recognized the true nature of God and man."[121] As Eliade notes, "Clearly, the 'inner light' that suddenly bursts forth after long efforts of concentration and meditation is well known in all religious traditions."[41]

Such experiences can also occur spontaneously. One survey suggests that as many as 5 percent of the American population may have had them. Moreover, such people may score exceptionally well on tests of psychological health.[64]

This is not to say that all experiences of inner light are the same. They are not. Nor is it to say that all religious traditions evaluate them in the same way. Some traditions regard them as indications of progress; for others they are seductive sidetracks to be noted and carefully passed by. Yet for still others, such as the Iglulik Eskimo shamans, they are regarded as essential and ecstatic.

Thus, after an Iglulik shaman has put a student through preliminary instruction and training, according to Rasmussen,

> the next thing an old shaman has to do for his pupil is to procure him anak ua by which is meant his "angákoq," i.e., the altogether special and particular element which makes this man an angákoq (shaman). It is also called his quamenEq, his "lighting" or "enlightenment," for anak ua consists of a mysterious light which the shaman suddenly feels in his body, inside his head, within the brain, an inexplicable searchlight, a luminous fire, which enables him to see in the dark both literally and metaphorically speaking, for he can now, even with closed eyes, see through darkness and perceive things and coming events which are hidden from others; thus they look into the future and into the secrets of others.
>
> The first time a young shaman experiences this light . . . it is as if the house in which he is suddenly rises; he sees far ahead of

> him, through mountains, exactly as if the earth were on a great plain, and his eyes could reach to the end of the earth. Nothing is hidden from him any longer; not only can he see things far, far away, but he can also discover souls, stolen souls, which are either kept concealed in far, strange lands or have been taken up or down to the Land of the Dead.[147]

For example, the Iglulik Eskimo Aua, whose remarkable career we have been following, finally experienced his *quamenEq* (shamanic enlightenment) alone in the wilderness. He had first trained in the company of his teachers but his quest remained incomplete. He therefore set out into the Arctic wilds to seek in solitude what had eluded him in society. There he was seized by wild mood swings, experiencing unprecedented fits of melancholy and joy.

> And then in the midst of such a fit of mysterious and overwhelming delight I became a shaman, not knowing myself how it came about. But I was a shaman. I could see and hear in a totally different way. I had gained my quamenEq, my enlightenment, the shaman-light of brain and body, and this in such a manner that it was not only I who could see through the darkness of life, but the same light also shone out from me, imperceptible to human beings, but visible to all the spirits of earth and sky and sea, and these now came to me and became my helping spirits.[147]

Thus did Aua, like his shamanic forefathers for perhaps hundreds or thousands or even tens of thousands of years before him, finally experience the inner light and vision that signified the end of his quest. This is the spirit vision that would enable him to "see" the cause and cure of his people's ills. For these people believed, quite literally, that "without vision the people perish," and shamans were the ones who took upon themselves the task of providing this vision.

Death and Rebirth

"It is only in the face of death that man's self is born," claimed Saint Augustine.[209] The extraordinary transformative power of a confrontation with death has been noted by both ancient religions and modern psychologies. For "a confrontation with one's personal death . . . has the power to provide a massive shift in the way one lives in the world. . . . Death acts as a catalyst that can move one from one stage of being to a higher one."[209]

In many cultures and religions, members must be willing to confront not only physical death but also ego death. This is the death of an old identity no longer appropriate to one's current stage of development. The old sense of self must die and out of its ashes must blossom a new identity appropriate to one's developmental or spiritual goal.

This experience of death and rebirth is a motif that echoes through the world's religions, cultures, and myths.[121] In diverse aboriginal cultures the so-called rites of passage are death-rebirth rituals acted out at important life transitions. For example, in puberty rites the childhood identities "die" and boys and girls are reborn and recognized as adults. The Christian who undergoes a deep conversion may have a sense of dying to the old bodily self and being "born again" in the spirit or in Christ. "Unless ye be born again . . ." is a common warning in religious traditions.

Shamans have heeded these warnings, and death-rebirth experiences are widely regarded as essential for shamanic mastery. Rasmussen writes:

> Before a shaman attains the stage at which any helping spirit would think it worth while to come to him, he must, by struggle and toil and concentration of thought, acquire for himself yet another great and inexplicable power: he must be able to see himself as a skeleton. Though no shaman can explain to himself how and why, he can, by

> the power his brain derives from the supernatural, as it were by thought alone, divest his body of its flesh and blood, so that nothing remains but his bones. . . . By thus seeing himself naked, altogether freed from the perishable and transient flesh and blood, he consecrates himself, in the sacred tongue of the shamans, to his great task, through that part of his body which will longest withstand the action of sun, wind and weather, after he is dead.[147]

These experiences may occur either spontaneously or as a result of willed imagination and may be interpreted metaphorically or literally. Shamans may interpret their death-rebirth experiences quite literally as actual physical events in which their bodies are first dismembered by the spirits and then constructed anew. Thus shamans may believe that

> they are cut up by demons or by their ancestral spirits; their bones are cleaned, the flesh scraped off, the body fluids thrown away, and their eyes torn from their sockets. . . . His bones are then covered with new flesh and in some cases he is also given new blood.[44]

The belief is that the practitioner has now been given a new, stronger body fit for the rigors of shamanic work.

This dismemberment experience is similar to that of the Tibetan tantric practice of *gChod*. Here practitioners cultivate detachment and compassion by visualizing their bodies being dismembered and offered to wrathful deities and hungry demons to eat. The major difference seems to be that whereas for the tantric these experiences are recognized as voluntary visualizations, for the shaman they are experienced as involuntary trials.

Similar experiences of dismemberment and reconstruction, of death and rebirth, have been observed among contemporary Westerners undergoing intensive psychotherapy or meditation practice. They occur most dramatically in either holotropic or LSD-assisted therapy sessions. The term *holotropic* means moving toward wholeness or aiming for totality. Holotropic therapy is a technique de-

vised by Stanislav and Christina Grof that combines hyperventilation, music, and bodywork. This powerful combination is capable of inducing significant altered states of consciousness and deep psychological insights. In fact, holotropic therapy may be one of the most powerful nondrug means of inducing therapeutic altered states.[69]

Studies of holotropic and LSD sessions have provided the most dramatic, detailed, and precise accounts we have of these fascinating and mysterious death-rebirth experiences. It will therefore be valuable to examine these accounts in some detail in order to fill out and understand the limited information available to us from shamanic traditions. For this we can do no better than to turn to the work of Stanislav Grof, whose several thousand clinical studies of these therapies are the world's most extensive.

The LSD or holotropically intensified death-rebirth is an experience of awesome power that shakes those who experience it to their psychological and spiritual core. Grof describes it as follows:

> Physical and emotional agony culminates in a feeling of utter and total annihilation on all imaginable levels. It involves an abysmal sense of physical destruction, emotional catastrophe, intellectual defeat, ultimate moral failure, and absolute damnation of transcendental proportions. This experience is usually described as "ego death"; it seems to entail instantaneous and merciless destruction of all the previous reference points in the life of the individual.
>
> After the subject has experienced the limits of total annihilation and "hit the cosmic bottom," he or she is struck by visions of blinding white or golden light. The claustrophobic and compressed world . . . suddenly opens up and expands into infinity. The general atmosphere is one of liberation, salvation, redemption, love, and forgiveness. The subject feels unburdened, cleansed and purged, and talks about having disposed of an incredible amount of personal "garbage," guilt, aggression, and anxiety. This is typically associated with brotherly feelings for all fellowmen and appreciation of warm human relationships, friendship and love. Irrational and exagger-

> ated ambitions, as well as cravings for money, status, fame, prestige and power, appear in this state as childish, irrelevant and absurd. There is often a strong tendency to share and engage in service and charitable activities. The universe is perceived as indescribably beautiful and radiant. All sensory pathways seem to be wide open and the sensitivity to the appreciation of external stimuli is greatly enhanced. The individual tuned into this experiential area usually discovers within himself or herself genuinely positive values, such as a sense of justice, appreciation of beauty, feelings of love, and self respect as well as respect for others.[68]

So powerful is the experience that words can seem inadequate to describe it. This emotional power has been wonderfully portrayed by artist Harriette Frances, who was a subject in one of the early LSD research studies. Her drawings, reproduced on the following pages, not only provide a graphic account of an LSD-induced death-rebirth, but also portray the amazing similarity of this twentieth-century process to ancient shamanic experiences.

The process of death and rebirth has probably been repeated numberless times throughout human history, but its interpretations have varied dramatically. A contemporary LSD subject might view it as the disintegration and reconstitution of the self-image or self-concept. Contemplatives might view it as a spiritual death and resurrection. Shamans, however, have traditionally taken it to be a literal destruction and reconstitution of their physical bodies. For them, the images of bodily dismemberment are interpreted quite literally. This literal, concrete interpretation of mental imagery is a theme we will see echoed throughout much of shamanism.

What are we to make of this recurrent experience of agonizing death, dismemberment, and destruction followed by a healing process of relief, reconstitution, and rebirth? Clearly this is a powerful, perennial experience that has been sought by many and has burst unsought on others. It appears to represent some deep, archetypal, and mysterious process of the human psyche, a process

with considerable healing potential. The following hypothesis is an attempt to understand this process in psychological terms.

The experience of death and rebirth, dismemberment and reconstitution, appears to be a psychological and/or spiritual transformative process most likely to occur at times of overwhelming emotional arousal and stress. This arousal activates psychological tensions and conflicts to unsustainable levels. The result is a crisis in which old patterning forces are no longer able to maintain the former psychological balance. The old psychodynamic forces, conflicts, habits, conditioning, organization, beliefs, and identity are overwhelmed and the psyche's organization temporarily collapses. The key result of this collapse, says Grof, is that "what is destroyed in this process is the old, limiting concept of oneself and the corresponding restricting view of existence and of the universe."[68]

This destabilizing process is projected, pictured, and experienced as images. These are so-called autosymbolic images, which symbolize one's own psychological state. Thus this initial phase of unbearable psychological tension and breakdown may be experienced symbolically but by both shamans and patients as visions of physical torture, bodily dismemberment, death, and decay or as scenes of war and destruction.

Out of this newly destructured chaos, reorganization and reconstruction occur. This reorganization takes place in a mind now partly freed of old limiting and distorting habits. Reorganization may be guided by archetypal forces and by the drive toward wholeness (holotropism) that so many psychologists and contemplatives have described as an inherent part of the psyche. The result may be a reconstructed psyche, identity, and consciousness which are less conflicted, less symptomatic, less bound to the past and more healthy, more integrated, more whole. The old identity has died and a new one has been born.

This reconstruction, reintegration, and wholeness are also reflected in the accompanying imagery. Thus the shaman may see the spirits reconstructing her body, the therapy patient may witness

FIGURE 4. The death-rebirth process is portrayed by Harriette Frances, a subject in one of the early LSD research studies. Her drawings demonstrate many of the key features of the LSD death-rebirth experience and their remarkable similarities to shamanic experiences. In the first drawing the artist portrays herself beginning to enter an altered state of consciousness as the LSD takes effect. Perception is altered and the environment takes on an unfamiliar appearance.

FIGURE 5. As her altered state deepens, she experiences falling downward through a whirlpool-like tunnel, past skeletal symbols of death and destruction, to a lower world.

FIGURE 6. In the lower world she experiences being pierced and tortured and is surrounded by images of death and decay.

FIGURE 7. She is torn apart and reduced to a skeleton but sees a light above her, which she struggles desperately to reach.

FIGURE 8. As she struggles to escape from this realm of all-consuming death and destruction, she feels herself being offered assistance.

FIGURE 9. She sees a bird, which for shamans is often a power animal and a symbol of spirit, and appeals to it for help.

FIGURE 10. Her body begins to re-form. This is the shamanic experience of being provided with a new body. This new body is believed by the shaman to be stronger and better fitted for future shamanic work.

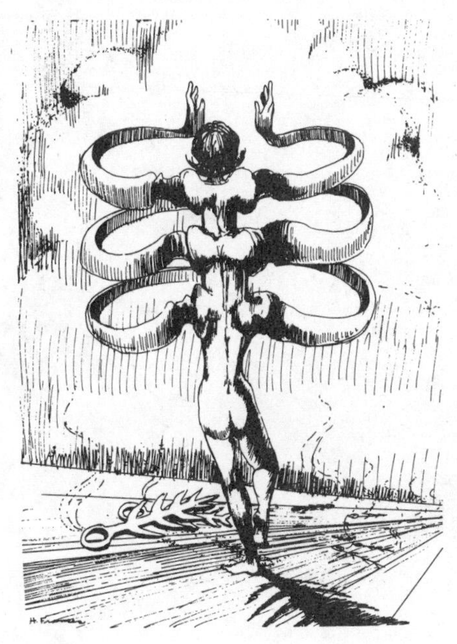

FIGURE 11. The repair of her body is completed.

FIGURE 12. She now experiences rebirth. Her body is completely reconstituted and she is surrounded by birds. She is left with an ecstatic sense of having been cleansed, rejuvenated, and revitalized and of having been through an experience of life-changing power and importance. Twenty years later the artist still regards this as one of the most significant experiences of her life.

images of birth, or the contemplative may experience herself as being "reborn in the spirit."

Such a process, involving major destruction of old conditioned patterns and self-images and reconstitution at a more effective, integrated level, might account for the dramatic benefits and breakthroughs that can follow death-rebirth experiences. These benefits and breakthroughs may include resolution of the disabling initiation illness in shamans, relief of chronic psychopathology in

FIGURE 13. A shaman wearing a tunic on which is portrayed part of the skeleton. This skeleton symbolizes the remarkable experience of death and rebirth that marked the shaman's initiation.

patients, and freedom from egoism and attachments in spiritual practitioners. Just how dramatic these benefits can be is evident from both ancient and contemporary accounts. Stanislav Grof concludes that "powerful experiential sequences of dying and being born can result in dramatic alleviation of a variety of emotional, psychosomatic, and interpersonal problems that have previously resisted all psychotherapeutic work."[69]

Likewise, some two thousand years ago Jesus spoke of the importance of this process in a metaphor that has echoed across centuries: "A grain of wheat remains a solitary grain unless it falls into the ground and dies; but if it dies, it brings a rich harvest."[17] The experience of death-rebirth can bring a rich harvest. As with many other psychological and spiritual transformations, it was the shamans who were the first to recognize and harvest it.

CHAPTER 7

Primitive Madman or Mystic in the Making? Conventional Views

It is the mind that maketh good or ill, that maketh wretch or happy, rich or poor.
EDMUND SPENSER

Perhaps the most controversial topic in shamanism concerns the psychological health of its practitioners. The range of descriptions and diagnoses that have been given these people is nothing less than extraordinary. Shamans have been labeled, pigeonholed, pathologized, denigrated, dissected, and dismissed in countless ways.

To start with some of the kinder diagnoses, the shaman has been described as a healed madman and a trickster. The labels hysteric, neurotic, epileptic, and schizophrenic have been applied liberally. The shaman has also been called a charlatan, a veritable idiot, and an outright psychotic. More recently, on the other hand, shamans have been eulogized and sanctified. Among other things, they have been called yogis, psi masters, and masters of death.

Traditionally the majority view has been that shamans are severely psychologically disturbed. Consequently both shamans and shamanism have often been dismissed as the unfortunate products of primitive minds, and seriously disturbed ones at that. The question of the shaman's psychological status is therefore no small matter; in fact, the status of this millennia-old tradition hangs on it. It will therefore be well worthwhile to take the time to care-

fully assess the evidence for the diagnoses most often given to shamans.

We must acknowledge at the beginning that there is no reason to assume that shamans are a homogeneous group. In fact, psychological testing suggests they are not.[44] For all we know they may no more display a single personality or neatly fit a single diagnosis than do all Western doctors. This may seem an obvious point but it is amazing how often people forget it.

In making this assessment we cannot simply examine the shamans' behavior alone. Rather, we need to consider the interaction between the shamans' behavior, our Western psychological and diagnostic viewing frames, and the psychological skills and cultural perspectives of the researchers making the diagnoses. Two shamanic behaviors in particular need to be carefully assessed since they have most often been interpreted as pathological. The first is the initiation crisis, the dramatic onset of painful symptoms and unusual experiences that mark the beginning of the shamanic life for some practitioners.

The second is the shamanic journey. Here the shaman enters an altered state of consciousness, then experiences herself as leaving the body and journeying to other worlds. The journey contains several experiences likely to arouse the suspicion of Western researchers—the altered state of consciousness that the shaman induces, the rich imagery and visions that accompany it, and the presence of spirits. The fact that shamans believe that these images, visions, spirits, and other worlds are as real as our ordinary waking reality only further heightens Western suspicions.

What about the observers who have made pathologizing interpretations of shamanic behavior? What about their possible blind spots and biases? Here we need to consider the possible biasing effects of Western cultural and psychological perspectives. We also need to take into account anthropologists' lack of psychological training and lack of personal experience in shamanic training and altered states.

Diagnostic Biases

Today's anthropologists have developed considerable sensitivity to the dangers wrought by the distorting lenses of cultural bias. When other peoples are judged by the beliefs and standards of our own culture, all too often their behavior is interpreted as barbaric, primitive, or pathological. This kind of bias seems to have occurred in the assessment of shamanism since

> the negative picture of the shaman, primarily (though not exclusively) found in the earlier anthropological literature, is the expression of a Zeitgeist, the spirit of the times, wherein the Western rationalistic-positive ideology was considered the norm against which other cultures and institutions were judged. Non-Western systems of explanation, where they deviated from these Eurocentric positivistic norms, were considered abnormal, a collective ignorance and error, in psychopathological terms, an expression of "poor reality testing."[98]

For example, a person in the West who reported seeing and being persecuted by spirits might well be diagnosed as psychotic, since these beliefs and experiences are not part of Western cultural reality. However, in shamanic cultures they are the norm. Indeed, the person who did *not* believe in spirits and the possibility of being persecuted by them would be considered strange. Thus, one of the central abilities of shamanism—the ability to interact with and control spirits—is considered normal and desirable in one culture but disturbed and dangerous in another. "What in shamanistic behavior may appear hysterical or psychotic to the Western psychiatrist is to the people concerned a time honored ritual."[108] Small wonder, then, that some researchers, blinded by their own cultural assumptions, could label the shamanic initiation crisis and shamanic journey as psychotic episodes.

Lack of psychological expertise may also have led to other pathological interpretations. For example, because they did not

know exactly what to look for, many anthropologists' reports lack crucial diagnostic information that would allow us to determine the precise nature of shamanic experiences and whether they are pathological. For example, the shaman's visionary experiences have been commonly described as "hallucinations" or "neurotic dreams" without more precise description or explanation. Likewise, the supposed epilepsy that sometimes occurs during initiation crises has been labeled as simply "fits," a description that makes accurate diagnosis impossible.

In addition there is another problem, which has only recently been recognized as a problem: most researchers have not themselves done shamanic practices. However, shamanic disciplines center on entering altered states of consciousness, and it can be extremely difficult to comprehend altered-state experiences without personal experience of that state.[179] When this lack of personal experience is combined with ignorance of the possible range and value of alternate states, the net effect can be dangerously distorting. Psychologist Richard Noll, who has done important work on this topic, points out that "devoid of the personal experience of ASCs (altered states of consciousness), yet quite familiar with the altered states of the diagnostic manual, the incredible sagas of shamans must indeed seem psychotic to an interpreter who only considers experiences in an ordinary state of consciousness to be valid, mentally healthy phenomena."[130] This is an example of what Michael Harner calls "cognicentrism," the tendency to interpret (and denigrate) alternate states from the limited perspective and experience of our own state.[73]

Interpretation of the meaning and significance of any behavior depends of course on the psychological perspective and theory from which it is viewed. What is a marker of health from one viewpoint may be seen as pathology from another. For example, one of the hallmarks of genuine mystical experiences is a sense of unity in which the boundaries between self and other dissolve. Many Eastern and some Western psychologists regard this as a

marker of exceptional psychological health.[193] However, traditional psychoanalysts often regard such experiences as unfortunate expressions of neurosis at best or psychosis at worst.

The tendency of psychoanalysts to regard mystical experiences as pathological is particularly important here, for it was psychoanalysis that was most often used initially to interpret shamanic experiences. Psychoanalysis has made enormous contributions to our understanding of mind and behavior, of course, but like any psychology it contains its share of limitations and blind spots. Particularly important is the fact that it was born out of a study of European psychopathology and consequently focused on sickness and early development. Thus, there has been a tendency for psychoanalysts to interpret even healthy behavior in terms of early or pathological development. As humanistic psychologist Abraham Maslow said, "It is as if Freud supplied to us the sick half of psychology and we must now fill it out with the healthy half."[116]

The anthropological result of this Freudian emphasis has been a bias toward interpreting the unusual (to Western eyes) behavior of other cultures as pathological, primitive, or regressive. Richard Noll concludes that the net result has been a "virulent influence of Freudian psychoanalytic tradition in culture and personality studies in nurturing unnecessary psychopathological interpretations of cross-cultural behaviors."[131] This is not to deny the many valuable clinical contributions that psychoanalysis has made; it is rather to emphasize that the inappropriate application of psychoanalytic views and theories to the peoples and behaviors of other cultures can lead to significant misunderstandings.

The risks of misunderstanding other cultures become particularly dangerous when the behaviors in question involve altered states of consciousness. Until quite recently Western psychology and anthropology recognized only a very limited range of normal states—mainly our normal waking, dreaming, and nondreaming sleep states. States falling outside this narrow range were automat-

ically assumed to be pathological. Richard Noll points out that "states of consciousness that are altered in some fashion are traditionally viewed as pathological merely because they deviate from . . . the 'ordinary state' against which all other states are contrasted."[130]

In recent years this view has changed dramatically. It has become clear that the range of potential healthy states of consciousness is considerably broader than previously imagined. Studies of other cultures, religious traditions, meditations, and yogas have revealed a startling plasticity of consciousness. States of exceptional concentration, calm, clarity, and perceptual sensitivity are among the many that have been identified.

However, these are new discoveries. Until recently, even states of exceptional joy, bliss, or compassion have all too often been interpreted as the unfortunate products of pathological or primitive minds. Mystical experiences, for example, have been interpreted as neurotic regressions, ecstatic states viewed as narcissism, and enlightenment dismissed as regression to intrauterine stages.[194] Likewise, a psychiatry textbook stated that "the obvious similarities between schizophrenic regression and the practices of yoga and Zen merely indicate that the general trend in oriental cultures is to withdraw into the self from an overbearingly difficult physical and social reality."[3]

In short, Western psychiatry has a long history of viewing mystics as madmen, saints as psychotics, and sages as schizophrenics. And this in spite of the fact that the great saints and sages may represent the heights of human development and have had the greatest impact on human history. "Who are . . . the greatest benefactors of the living generation of mankind?" asked Arnold Toynbee. To this he answered, "I should say: Confucius and Lao Tze, the Buddha, the Prophets of Israel and Judah, Zoroaster, Jesus, Mohammed and Socrates."[185]

This historical argument against equating mystical and pathological states now has scientific support. Several hundred research

studies have made it clear that the altered states induced by meditation and yoga, for example, are unique and should in no way be confused with psychopathology.[164] As Ken Wilber argued most emphatically, these states can be equated with pathology "only by those whose intellectual inquiry goes no further than superficial impressions."[200]

In summary, it appears that religious experiences and states of consciousness have been viewed all too often as pathological because of cultural bias, lack of psychological expertise, psychoanalytic emphasis on pathology, and ignorance of the potential range and value of certain altered states. In recent years this situation has begun to change. The states and practices of Buddhist meditation and Hindu Yoga, for example, have begun to be appreciated as valid and valuable. However, a similar shift has only just begun to occur with regard to shamanism. Older views of this tradition as merely the product of psychologically disturbed individuals still prevail. Let us therefore examine the evidence for and against the various pathologies and diagnoses that have been most often attributed to shamans. The most common of these diagnoses have been, to use the old and imprecise language found in anthropological literature: epilepsy, hysteria, and schizophrenia. Let us examine the evidence for and against each of these venerable diagnoses and then consider more recent interpretations.

Epilepsy

The conclusion that shamans are epileptics is due to descriptions of their "fits" during initial crises. These fits have rarely been observed directly by anthropologists; the information has usually come from shamans' recollections many years afterwards. This alone would make precise diagnosis difficult, since recollections of past illness can be notoriously inaccurate. The situation is exacerbated because anthropologists have not known the correct ques-

tions to ask in order to make accurate diagnoses. The net result is a collection of descriptions so vague and so unhelpful that it is impossible to determine whether the condition was in fact epilepsy, let alone what type of epilepsy might have been involved.

One anthropologist observed a series of fits in a woman who desired to become a shaman but was rejected by her tribe. He concluded that

> the most typical picture of hysterical character, with strong sexual excitement, was beyond any doubt: she was lying on the stove-bed in a condition varying between great rigidity ("arch") and relaxation; she was hiding herself from the light . . . there was temporary loss of sensitiveness to a needle . . . at times continuous movements with the legs and basin were indicative of a strong sexual excitement. . . . Her cognition of reality was rather doubtful, for during her fit she did not recognize persons being around her. However, from time to time, or at least at the end of her fits, she was quite conscious of her surroundings and before a fit she looked for isolation and for certain comfort for herself during the fit.[165]

This description is one of the most detailed in the literature, yet it is not detailed enough to allow certain diagnosis. The description is consistent with "hysterical epilepsy," but definite diagnosis would require a more precise description of the attack, a description of the patient's experience, and ultimately laboratory data.

What then are the possible causes of shamanic "fits"? Possible diagnoses would include various types of epilepsy, including generalized and temporal lobe epilepsies; hysterical seizures; and emotional agitation.

Generalized, or grand mal, epilepsy is the classic form of convulsion. The patient loses consciousness and falls to the ground. After a few seconds, generalized muscle contractions occur, followed by intense jerking movements of the whole body. The movements gradually become less frequent and finally cease, leaving the patient comatose and flaccid. Consciousness then gradually returns,

although the patient often remains confused and drowsy and has no memory of the attack.

Of greater possible significance to shamanic pathology is temporal lobe epilepsy. This form of the disorder is particularly intriguing because it elicits not only changes in behavior but also dramatic and unusual experiences. During an attack a patient may experience hallucinations, intense emotions ranging from fear to ecstasy, and feelings of unreality. During this time the patient may display unconscious automatic movements that are quite out of place.

Both the generalized and temporal lobe attacks are forms of organic epilepsy—that is, they are due to some type of brain abnormality, and thus they tend to recur over long periods of time. However, the accounts of shamanic "fits" usually imply that the attacks occurred only during a time of emotional agitation—the initial shamanic crisis—and then disappeared spontaneously. This fact suggests that the fits were not organic in origin and hence were neither generalized epilepsy nor temporal lobe epilepsy.

This leaves two other major possibilities: hysterical epilepsy and emotional agitation. Hysterical epilepsy is a form of what is technically known as "hysterical neurosis, conversion type." Here psychological conflict is expressed as, or converted to, behavior that mimics an epileptic attack. It seems possible that some shamanic fits are of this nature. The fact that the fits occur during times of psychological stress, often disappear afterwards, and are expected of would-be shamans all suggest a psychological cause. Another possibility is that some of the "fits" are simply episodes of intense emotional agitation rather than any true or even hysterical epilepsy.

In summary, then, available descriptions are so vague that it is impossible to make any definitive statement about the occurrence of epilepsy in shamans. However, there seems to be little evidence for organic epilepsy. Whatever fits do occur may be psychological in origin. Not all shamans experience fits; moreover, epilepsy could not account for other shamanic experiences such as the shamanic

journey. Consequently, it is clearly incorrect to label all shamans as epileptics or to imagine that shamanism can be either explained or dismissed on the basis of epilepsy.

HYSTERIA

The second condition that has often been used to diagnose and dismiss shamanism is hysteria. This is actually an old term for a variety of disorders that are now called hysterical neuroses.[4] These are divided into two major types, conversion disorders and dissociative disorders. Conversion disorders occur when a person unconsciously converts psychological conflicts into physical symptoms. As previously discussed, epilepsy-like symptoms are one physical expression that such conversion of psychological disturbances can take.

In hysterical neuroses of the dissociative type, the symptoms are psychological rather than physical. The key element is loss of conscious awareness and control of certain mental processes such as memory, perception, and identity. Dissociative disorders include multiple personality disorder, depersonalization, and trance states. In *multiple personality disorder* there exist within the individual two or more distinct personalities that alternate in control of the person's identity and behavior. In *depersonalization* there is a persistent or recurrent sense of detachment and alienation from one's experience. *Trance states* are altered states of consciousness with diminished or selectively focused attention.

We will now consider hysterical dissociative disorders and examine to what extent they account for shamanic experiences. Three types of shamanic experience have been labeled "hysterical": the initial crisis, mediumship, and the shamanic journey. We will look at each of these in turn.

With its wide range of bizarre experiences and behaviors, it is not surprising that the shamanic initiation crisis has been labeled hysterical. The constellation of dramatic changes in consciousness,

identity, and behavior that can accompany it might perhaps be classifiable as an unusual form of hysterical dissociation. However, again the major problem is that the descriptions we have of initiation crises are usually too imprecise to allow accurate diagnosis. Consequently, all we can say is that dissociation might play a role in initiation crises.

The second aspect of shamanism that might reflect dissociation is the process of mediumship, or channeling, as it is now known. During this process one or more spirits seem to speak through the shaman, whose state of consciousness may vary from full alertness to complete absense of personal awareness. During this absence the spirit(s) may seem to displace the personality of the shaman, whose body posture, behavior, mannerisms, and voice may change dramatically.

This type of phenomenon has occurred throughout diverse cultures and times. In the West one of the earliest and most famous examples was the Greek oracle at Delphi who was consulted by peasants and kings. Spirit messengers were much in vogue around the end of the nineteenth century, when the process was known as mediumship. Interest has recently surged once again under the name of channeling.

Western psychiatry tends to regard this phenomenon, whatever its name, as a form of dissociation. Witness the *Comprehensive Textbook of Psychiatry,* which says that "a curious and not fully explored or understood form of dissociation is that of the trance states of spirit mediums who preside over spiritual seances."[129]

There is an interesting clash of world views here. For Western psychiatry, mediumship is a form of dissociation in which the "spirits" are assumed to be splintered fragments of the psyche. For the shaman, on the other hand (and the Western medium or channeler), the "spirits" are experienced as, and usually believed to be, distinct entities possessing knowledge and wisdom separate from (and often greater than) that of the medium. To decide definitively between these two views may seem a simple matter.

However, as we will see in a later chapter, a little reflection soon shows that the decision is more tricky than it first appears.

For now, suffice it to say that a number of careful studies suggest that mediumship/channeling may be a complex phenomenon which, though producing much nonsense, can also sometimes produce meaningful, even profound, information.[79, 102] To simply label it as "hysteria" would be an unfortunate error preventing us from exploring an unusual capacity of mind. Clearly it deserves careful research.

A third phenomenon that might be considered a form of dissociation is the shamanic journey. During the journey the shaman enters a trance, becomes less aware of the environment, and journeys to other worlds to contact a rich range of spirit beings and visionary experiences.

Western psychiatrists might argue that the journey is indeed a form of dissociation since it involves entering a trance and trances are listed as one form of dissociation. The implication is that these trances are necessarily pathological. Shamans, their tribespeople, and many anthropologists would disagree. For the tribe, the shamanic journey is indeed a ray of hope by which healing and help can reach this world from the sacred realms.

There seem to be several arguments against including the shamanic journey under the category of dissociative disorders. First, the journey is not only culturally sanctioned but culturally valued, and to label it as a disorder may be to "fail to distinguish clinic and culture."[210]

Moreover, the shaman has control over the trance, entering and leaving it at will. This is quite different from the classic dissociative disorders, which appear to overtake and control their victims. Thus it has been pointed out that "the Siberian shaman may fall into a state of partial hysterical dissociation like the hysteric in, say Britain, but this state he voluntarily seeks and in doing so he obtains authority and respect from the tribe."[210]

Another consideration is that the shamanic journey does not

seem to function necessarily as a psychological defense mechanism. In the clinical dissociative disorders, the dissociation functions as a defense mechanism by reducing and distorting consciousness in order to avoid the awareness of psychological pain and conflict. The shamanic journey seems to do almost the opposite. The shaman deliberately opens herself, either to her own pain and suffering or to that of her people, or even to that of the spirits in other worlds, and thereby attempts to find a resolution to that pain.

This is not to deny that the journey—or almost any other shamanic behavior, for that matter—can sometimes be used as a psychological defense. Personally I have enormous faith in people's ability to use almost anything for defense. However, this is very different from saying that the journey serves primarily or exclusively as a defense.

It seems that there are several cultural and clinical arguments against viewing the shamanic journey as a dissociative disorder. There may also be significant dangers associated with applying this diagnostic label.

The first danger is that the label has, of course, a pathological connotation. It reinforces the idea, already prevalent in the literature, of the shaman as necessarily disturbed.

A related danger is the trap of reductionism. Once a diagnostic label and mechanism such as dissociation are suggested, there is a grave risk of reducing the entire process—in this case the shamanic journey—to nothing but dissociation. Thus a rich, complex, and culturally valued process, when slotted into a Western diagnostic category, can easily be diagnosed and dismissed as nothing but a curious cultural variation of a common defense mechanism.

These dangers of pathologizing and reductionism extend beyond shamanism to religion in general. If the shamanic journey and its trance are reduced to dissociation, this reinforces the tendency to diagnose and dismiss all mystical states of consciousness—even though for millennia these experiences have often been regarded as the *summum bonum,* the highest goal and highest good of

human existence. The net effect is to lose awareness of the possible uniqueness and value of these states, to cut short open-minded research, to explain the unknown in terms of the known and the unfamiliar in terms of the familiar, and thereby to assume that we have nothing to learn from the great spiritual heroes and their practices.

In summary, then, the existence, extent, and nature of "hysteria" in shamanism are unclear. Hysterial conversion and dissociation may conceivably account for some "fits" and other abnormal behaviors during the shamanic initiation period. However, it is difficult to be sure, since our information about what shamans really experience during this period is imprecise at best.

Hysterical dissociation might also be involved in two other shamanic behaviors, namely spirit possession and the shamanic journey. However, to diagnose these as nothing but dissociative disorders seems to risk imposing Western cultural and diagnostic perspectives, thereby reducing and pathologizing these rich phenomena to mere diagnostic categories. Therefore it seems more appropriate to focus on gathering more precise data on the actual phenomena themselves than to diagnose and dismiss them.

Schizophrenia and Other Forms of Psychosis

The epileptic, neurotic, and hysteric may be disturbed individuals, but at least they retain contact with consensus reality. The psychotic, however, lives in a world apart, lost in private fantasies and unable to recognize them as the illusions and delusions they are. To an outsider the psychotic's experiences seem bizarre and incomprehensible.

Even though shamans' experiences may make perfect sense to them and their tribespeople, they may seem completely bizarre and incomprehensible to someone from another culture. It is not surprising that some Westerners have therefore decided that shamans

are psychotic and schizophrenic. For example, one researcher described the Mohave shaman as "an outright psychotic,"[36] and a psychiatrist concluded that schizophrenia and shamanism have in common "grossly non-reality-oriented ideation, abnormal perceptual experience, profound emotional upheavals, and bizarre mannerisms." Indeed, the only difference that this psychiatrist could see between shamanic and Western schizophrenic episodes was the degree to which the two cultures accepted them.[169]

The shamanic experiences that have seemed most bizarre to the Western mind and have led to diagnoses of schizophrenia have been the initial crisis and the visionary experiences during the shamanic journey. Consequently, we need to examine both of these experiences in order to assess the validity of the claim that shamans are psychotic.

Unlike the initial crisis, the shamans' experiences and states of consciousness during the journey can be assessed with some degree of accuracy since we possess many detailed accounts of them. These accounts include descriptions by observers as well as descriptions by the shamans themselves. In addition we now have accounts by Westerners who have undertaken shamanic training and described their own journeys. When these descriptions are compared to those of schizophrenia, as we will see in chapter 19, differences become clearly apparent. Consequently it is no longer appropriate to suggest that shamanic journey experiences are evidence of schizophrenia.

The situation is much less clear in regard to the shaman's initial crisis. As previously discussed, we have little firsthand data on these crises and what we have is sketchy at best. It is therefore impossible to reach any definitive diagnosis. However, two questions need to be addressed: whether the behavior during the crises is consistent with psychosis; and, if it is, whether it is consistent with schizophrenia.

The diagnosis of psychosis during the initial crisis has been based on the shaman's experience and behavior. At this time the

shaman-to-be may experience herself as being tormented and controlled by spirits. She may also exhibit considerable confusion, emotional turmoil, withdrawal from society, and a range of unusual and even bizarre behavior such as going naked, refusing food, and biting herself. These beliefs and behaviors are bizarre by Western standards, and the belief that one is being tormented by spirits would certainly be considered delusional in our culture.

However, belief in spirit possession and persecution is not considered delusional in the shamanic culture but fully consistent with the cultural world view. Moreover the shaman is not alone in having these experiences. At one time or another many people in the tribe may feel persecuted. What is unique about the shaman, is not that she complains of persecution by spirits but that she learns how to master and use them.

Given the limited data and the cultural setting, then, we cannot say for sure whether shamanic initiation crises sometimes include psychotic episodes. All we can conclude is that the bizarre behavior, emotional turmoil, confusion, and incoherence could be consistent with a psychotic episode. Therefore, it is possible that some would-be shamans who are compelled to their profession by an initial crisis may undergo a temporary psychosis. However, there is no clear evidence that this psychosis persists past the initiation phase, and for several reasons it is most unlikely that the condition is schizophrenia.

For readers interested in a more technical discussion of the possible diagnoses of the initiation crisis, see the following section, "Types of Psychoses That Might Occur During the Initiation Crisis."

What can we conclude about the oft-repeated claims echoing through decades of literature that shamans are healed madmen at best or actively psychotic and schizophrenic at worst? The experiences most often diagnosed as psychotic have been shamanic journeys and initial crises. Of the shamanic journey we can clearly say that it is a unique experience that should in no way be confused with psychosis.

The initial crisis is less clear. Some of the shamans who undergo such a crisis might suffer a temporary psychotic episode. However, it is important to note that only a small percentage of shamans undergo an initial crisis, and of these probably only some experience psychosis. This means that only a very small percentage of all shamans suffer a psychosis. Moreover, this psychosis is short-lived and seems unlikely to be a form of schizophrenia. In fact, the shaman may end up as one of the most psychologically healthy members of the tribe.

This is not to say that all shamans are models of mental health or model citizens. Some engage in all manner of trickery and deceit. However, contrary to decades of speculation, the vast majority of shamans cannot be diagnosed as mentally ill or labeled as epileptic, hysterical, schizophrenic, or psychotic. In short, shamanism can no longer be dismissed as the confused production of primitive or pathological minds.

Types of Psychoses That Might Occur During the Initiation Crisis

If a psychotic episode does occur during the initiation crisis, there seem to be four possible diagnoses that might be applied. The first is a brief reactive psychosis. As the name suggests, this is a brief episode (lasting from a few hours to a month) occurring in response to stressful situations, often marked by considerable emotional turmoil, yet with eventual full recovery.[4]

Other possible diagnoses are schizophrenia and its short-lived variant, schizophreniform disorder. Current diagnostic practices require continuous signs of psychological disturbances for at least six months before a diagnosis of schizophrenia can be made. Where disturbances are shorter but the clinical picture is otherwise consistent with schizophrenia, the diagnosis of schizophreniform disorder is made.

The fourth possibility is an atypical psychosis. This diagnosis is given when a psychotic episode does not meet the diagnostic criteria for specific psychotic disorders such as schizophrenia or when there is inadequate information to make a specific diagnosis.

What is the evidence for and against each of these diagnoses? Given how limited and unreliable the clinical data are, it is impossible to make a definitive diagnosis, but we can consider the possibilities as follows.

The American Psychiatric Association's *Diagnostic and Statistical Manual* suggests that the diagnosis of atypical psychosis, or "psychotic disorder not otherwise specified," should "be used for psychosis about which there is inadequate information to make a specific diagnosis."[4] This certainly fits the shamanic situation. Thus we could simply say that if a psychotic episode does occur during the initiation crisis, it can be considered an atypical psychosis.

However, the initial episode also appears to be consistent with brief reactive psychosis. The symptoms and behavior are compatible, and the episode is short-lived with good recovery. Either atypical psychosis or brief reactive psychosis might therefore be appropriate diagnoses.

However, it is schizophrenia that has been the most common diagnosis. In part this may reflect a lack of psychiatric sophistication among researchers. Nonpsychiatrists are often unaware of the many varieties of psychosis and may assume that all psychoses are schizophrenia. However, because of the brief duration of the initial illness and its successful outcome, schizophrenia seems to be the least likely diagnosis.

There are other data that argue against either a schizophrenic or schizophreniform diagnosis. To begin with, many shamans have seemed not at all schizophrenic to anthropologists. Likewise, native peoples often make sharp distinctions between shamanic crises and mental illness. Moreover, shamans often seem to end up not only psychologically healthy but exceptionally so. This is in marked contrast to schizophrenics, many of whom deteriorate progressively

over the years. Indeed, the exceptional psychological well-being of shamans also argues against most of the other diagnoses, such as epilepsy and hysteria. While some patients may spontaneously recover from any of these disorders, one would hardly expect them to end up as the most able members of society.

Shamans end up serving the community—indeed, this is one of their defining characteristics—while schizophrenics rarely make major contributions. Several researchers have pointed to a correlation between psychological health and service.[193] Healthy people tend to devote themselves more to aiding others, and this may be a further argument against seeing the shaman as psychologically distressed.

It would be very helpful in making definitive assessments of the health of shamans to have good psychological test data. Unfortunately there are almost none available. Much has been made of a Rorschach study of Apache Indians that found no evidence that shamans are severely neurotic or psychotic,[22] but this study was flawed in several ways and so the evidence it provides is weak.[44] At the present time psychological tests are therefore of little help in evaluating the shaman's personality or psychological health.

CHAPTER 8

Psychotic Emergency or Spiritual Emergence? Recent Views

Of external facts we have had enough and to spare, more than the squirrellike scholars will ever be able to piece together into a single whole, enough to keep the busy popularizers spouting in bright-eyed knowledgeability the rest of their days; but of the inner facts—of what goes on at the center where the forces of our fate first announce themselves—we are still pretty much in ignorance.

WILLIAM BARRETT

Despite decades of attempts to pigeonhole them, shamans simply do not slip neatly into traditional psychiatric diagnoses and categories. Their initiation crises can indeed be considered times of psychological crisis and sometimes perhaps even of brief psychosis. Yet their visionary journeys and altered states of consciousness are under control, helpful to others, and clearly distinguishable from the schizophrenic hallucinations with which they have so often been compared.

Much has been made of the initiation crisis, and it is important to remember that it occurs in only a small percentage of shamans. Perhaps what is most important is not the crisis itself but what comes out of it. For the shaman "is not only a sick man," said Eliade, "he is a sick man who has been cured, who has succeeded in curing himself."[41] From this perspective, "shamanism is not a disease but being healed from disease."[2]

In fact, shamans often end up as the most highly functional members of the community and, according to Eliade, "show proof of a more than normal nervous constitution."[41] They are commonly described as displaying remarkable energy and stamina, unusual levels of concentration, control of altered states of consciousness, high intelligence, leadership skills, and a grasp of complex data, myths, and rituals. So, although the symptoms and behavior of the shamanic initiation crises are unusual and even bizarre by both Western and tribal standards, shamans not only recover but may function exceptionally well as leaders and healers of their people.[41, 149, 153]

What can we make of this curious combination of initial disturbance and subsequent health? Mainstream psychiatry rarely recognizes the possibility of positive outcomes from psychosis; the diagnostic manual does not even mention it. We are left to ask whether there are any data and diagnoses that could encompass *both* the initial pathology and the subsequent recovery.

The answer is yes. Shamans are not the only people observed to be better off after a psychological disturbance than before it. Over 2000 years ago, Socrates declared that "our greatest blessings come to us by way of madness, provided the madness is given us by divine gift."[114] More recently the eminent psychiatrist Karl Menninger observed that "some patients have a mental illness and then they get weller! I mean they get better than they ever were. . . . This is an extraordinary and little realized truth."[114]

In our own time a surprisingly large number of mental-health professionals have made similar observations. I say surprising because the possibility is barely mentioned in traditional psychiatric texts. Yet a significant number of researchers, some quite eminent, have recognized that psychological disturbances, even including psychoses, may function as growth experiences that result in greater psychological or spiritual well-being. Examining these disturbances may therefore shed light on shamanic initiation crises.

The general process is one of temporary psychological disturbance followed by resolution and repair to a higher level of func-

tioning than before the initial crisis began. From this perspective what seemed at the time to be purely a crisis of disturbance and disease can later be reinterpreted as a stage of development and growth. These crises have been given many names, each of which illustrates a different perspective and piece of information about the process. For example, disturbances with positive growth outcomes have been described as "positive disintegration," "regenerative processes," "renewal," and "creative illness."[33, 43, 137]

Some crises and psychoses are specifically associated with mystical or transpersonal experiences. These have been described as "mystical experiences with psychotic features," "divine illnesses," "spiritual emergencies," and "transpersonal crises."[67, 107, 114]

Psychological Disturbance as Developmental Crisis

What these names and descriptions make clear is that a period of psychological disturbance may sometimes be part of, or at least be followed by, significant growth and development. Consequently some—but only some—psychological disturbances can now be seen as developmental crises rather than as merely pathological processes.

Developmental crises are periods of psychological stress and difficulty that can accompany life transitions and turning points. They may be marked by considerable psychological turmoil, sometimes even of life-threatening proportions. These transitions can occur spontaneously, as in the well-known cases of adolescent and mid-life crises, or may be induced by growth-accelerating techniques such as psychotherapy and meditation.

These crises occur because psychological growth rarely proceeds simply and smoothly to greater well-being, clarity, and maturity. Rather, growth is usually marked by transition periods of confusion and questioning or, in extreme cases, by periods of disorganization and despair. Thus the twin lions that guard the gates of Eastern temples are sometimes said to represent confusion and

paradox; the person who would have true wisdom must be willing to pass through both.

This is why it is said that for a person seeking true wisdom, clarity can become a trap. When we develop an understanding of ourselves and the world, we tend to hold on to it desperately. We cling to our old understanding because it saves us from having to face the ever-changing novelty and uncertainty of life. We cling to it not knowing that the world is a mystery and that, paradoxically, the sense of not knowing is a necessary prelude to the dawning of wisdom. For clarity "dispels fear, but also blinds," and the person who holds fast to it will no longer learn.[31]

If these crises are successfully negotiated, then the disorganization and turmoil may turn out to be the means by which constricting, outdated life patterns are cast off. Old beliefs, goals, identity, and lifestyle may be reassessed and released and new, more life-affirming modes adopted. It seems, therefore, that psychological pain and confusion can be symptoms of psychological disease and decline on the one hand or of developmental transitions and growth on the other.

These crises can be precipitated by stress or spurred by psychological or spiritual practices. They can also occur spontaneously, expressing inner forces that compel development whether the individual wants it or not. These developmental forces have been described by such terms as individuation, self-actualization, and transcendence. Their result is a dynamic tension between the forces of growth and the seductiveness of the familiar, between the pull of transcendence and the inertia of routine. As John Perry, a Jungian psychiatrist, observed:

> Spirit [is] constantly striving for release from its entrapment in routine or conventional mental structures. Spiritual work is the attempt to liberate this dynamic energy, which must break free of its suffocation in old forms. . . .
>
> During a person's developmental process, if this work of releasing spirit becomes imperative but is not undertaken voluntarily

> with knowledge of the goal and with considerable effort, then the psyche is apt to take over and overwhelm the conscious personality. . . . The individuating psyche abhors stasis as nature abhors a vacuum.[137]

In other words, rather than tolerate stagnation, the psyche may actually create crises that force development. Such can certainly be the case with shamans. Many are not the least bit pleased by the prospect of their new profession and resist the initial signs and symptoms with all their might. However, resistance is no easy matter, and many tribal myths hold that the person who resists the call will sicken, go mad, or die.

When the forces of growth overwhelm the forces of inertia, a developmental transition or crisis occurs. The symptoms of this crisis may vary depending upon the individual's personality and maturity. They may range from primitive pathology at one extreme to transpersonal or spiritual concerns at the other.[204] In the latter case the crisis has come to be known as a transpersonal crisis, spiritual emergency, or spiritual emergence.[66, 67, 70] It is these that seem closest to, and most helpful in understanding, the shamanic initiation crisis.

The study of transpersonal crises is still in its infancy. Although they have been described for centuries as complications of spiritual practices, careful examination and systematic treatment have only just begun. The following classification is therefore preliminary and will presumably be refined in the years to come. In the meantime it gives us a way of separating out different types of spiritual emergency and of throwing light on different forms that shamanic initiation crises may take.

Forms of Spiritual Emergency

The following are currently recognized forms of spiritual emergency most relevant to shamanism and its initiation crises: mystical

experiences with psychotic features; shamanic journeys; possession; renewal; kundalini; and psychic opening.

Mystical experiences with psychotic features are usually short-lived episodes that have a better prognosis than other psychoses.[114] This combination of mystical and psychotic experiences seems consistent with the bizarre behavior yet mystically meaningful experiences of some shamanic crises.

Spiritual emergencies of the *shamanic journey* type are emergencies whose symptoms echo themes commonly encountered in both shamanic initiations and journeys. As Stanislav and Christina Grof observe:

> Transpersonal crises of this type bear a deep resemblance to what the anthropologists have described as the shamanic or initiatory illness. . . . In the experiences of individuals whose transpersonal crises have strong shamanic features, there is great emphasis on physical suffering and encounter with death followed by rebirth and elements of ascent or magical flight. They also typically sense a special connection with the elements of nature and experience communication with animals or animal spirits. It is also not unusual to feel an upsurge of extraordinary powers and impulses to heal. . . . Like the initiatory crisis, the transpersonal episodes of a shamanic type, if properly supported, can lead to good adjustment and superior functioning.[66]

The similarity of these experiences—death-rebirth, magical flight, animal spirits, impulses to heal—to classic shamanic experiences is striking. Thus it seems that shamanic initiatory crises may reflect a deep psychological process, not limited to particular cultures or times. This process seems capable of exploding from the depths of the psyche in contemporary Westerners surrounded by cars and computers as well as in ancient shamans in tepees and igloos. Clearly some deep, perhaps archetypal, pattern is being played out here. The Grofs therefore conclude that "individuals whose spiritual crises follow this pattern are thus involved in an

ancient process that touches the deepest foundations of the psyche."[66] Therefore we may have much to learn from ancient shamanic wisdom about the appropriate handling of these crises.

Experiences of *possession* have been described throughout history and may be a major feature of the shamanic crisis. Today they may occur either spontaneously or in religious or psychotherapeutic settings. The experiences battling with or being overwhelmed by rage and hatred can be of hideous intensity. So powerful, repugnant, and alien do these emotions feel that they seem literally demonic, and the victim may fear he is engaged in a desperate battle for his very life and sanity. These experiences are so dramatic that even some psychiatrists have been led to the same conclusions.[135] Others adopt a more psychological perspective and assume that the possession is an expression of powerful archetypal patterns that can be treated therapeutically. Indeed, the Grofs claim that "with good support, experiences of this kind can be extremely liberating and therapeutic."[66]

Psychiatrist John Perry has described the *renewal process* as an experience of profound, all-encompassing destruction followed by regeneration. Individuals going through this process are overwhelmed by images in which they see both themselves and the world being destroyed. Yet this destruction is not the end but rather is a prelude to rebirth and regeneration. Out of the images of ruin comes an experience of personal renewal and rebirth and of the regeneration of the world. Images of death and rebirth are of course common in the shamanic crisis.

The renewal process may entail considerable stress and conflict; it may even reach psychotic proportions. Psychiatrists do not usually distinguish this particular process from other psychoses and usually suppress all of them with drugs. However, Perry claims that

> if a person undergoing this turmoil is given love, understanding and encouragement, the spiritual crisis soon resolves itself without the need for interruption by suppressive medication. The most frag-

> mented "thought disorder" can become quite coherent and orderly within a short time if someone is present to respond to it with compassion. Such a relationship is far better than a tranquilizer in most instances.[137]

The fundamental change in this "renewal process" is said to be a dissolution of the old, outdated self-image and its renewal, rebirth, and replacement with a new, more appropriate image. As such this renewal process is thought to be a cycle of potentially beneficial growth.

The awakening of *kundalini* is a process that has been most fully described in India, although important parallels exist in many cultures and religious groups. According to Indian tradition, kundalini is the creative energy of the universe. Humans partake of this energy but it usually lies dormant and unrecognized. However, under the prodding of spiritual practice, and occasionally spontaneously, the kundalini may be aroused and unleash enormous, even overwhelming, physical and psychological energy. The result is a rich array of intense physical, psychological, and spiritual experiences that may be ecstatic or frightening. These can manifest physically as tremors, spasms, and shaking or psychologically as (for example) intense emotions, agitation, heat, energy, pain, bright lights, and vivid imagery. These examples are but a small sample of a wide range of possible physical, psychological, and spiritual symptoms that, if not correctly diagnosed, would be regarded as unrelated psychological disorders. Kundalini crises are beginning to occur more often in the West as more and more people begin intensive meditative and yogic practices. Kundalini might possibly account for the unusual symptoms and intense agitation of some shamanic crises.

Psychic opening, the last type of spiritual emergency, is probably the most difficult for those of us reared in the Western scientific culture to accept. In this experience, individuals feel they have suddenly become susceptible, sometimes quite against their will, to

one or more psychic abilities. These may include out-of-body experiences, visions, and mediumship or channeling—all experiences that are common among shamans. Setting aside for a moment the question of the validity of these experiences, it is clear that people can experience significant difficulty as a result of them. They may feel overwhelmed by a flood of unusual experiences and fear that they are losing their sanity.

These, then, are some forms of spiritual emergence most relevant to shamanic initiation crises. Given our limited knowledge, there seems no reason to assume that there is only one type of shamanic crisis. In the future it may be possible to map the various types according to this classification.

Reductionist and "Elevationistic" Error

There are two opposite types of diagnostic error that can be made here. One is reductionistic: to fail to recognize a spiritual emergency and instead view it as purely pathological. The other is "elevationistic": to mistake a pathological process such as schizophrenia for a primarily spiritual emergency.

These divergent diagnoses reflect divergent attitudes toward religious experiences. At one extreme are those people for whom all religious and mystical experiences are nothing but self-deception at best. At the other extreme are those who elevate all psychopathology to larger-than-life forms of growth and healing. This is the attitude that views all psychoses as growth processes and mental illness as a myth even though it fills almost half the hospital beds in the country.

Although the topic remains controversial, there is considerable evidence that *both* pathological and religious-mystical experiences exist and that neither can be wholly reduced to, or explained in terms of, the other. To confuse the two is to fall into what Ken Wilber has eloquently called "the pre-trans fallacy."[202] This is the

fallacy in which pathological regressions to preegoic stages of development are confused with progressions to transegoic levels, in which the preegoic repressions of schizophrenics are confused with the transegoic realizations of saints.

This is not to say that distinguishing these two types of experience is always easy. The precise criteria for doing so are only now being developed and the task is complicated by the existence of hybrid forms in which both mystical and pathological experiences coexist.[114] Clearly, spiritual practices and awakenings (to use religious terms), or transpersonal techniques and states of consciousness (to use psychological terms), may revive and exacerbate unresolved conflicts. This is not necessarily bad, since the process can bring to the surface issues and difficulties requiring attention and healing. The result may be a healing of specific conflicts and better personality integration.[67]

Treatment of Spiritual Emergencies

It seems that if these spiritual emergencies are recognized and treated appropriately, they may sometimes prove to be valuable growth experiences; hence their other name of "spiritual emergence." However, if they are suppressed by traditional—especially pharmacological—treatments, the growth process may be aborted.

Several factors have been found to be helpful in treating spiritual emergencies. The first is a trusting relationship in which the patient feels cared for and safe. The second is a positive attitude in which the patient expects that the process will prove valuable and may ultimately be transforming and healing. Such attitudes in patients favor good therapeutic outcomes.[119] Openly expressing the emerging experiences can be helpful and can be facilitated by a variety of psychotherapeutic techniques.[70]

It can now be seen how the shamanic crisis fits into this scheme. The crisis contains symptoms and behaviors that appear

bizarre and even pathological. However, the outcome may be positive when the shaman-to-be is recognized as such by the tribe and receives culturally appropriate support, guidance, and "therapy." This support includes a relationship with an experienced shaman, a positive reinterpretation of the disturbance as part of a shamanic awakening, and shamanic practices that enable the novice to work with the emerging experiences. With this assistance the shaman may not only recover from the initiation crisis but may emerge strengthened, matured, and enabled to help others. In short, for centuries shamanic cultures have provided the types of support that contemporary psychologists are now finding helpful for spiritual emergencies.

Since developmental crises tend to bring unresolved conflicts to the surface, it follows that shamanic initiation crises may be a mix of progressive and regressive forces, signs of growth and symptoms of pathology, and a comprehensive account will recognize both. However, at the very least it no longer seems appropriate to dismiss shamans and their initiation crises as invariably and purely pathological. Something much richer, more complex, and more beneficial seems to be going on and deserves open-minded respect and research.

It appears that spiritual emergencies may be newly recognized forms of perennial developmental crises. This developmental perspective allows us to view both shamanic crises and contemporary spiritual emergencies as related and difficult but potentially valuable maturation crises. This perspective also helps us to recognize the psychological disturbance as well as the potential for growth. As such it denies neither the pain nor the potential development and even transcendence latent within it.

This developmental perspective also throws new light on appropriate treatment. On the one hand it calls into question that traditional psychiatric strategy of routinely using drugs to suppress spiritual emergencies. On the other hand it suggests supportive in-depth psychotherapeutic work for these patients and traditional

shamanic healing approaches for shamanic crises. Awareness of the existence of these spiritual emergencies may help us to identify and treat them appropriately. This awareness may also help us appreciate the healing wisdom embodied in the shamanic tradition and its practitioners.

CHAPTER 9

Shamanic Trickery

Truth is so very precious, man is naturally economical in its use.

MARK TWAIN

To add insult to injury, shamans have not only been diagnosed as psychologically disturbed but have also been dismissed as charlatans. However, whereas the evidence for psychological disturbance is debatable, the evidence for deceit and trickery is clear.

Since the reputation of shamans rests largely on their ability to display supernatural powers, it is not surprising that they may be tempted to lend the supernatural a helping hand. This they may do in many ways. For example, they may bribe spies to provide personal information about patients, which can be later revealed with appropriate dramatic flourish. The spies may also assess the patient's health in order to help the shaman determine whether to take on the case. This is no small decision, since if the patient should die, the shaman may lose his reputation—and in some tribes his life.[153]

TRICKS OF THE SHAMAN'S TRADE

Shamans are not averse to using tricks to add a little dramatic flair to their treatments. When sucking spirit intrusions from a patient's body, a shaman may dramatically spit out an object (such as a worm or a bloody tuft of hair) that he had previously hidden in his mouth. Likewise, the Eskimo shamans of St. Lawrence Island in Alaska may pretend to crush a stone to sand and then re-form it

back into a stone.[195] Long observation of Eskimo shamans led the anthropologist Bogoras to conclude:

> There can be no doubt, of course, that shamans, during their performances, employ deceit in various forms, and that they themselves are fully cognizant of the fact. "There are many liars in our calling," Scratching Woman said to me. . . .
>
> Of course, he was ready to swear that he never made use of any of these wrong practices. "Look at my face," he continued; "he who tells lies his tongue stutters. He whose speech, however, flows offhand from his lips, certainly must speak the truth." This was a rather doubtful argument, but I refrained from making any such suggestions.[19]

Shamans may also pretend to do physical battle to vanquish evil spirits. Rasmussen observed such a case and reported it as follows:

> During our stay at South Hampton Island I was witness to such a case, where a Shaman named Saraq went out to fight against evil spirits, but I discovered that he had taken some Caribou blood with him beforehand and rubbed himself with this without being discovered by anyone else. When he came in, he stated that the shaman who had been out with him had been unable to hold the evil spirit, but he, Saraq, had grasped it and stabbed it, inflicting a deep wound. It had then made its escape, but the wound was so deep that he could not conceive of the possibility of it surviving. All believed his report, all believed that he had driven the evil spirit which had been troubling the village, and no one was afraid any longer.[147]

Acquiring such tricks may be part of the shaman's training. For example, in the course of his training a Kwakiutl shaman from the Vancouver area of Canada learns

> a curious mixture of pantomime, prestidigitation, and empirical knowledge including the art of simulating fainting and nervous fits,

> the learning of sacred songs, the technique for inducing vomiting, rather precise notions of auscultation and obstetrics, and the use of "dreamers," that is, spies who listen to private conversations and secretly convey to the shaman bits of information concerning origins and symptoms of the ills suffered by different people. Above all, he learned the *ars magna* of one of the shamanistic schools of the Northwest Coast: the shaman hides a tuft of down in a little corner of his mouth, and he throws it up, covered with blood, at the appropriate moment—after having bitten his tongue or made his gums bleed—and solemnly presents it to his patients and the onlookers as the pathological foreign body extracted as a result of his sucking and manipulations.[109]

These are harmless tricks that might even be helpful inasmuch as they bolster faith in the shaman's therapeutic abilities and inspire a strong placebo response. However, not all shamanic trickery is so benign. Some shamans have been reported to give toxins or psychedelics to their patients in order to make the disease and its cure all the more dramatic.[153] A Jivaro shaman may bewitch disliked neighbors and then refer them to his shaman partner for treatment.[74] Shamans may even attempt to kill. Rasmussen reports:

> If now a shaman desires to injure a person by magic, someone whom he does not like and of whom he has grown envious, he will first endeavor to obtain some object belonging to the person concerned; this he takes and speaks ill over it and keeps on speaking ill over it hoping thus to pass on the evil to the person he desires to hurt and should he discover a powerful destructive force, which may lie concealed in a grave, then he must rub the object he is speaking ill over into the grave. This may give rise to sickness, madness or enmity ending in homicide.[147]

Small wonder, then, that shamans have been ambivalent figures, revered and sought for their healing abilities while feared and hated for their harmful powers.

It is clear that shamans may engage in all manners of trickery. Five major questions arise from this:

1. Do all shamans engage in trickery and deceit?
2. Is part of the trickery done not purely for the shaman's benefit but for the benefit of the patient and tribe? In other words, is some of the trickery a kind of pious fraud?
3. Are shamanism and shamanic practices *entirely* ineffective and fraudulent, as some people have claimed, or are some of the practices valuable and effective in their own right?
4. Do shamans use more trickery than other healers and professionals?
5. Do shamans deceive themselves?

Let us examine each of these in turn, beginning with the question of whether all shamans engage in trickery and deceit. The answer is that we don't know. Clearly trickery is widespread, but many anthropologists have been impressed by the sincerity of shamans and their desire to help. There is also the question of whether trickery should be regarded as fraudulent when the shaman believes that using it may help the patient.

Expectations of Healing

This raises the question of how much shamanic trickery may be useful to patients and used by the shaman for benevolent motives. One of today's major research discoveries is the extent to which nonspecific factors such as faith in the physician may exert a powerful healing or placebo effect. The environment, the physician's status, and the rituals involved in giving and taking medicine can be almost as important as the drug itself. Today's psychiatrists who prescribe drugs to reduce depression or anxiety are well aware

that they had better exude confidence if the drug is to have maximum effect, for the expectations of both patient and therapist tend to become self-fulfilling prophecies.

Sharp observers that they are, shamans may have reached the same conclusions. They may therefore choose to radiate confidence to remove their patients' doubts and perhaps also their own. Rasmussen, for example, describes a shaman who stated that "I believe I am a better shaman than others among my countrymen. I will venture to say that I hardly ever make a mistake in the things I investigate and what I predict. And I therefore consider myself a more perfect, a more fully-trained shaman than those of my countrymen who often make mistakes."[147]

The shaman's tricks and abundant self-confidence may therefore increase patients' expectations, and therefore likelihood, of being cured:

> Plainly, the shaman's tricks serve as a symbol of his healing power. They impress the audience with his magical skill and knowledge, and provide a concrete visible representation in the form of a worm, or bloody down of the patient's illness. In that the tricks reinforce the belief of the patient and the community in the shaman's power, they add tremendously to the force of his suggestion and the patient's expectant faith in the healing process.
>
> We need have no doubt that the healing rituals, relying heavily as they may do on the power of suggestion, are effective. Their value in aiding the recovery of emotional and physical illnesses has been repeatedly observed and amply recorded.[195]

It is therefore possible that shamans may use some of their tricks quite consciously to increase their therapeutic impact. A special case of this occurs when shamans regard their activities from an altered state of consciousness. For example, a shaman may pull out a worm he has hidden in his mouth and announce that it is the patient's illness. An outsider would, understandably enough, probably regard the shaman as an outright charlatan. The shaman in an altered state, however, may have a very different view of the

procedure. In his visionary state he may see the illness sucked into the object in his mouth so that this object has now, at least from his perspective, both ordinary and supernatural aspects to it. As Michael Harner explains:

> He then "vomits" out this object and displays it to the patient and his family saying "now I have sucked it out. Here it is." The non-shamans think that the material object itself is what has been sucked out and the shaman does not disillusion them. At the same time, he is not lying because he knows that the only important thing about the tsentsak (spiritual force or helper) is its supernatural aspect, or essence, which he sincerely believes he has removed from the patient's body. To explain to the layman that he already had these objects in his mouth would serve no fruitful purpose and would prevent him from displaying such an object as proof that he had affected the cure.[78]

So, from the shamans' perspective, some of the "tricks" they use are regarded as essential parts of the healing process, done primarily for the benefit of the patient.

Beyond Trickery

The question arises whether trickery and deceit are all there is to shamanism. Some people have certainly thought so and have dismissed shamans as nothing more than tricksters and outright charlatans. Of course there may be some who fit this picture, but several lines of evidence suggest that shamanism can't be dismissed as only trickery.

First there is the enormous durability of the tradition. Shamanism has survived in various forms for millennia and it is hard, though not impossible, to imagine that a tradition would have survived for so long in so many cultures unless there were some genuine and effective components to it. When we remember that

Western scientifically based medicine has a history of only a century or so and psychotherapy even less than this, then the durability of shamanism becomes all the more impressive.

A number of anthropologists have been impressed by the apparent sincerity of many shamans, and some of their psychological and pharmacological techniques make good sense from a Western scientific perspective. Indeed some of the techniques such as the shamanic journey have proved to be powerful tools for Westerners as well as native shamans.

Finally, it should be noted that shamanism presents a coherent world view that explains the cause and cure of illness. Within this world view the shaman's practices seem logical and appropriate to both the shaman and the patient. This is important since a shared world view and understanding of the cause and cure of illness held by both patient and therapist may provide a healing myth and curative context that foster the placebo effect and healing. What may be most important is not that the healing myth be true, but that it be plausible to both patient and therapist.[50]

Do shamans deceive any more than other healers or other professionals? Certainly the desire to impress others is universal and few of us could claim that we never use dubious means to bolster our personal and professional image. "There is hardly a legitimate everyday vocation or relationship whose performers do not engage in concealed practices which are incompatible with fostered impressions."[60] Nor is the shaman alone in using placebo effects both consciously and unconsciously. It has been said that "the history of (Western) medical treatment for the most part until relatively recently is the history of the placebo effect."[162] A considerable amount of the effectiveness of current psychotherapy may be due, not to the cherished theories and techniques of the therapist, but to her caring, empathy, and authenticity and the warmth of the relationship. Some have claimed that in this regard shamanism and psychotherapy have much in common[195]—a claim that is disputed, of course, by many psychotherapists.

Self-Deception and Healing

Shamans and psychotherapists may both deceive themselves. Both may mistakenly believe that their cures are due to specific techniques such as unearthing and interpreting childhood traumas in psychotheraphy, or extracting and battling spirits in shamanism. However, in point of fact much of their effectiveness and healing power may stem simply from the warmth and support of a caring relationship.[209]

Both shamans and therapists must confront the fact that their techniques are by no means as powerful and universally effective as they would like. Both are repeatedly confronted by distressingly large numbers of patients and illnesses that they cannot help, and both may sometimes lose faith in the effectiveness of their craft.

Yet shamans, like therapists of all kinds, are motivated to maintain faith in their trade by powerful social and psychological forces. After all, they have invested significant amounts of time and money in their training, and their income and status depend on it. Faced with this unpleasant conflict, both shamans and psychotherapists may resort, consciously or unconsciously, to self-deception to bolster their faith in their own effectiveness.[195] These self-deceptions may include a variety of psychological defense mechanisms such as rationalization, repression, and selective memory. With the help of rationalization, the failure to cure may be explained away by attributing it to such difficulties as the patient's resistance or the spirits' malevolence. Repression and selective memory may enable shamans and therapists to forget their failures while recalling with vivid clarity their cures, or at least the legitimate reasons why they were unable to cure.

These defenses are likely to be supported by the needs and demands of the patients and society. People anxious for help are likely to project healing ability onto the healer in a desperate attempt to believe they can be cured. "It is difficult for a healer to doubt his own worth if he is constantly assured of it by his patients,

their relatives and the whole community. If the social consensus is that someone has the power to heal, then he is a healer."[195]

In summary, it appears that shamans may use liberal trickery and deceit but that they are hardly unique in this. Conscious and unconscious bolstering of one's professional image seems to be part of human nature and to occur in most professions. Moreover, shamans may personally believe in some of the techniques that seem like outright trickery to outsiders, and it is possible that shamans may deceive themselves almost as much as they do their patients. In addition, the shaman's trickery may not be entirely self-serving. Patients who believe they can be healed, even when that belief has been fostered by a healer's deceit, may be more likely to recover than those who do not believe. As Henry Ford said, "Those who believe they can do something and those who believe they can't are both right." While it is clear that shamans may indulge generously in trickery, it is also clear that shamanism cannot be dismissed as only trickery.

PART III

The Shaman's Universe

C H A P T E R 1 0

Many Worlds and Many Spirits

We do not see things the way they are but as we are.

JEWISH PROVERB

In order to understand shamans' experiences we need to understand their universe. What is the nature of this cosmos that shamans believe they can penetrate, explore, and even overpower? What, in short, is their cosmology? Fortunately, a general outline will serve our purposes; we need not go into the many details and cultural variations that Eliade has described so meticulously.

MANY WORLDS

The shaman's universe is three-tiered, comprising an upper, middle, and lower world. The upper and lower worlds may themselves be multilayered. What makes shamans "cosmic travelers" is their experience of being able to traverse these multiple worlds and levels. As Eliade points out:

> The pre-eminently shamanic technique is the passage from one cosmic region to another—from earth to the sky or from earth to the underworld. The shaman knows the mystery of the breakthrough in plane. This communication among the cosmic zones is made possible by the very structure of the universe.[41]

"The very structure of the universe" to which Eliade refers is its interconnectedness. The three worlds and many levels are believed to be linked by a central axis, the *axis mundi,* or world axis. Eliade points out that this axis is described in diverse myths in which

> the essential schema is always to be seen, even after the numerous influences to which it has been subjected; there are three great cosmic regions, which can be successively traversed because they are linked together by a central axis. This axis, of course, passes through an "opening," a "hole"; it is through this hole that the gods descend to earth and the dead to the subterranean regions; it is through the same hole that the soul of the shaman in ecstasy can fly up or down in the course of his celestial or infernal journeys.[41]

The central axis takes three main forms, all of them common to diverse cultures and myths, both shamanic and nonshamanic. The first is the "cosmic mountain" at the center of the earth. The second is the "world pillar" that may hold up the sky. The third is the highly symbolic "world tree," symbol of life, fertility, and sacred regeneration, which the shaman climbs to other worlds. Whatever form it takes, the world axis is the cosmological symbol of the connection between worlds—a connection that the shaman, alone among humans, is able to traverse.

But the shaman's worlds and levels are more than interconnected; they are believed to interact with one another. Shamans believe that these interactions can be perceived and affected by one who knows how to do so and that the shaman, like a spider at the center of a cosmic web, can feel and influence distant realms. The shaman was thus a forerunner of later Chinese sages who claimed that "Heaven, Earth and the ten thousand things form one body."

All parts of this interconnected universe are usually regarded as alive and conscious to some degree. In contemporary philosophical language these would be the doctrines of hylozoism and ani-

mism. *Hylozoism* is the belief that all objects are imbued with life. *Animism* is the belief of tribal people that every object is invested with a mind or soul. When this same belief is held by Westerners, it is called *panpsychism*. Needless to say, the doctrine of panpsychism is most unfashionable in these materialistic times. Historically, however, it has had some notable Western supporters, including first-rank philosophers such as Leibniz, Schopenhauer, and Whitehead.

As metaphysicians, shamans tend to be realists. That is, where Westerners might regard the upper and lower worlds the shamans traverse as mental constructions, the shamans regard them as independently existing realms. Michael Harner points out that for the shaman, "the mind is being used to gain access, to pass through a door into another reality which exists independently of that mind."[76] This is another example of the literal, objective, and realist interpretation of experience so characteristic of the shamanic world view.

For the shamans' tribespeople this multilayered cosmos is a belief, a myth, and an article of faith. For the shamans it is a direct experience. They alone traverse these layers and turn a cosmology into a personal road map. They alone, says Eliade, transform

> a cosmotheological concept into a *concrete mystical experience*. This point is important. It explains the difference between, for example, the religious life of a North Asian people and the religious experience of its shamans; the latter is a *personal and ecstatic experience*.[41]

Since the shamans alone experience the realms described in tribal myth and cosmology, the question arises as to whether their journeys and descriptions also shaped these myths and cosmology. To put the question more generally, and to make it a very important one, to what extent do spiritual practitioners *create* their tradition's cosmology from their experience and to what extent is their

experience *created by,* or at least molded by, their cosmology? To what extent do religious practice and experience create beliefs and to what extent do beliefs create religious experience? Which is chicken and which is egg, or are they mutually interdependent?

Eliade argues that cosmology determines shamanic experience. While he acknowledges that a number of epic stories may have been fostered by accounts of shamanic journeys, he denies the impact of these journeys on cosmology. "The shamans did not create the cosmology, the mythology, and the theology of their respective tribes; they only interiorized it, 'experienced' it, and used it as the itinerary for their ecstatic journeys."[41]

On the other hand, Michael Harner notes that what defines shamanism are its techniques and that the experiences these techniques elicit allow practitioners to reach their own conclusions and cosmology.

> Shamanism ultimately is only a method, not a religion with a fixed set of dogmas. Therefore people arrive at their own experience-derived conclusions about what is going on in the universe, and about what term, if any, is most useful to describe ultimate reality.[76]

This suggests that personal shamanic experiences can shape personal beliefs and therefore possibly also cultural ones. However, it is obvious that shamans must bring some prior beliefs and cosmology to their practice. Why would a shaman learn to journey to the upper world if she did not already believe there was one? There are wide cultural variations in myths, and shamans tend to have experiences consistent with the myths of their culture. This is similar to the way in which psychotherapy patients tend to have experiences and dreams consistent with the beliefs of their therapists. Thus it seems that in the short term shamanic experience is definitely shaped by cultural cosmology. Perhaps in the long run the reverse also occurs and shamanic experience shapes the image of the cosmos.

Many Spirits

The shaman's universe is filled with life, awareness, and spirits. These spirits—ever-present, powerful, and potentially malevolent—exert an enormous influence on tribal cultures. Whatever happens, good or bad, fortunate or unfortunate, success or failure, is likely to be attributed to the spirits.

Yet ordinary people are largely helpless victims of these spirits. They have little control over them save to blindly follow the taboos handed down across generations, to pray, to sacrifice, or to ask the shaman to intercede on their behalf. It is the shaman alone who can control spirits. Indeed, for many anthropologists this control is one of the shaman's defining characteristics.

In order to control the spirits, the shaman must first learn to see them. Therefore, before we examine the nature of these spirits it will be valuable for us to examine the ways in which the shaman learns how to perceive them.

Spirit Vision

Since the spirits are usually invisible to the untutored eye, a major part of shamanic training involves acquiring the power of "spirit vision" by which they can be recognized. This explains, says Eliade, "the extreme importance of 'spirit visions' in all varieties of shamanic initiations."[41]

Given the importance of this spirit vision, it is not surprising that considerable effort may be invested in acquiring it. We have already discussed diverse aspects of shamanic training, many of which may foster spirit vision. A variety of specific techniques may be used, some of which are extrémely demanding. For example, the Jivaro Indian initiate of South America may spend days fasting and ingesting drugs until finally a spirit is seen. In another tribe the instructor rubs herbs on the eyes of the apprentice; then:

> For three days and nights the two men sit opposite each other, singing and ringing their bells. Until the eyes of the boy are clear, neither of the two men obtains any sleep. At the end of the three days the two again go to the woods and obtain more herbs. . . . If at the end of seven days the boy sees the wood-spirits, the ceremony is at an end. Otherwise the entire seven day ceremony must be repeated.[110]

The spirits are usually sought under specific conditions such as reduced lighting and altered states of consciousness, conditions that enhance awareness of visual imagery. Trance and drug states can intensify images, and darkness enhances sensitivity to them.

What are we to make of the shamans' training and development of spirit vision? One psychological explanation might be that the shaman learns to organize and interpret the flux of visual images seen during trances. Even in an ordinary state an almost continuous flux of images can be seen when the eyes are closed. In altered states these images can become clearer, more meaningful, and more archetypal.

Shamans may be particularly likely to organize this flux into spirits and other images consistent with their expectations. A study of Zinacanteco natives of Mexico showed a number of perceptual differences between shamans and nonshamans.[166] In this study the experimenter showed a series of blurred, out-of-focus photographs and asked the natives what they saw. Shamans were much less likely than nonshamans to say "I don't know" even when the photographs were blurred to the point of being completely unrecognizable. Moreover, when the experimenter offered suggestions as to what the image might be, shamans were more likely than nonshamans to ignore the suggestions and to give their own personal interpretation.

These findings suggest that shamans may be especially able to create meaningful patterns from unclear data—that is, they tend to organize ambiguous experiences into coherent meaningful images.

These images are particularly likely to reflect the shamans' own personal categories. This suggests that shamans may be particularly adept at finding what they expect to see. Consequently they may be especially skilled at finding spirits amidst the many images they encounter during their seances. Of course it remains for future research to confirm these findings and to see whether they hold true for shamans in other parts of the world.

Psychologist Richard Noll has suggested that shamans may also be intense fantasizers.[132] Studies of excellent hypnotic subjects suggest that some 4 percent of the general population may be so-called "fantasy-prone" personalities. These are people who "fantasize a large part of the time, who typically 'see,' 'hear,' 'smell,' 'touch,' and fully experience what they fantasize."[205]

Perhaps some shamans are "fantasy-prone" personalities who are able to organize and learn from their intense images in ways that are both personally and socially beneficial. They may be particularly adept at creating and recognizing images of spirits. This is not to say that this can account for all experiences of spirits or that spirits are necessarily only visual images. We will discuss this tricky question of the nature of spirits shortly. But whatever the nature of spirits, shamans clearly exemplify the words of the great sixteenth-century physician Paracelsus: "Everyone may educate and regulate his imagination so as to come thereby into contact with spirits, and be taught by them."[133]

The novice's task of learning to see the spirits involves two stages. The first is simply to catch an initial glimpse of them. The second is to deepen and stabilize this glimpse into a permanent visionary capacity in which the spirits can be summoned and seen at will. As Eliade says of the initial training, "All this long and tiring ceremony has as its object transforming the apprentice magician's initial and momentary and ecstatic experience . . . into a permanent condition—that in which it is possible to see the spirits."[41]

This shamanic task is but a specific example of a challenge that faces mystics of all traditions. All of them, after their initial

penetration into transcendental realms, must further develop and stabilize this ability. They must learn, as Huston Smith so eloquently stated, to transform flashes of illumination into abiding light.[175] In less poetic but more psychological terms we might say that their task is to transform a peak experience into a plateau experience, or a transitory altered *state* of consciousness into an enduring altered *trait* of consciousness.

Even this altered trait is not the highest goal for some traditions. For beyond the capacity to enter transcendent states at will lies a condition in which transcendental awareness permeates the ordinary waking state. This is the *sahaj samadhi* of yoga, the "eyes-open samadhi" of Zen, or the Christian mystic's state of deification.[62] This phenomenon is interesting, both in showing the evolution and higher reaches of spiritual training, and in pointing to a similar skill in shamanism. There is no evidence that shamans practice these samadhis. However, there are suggestions that mature shamans may eventually develop in their ordinary state abilities—such as spirit vision—that initially they could perform only in altered states.[7]

Types of Spirits

The types of spirits that the shaman may see and summon are many—animal and human, lesser and greater, within and beyond the shaman's power to control. As Eliade points out, the shaman is "a man who has immediate concrete experiences with gods and spirits; he sees them face to face, he talks to them, prays to them, implores them—but he does not 'control' more than a limited number of them."[41]

Those he controls are his helping spirits. Many of these are seen as animals, sometimes called power animals. According to Eliade, "They can appear in the form of bears, wolves, stags, hares, all kinds of birds,"[41] and numerous other forms as well.

Remarkably similar encounters can occur during psychotherapy. A number of therapists use guided visualization techniques to evoke images of "power animals" or "spirit guides" and then encourage the client to interact with and learn from these guides. As visualization therapies become more popular, such experiences are becoming more common, and a number of therapists have reported that they can be very helpful.[56]

Encounters with "spirit guides" also occur spontaneously in psychedelic therapy. According to Stanislav Grof, they can be "most valuable and rewarding phenomena."[69] It is remarkable how often ancient shamanic experiences are echoed in contemporary psychedelic ones. This suggests that shamans have long accessed and mined deep archetypal realms of the psyche that remain hidden to most people.

Functions of Spirits

Whatever their form, the spirits may assist the shaman in any of four ways: with journeys, by providing strengths and abilities, by teaching, and by possessing the shaman.

The spirits may travel with the shaman on ecstatic journeys, accompanying or even carrying her to the sky. They may defend her from threats and battle on her behalf. Their strength may become hers if she voluntarily merges with them and thereby partakes of their powers and capacities. She may see herself turned into an eagle and soar into the sky or become a tiger and feel infused with its power. After returning from the journey she may perform her "power animal dance," moving and sounding like the animal, as a way of experiencing and maintaining its presence.

The following example of finding a power animal was reported by a participant in a shamanic workshop. It demonstrates both the experiential power of these encounters and the fact that they are accessible to contemporary Westerners.

> This was a journey to the lower world to meet and request assistance from power animals. I began my journey by entering a cave in Hawaii and went down a tunnel until I reached the lower world which first appeared as a small green globe. On landing I found myself in a lush green jungle filled with animals.
>
> I was immediately drawn to a lion. I appealed to him to be with me during the workshop and to let me share his powers, his strength, suppleness, keen sensitivity and agility.
>
> I then asked him what I needed to know or do. Immediately the lion leaped at and into me and merged with me so that my shamanic body was human/lion and I felt its power. This sense of power was very helpful since it seemed to counteract a sense of contraction connected with feelings of fear and guilt that I had been experiencing.
>
> At the end of the journey I returned up the tunnel into the cave and then back into the workshop room. Yet there was a clear sense that the lion returned with me. I was left feeling healed, empowered and strengthened.

What are we to make of these reports of merging with power animals? Psychologically the process makes good sense and has been widely used in both East and West, in ancient religions and modern psychology. A number of psychological mechanisms might be involved. These include permission giving (being given permission to feel powerful, effective, and so on), "acting as if" (one had a particular desired quality), role playing, belief, and identification. Whatever the mechanism, it is clear that visualizing oneself merging with a powerful benevolent figure can be surprisingly empowering. Therapists report good success with this technique.[45, 187]

Perhaps the most dramatic example among religious traditions is the so-called "deity yoga" of Tibetan Buddhism. Here the yogi visualizes himself first creating and then merging with a godlike figure who embodies virtue upon virtue: unconditional love, boundless compassion, profound wisdom, and more. After merging, just like the shaman and her power animal dance, the

yogi attempts to move, speak, and act as the deity. In other words, after merging with their allies, both shaman and yogi attempt to embody, experience, and express their allies' qualities. The difference is that for the shaman the power animal ally is regarded as real, whereas for the yogi the deity is ultimately regarded as a mental creation and projection. The potential power of these visualizations is suggested by the fact that the Tibetans regard deity yoga as one of the most powerful and advanced of their vast array of practices. In what may be the world's most dramatic claim for effectiveness, they claim that with deity yoga a practitioner can become a Buddha in a single lifetime rather than in the "three countless eons" it would otherwise take.[82]

Thus the practice of merging with a power figure is widely recognized as a technique of great potency. This is another example of twentieth-century psychologists rediscovering techniques that shamans may have used for more than twenty centuries.

The spirits may also instruct and teach. In fact, "during the period of initial contact the spirits function above all as teachers."[168] This teaching is most likely to occur during altered states such as dreams, trances, and journeys and during the curious process of mediumship.

Mediumship or Channeling

Mediumship, or channeling as it is now known, is common among shamans, who may have been the world's first mediums. A survey of 21 cultures where shamans engage in soul flight showed that in over half of these cultures shamans also act as mediums.[140]

The process of mediumship/channeling involves a supposedly spiritual entity speaking through the medium or channel. The medium's state of consciousness may vary from full awareness and complete memory of the process to complete unawareness and amnesia. The medium's voice, expression, accent, posture, and be-

havior may all change, suggesting that the original person and personality have been replaced by one quite different. The effect can be most dramatic.

Mediumship is a worldwide phenomenon and its impact has been remarkable. It has played a major role in world religions, and in a survey of 188 cultures it was found in over half of them.[21] There are many famous examples, of which the best known is probably the Greek Oracle at Delphi. For over 1000 years the Delphi temple priestesses regularly became possessed, supposedly by the god Apollo, and dispensed advice to princes and paupers alike.

King Croesus, whose enormous wealth inspired the saying "rich as Croesus," was one of the oracle's more famous customers. Greedy for yet more wealth, he wanted to know whether to attack his neighbors. The oracle's sage advice was, "After crossing the [river] Halys Croesus will destroy a great empire."[79] Much inspired, Croesus crossed the river and in fact did destroy a great empire: his own.

The oracle was also approached for military strategy to defend against the marauding Etruscans. The oracle's advice was to "use as few ships as possible." Displaying admirable faith in the oracle, the people sent out a mere five ships against the entire Etruscan fleet. Not wishing to be embarrassed by seeming to need a larger force, the Etruscans also sent out only five ships. These were promptly sunk. The Etruscans immediately sent out another five. These were also sunk. The scenario was repeated a third and fourth time. Finally the Etruscans retired from the scene.[79]

It was also the oracle who dubbed Socrates the wisest man in Athens, much to Socrates' surprise. Of course, not all the oracle's advice was so dramatic or effective. Yet the oracle had a track record respectable enough to stay in business for over a thousand years and had a major impact on Greek history.

Mediumship has been important in many religions. There are references to it in both the Old and New Testament and it played a

significant role in Jewish mysticism.[81] Some extremely influential religious texts, regarded as profound by many brilliant minds over many centuries, were apparently produced in this way. Examples include parts of the Koran and Tibetan Buddhist scriptures.[79]

Mediumship has once again become popular in the West, where it is now known as channeling. Of the many books on the subject the most thorough are probably *Channeling*[102] and *Tongues of Men and Angels*.[79] Contemporary channeling shows both differences and similarities compared to earlier times. Today's channeled productions include literary, musical, metaphysical, spiritual, and psychological works. The emphasis on psychology is new, as are a number of the supposed sources. In ancient times gods, goddesses, and angels were busy being channeled; in the nineteenth century American Indians, Orientals, and deceased spirits were much in vogue. Today, however, spiritual masters, more-evolved beings on other planes, and extraterrestrials are all the rage.

The range of quality of channeled materials is enormous. They include the abysmal and trite, the ego-serving and self-aggrandizing, as well as the clearly erroneous and ridiculous. Some of the more amusing examples include "Leah, a sixth density entity from the planet Venus six hundred years in the future"[158] and Mademoiselle Helene Smith. Among other experiences, Mademoiselle Smith journeyed with her spirit guide Leopold to Mars, "whence she returned with colorful descriptions of the Martian countryside and samples of the inhabitants' writing and language."[129] This is considerably more than either Soviet or American space probes have been able to do. Productions such as these led Ken Wilber, one of today's best-known writers on psychology and religion, to state, "Higher intelligences have got to be smarter than the drivel most of these channels bring through."[203]

Yet channeled works also include, though much more rarely, favorably reviewed literary works, extraordinarily complex and coherent (though not necessarily verifiable or correct) metaphysics, and helpful—even profound—spiritual works.

The most famous literary productions were those of either (depending on your belief system) Pearl Curran, a little-educated St. Louis housewife, or of Patience Worth, the spirit of a seventeenth-century Englishwoman. Pearl/Patience could perform a variety of remarkable feats. She could dictate a poem on a specified topic faster than a scribe could write it in shorthand. She could even alternate lines from two different poems as she did so; the first line from poem one, the second from poem two, the third line from poem one, and so on. Author Edgar Lee Masters witnessed one such writing session and shook his head in disbelief, saying, "It simply can't be done."[79] Altogether, Pearl/Patience channeled over twenty volumes of poetry, novels, and advice that were widely published and favorably reviewed.

Among the many contemporary spiritual works, one of the most interesting is a three-volume set with the unlikely name *A Course in Miracles*.[6] This is a Christian mystical text channeled by a reluctant and astounded Jewish professor of psychology at Columbia Medical School. "Having no belief in God," she said, "I resented the material I was taking down, and was strongly impelled to attack it and prove it wrong."[172]

But no matter how negative the reluctant scribe felt about the work, others have felt just as strongly positive. The first book review stated that "the three books comprise one of the most remarkable systems of spiritual truth available today."[172] Likewise, a Stanford University professor called it "perhaps the most important writing in the English language since the translation of the Bible."[172] Ken Wilber's comments about channeled "drivel" suggest that he is no great fan of channeling. Yet he has commented that "the *Course* is clearly inspired. Its insights are genuinely transcendental. . . . I known of no other channeled material that even comes close to it."[203]

Not everyone admires the *Course,* and it has been assailed by some Christian fundamentalists and theologians. Yet it has sold over half a million copies and is being translated into over a dozen

languages. In content it seems to embody the perennial philosophy (the common philosophical and spiritual core found at the heart of the world's great religions) expressed in Christian form. Add to this several famous Tibetan Buddhist texts and parts of the Koran, and it becomes clear that a small number of channeled spiritual works may be of extraordinary profundity.

Skeptics would deny that channeled productions are ever significant or profound. For the true skeptic, all such productions "consist solely of strings of loosely associated gobbets of naive ideas" produced by people "of hysterical personality, displaying dissociative features" and in many cases "all the hallmarks of schizophrenia."[148] Certainly most channeled productions are trite or nonsensical but this does not prove that all of them are. Skeptics tend to carefully ignore the difficult cases such as the classic channeled religious texts and the writings of Pearl Curran.

Clearly, mediumship is no simple matter. Meaningful and profound productions occur even though they are far rarer than trivial and nonsensical ones. The phenomenon cannot be simply dismissed as pure nonsense or pathology.

Unfortunately, most people take extreme positions. On the one hand are the true believers who doubt not a single word of their favorite spirit guide or god. On the other hand are the true skeptics for whom every word is false and who dismiss channeling, often after only superficial study, as self-deceit at best or psychosis at worst. Either approach serves as a pleasant psychological anesthetic that saves one from having to investigate and think about the issue in greater depth.

Yet channeling is clearly a complex curious phenomenon from which, at the very least, we stand to learn much about little-known capacities of mind. There seems no reason to assume there is only one type of channeling. For all we know, it may turn out to be a complex process involving different mechanisms and sources in different cases.

Many theories, none of them entirely satisfactory, have been

suggested to account for channeling. These range from fraud to dissociation to possession by true spiritual entities. Needless to say, it is easier to suggest processes involved in producing trivial nonsensical works than profound ones. Fraud may account for some cases but hardly all, and some channels are reluctant and confused by the whole process.

Dissociation is perhaps the most common explanation. In this process aspects of the psyche are split off from conscious awareness and ego control. Such aspects may then function independently as subpersonalities or as more or less full-fledged separate personalities, as in cases of multiple personality. Such personalities may project thoughts into egoic awareness, and these thoughts are then perceived by the ego or conscious personality as coming from outside itself.

Multiple personalities provide a dramatic example of dissociation and divided consciousness. However, the implications of research on dissociation are much more subtle and extensive. They suggest that all of us live with some degree of dissociation and that "the unity of consciousness is illusory."[80]

The implication is that anyone—ancient shamans, modern channelers, and all the rest of us—may be capable of receiving information from aspects of our own psyches that lie outside conscious awareness. This information may seem to come not from our mind but from another entity, a fact that can be easily demonstrated with hypnosis. Some of the communication may consist of information and memories that the conscious personality has long forgotten. When this occurs the effect can be particularly dramatic and provide apparently impressive evidence that the message must come from another entity.[158]

Purely psychological mechanisms may be sufficient to account for many, if not all, superficial channeled productions. There seems little need to invoke spirits, or any other type of nonhuman entity for that matter. In addition, the long-standing scientific principle of parsimony argues for keeping explanations as simple as possible.

Most psychological explanations of channeling stop here. Unfortunately, very little experimental research has been done on channeling. An interesting beginning was made by Sarah Thomason, a professor of linguistics at the University of Pittsburgh. She analyzed the voices of eleven different channelers and found a number of contradictions and peculiarities in speaking styles.

Several of her findings were highly suspicious. For example, two entities were said to sport British accents yet claimed to be thousands of years old. However, British accents as we know them have probably not existed for more than one thousand years at most. Another entity used inconsistent pronunciation, which became more inconsistent and more American the more excited he became. According to Thomason, this is a real giveaway and "just the opposite of what one would expect, if he were a non-native speaker of American English."[183]

Other findings were puzzling. The well-known "entity" Lazaris, who does telephone interviews and has a waiting list more than two years long, was a case in point. "Lazaris' accent sounds fake to me," said Thomason, "but there are no obvious inconsistencies in his sound pattern." The phenomenon of channeling is clearly in need of further research.

This still leaves us with the problem of accounting for the occasional profound channeled work. While it is easy to conceive of a subpersonality producing trivial nonsense, it is more difficult to imagine it creating major literary or spiritual works apparently far beyond the channel's level of knowledge and skill. However, it is possible to imagine such creations coming from the psyche if we can conceive, as many Eastern and some Western psychologies do, that there may be aspects of the psyche that are "superior" or "transcendent" to the ego or conscious personality. Indeed, some channels find that over time they eventually come to experience their spirits, not as separate entities, but rather as aspects of their own mind and unacknowledged wisdom.[115]

If we are to be completely honest, we must admit that none of

these suggestions actually disproves or rules out the possibility that spirits, whatever they may be, are the actual source of some channeled materials. Therefore, to be honest and complete, we should briefly examine the nature of "spirits." It is to this tricky question that we now turn.

The Nature of Spirits

What is a spirit? The Oxford Dictionary defines it as "a supernatural, incorporeal, rational being or personality, usually regarded as imperceptible at ordinary times to the human senses, but capable of becoming visible at pleasure, and frequently conceived as troublesome, terrifying or hostile to mankind." This has probably been the most common view of spirits throughout human history. However, if we set aside historical notions such as these, as well as our own preconceptions, we need to ask questions such as: are spirits part of or separate from the medium or shaman, are they mental or nonmental, material or immaterial, and are they expressions of health or pathology? In short, what is the psychological and ontological status of spirits?

We may be able to shed light on these questions by examining shamans and their spirits along with related data from other traditions. To do this we need to look first at exactly what it means to experience a spirit. Essentially it is an experience of interaction with what is felt to be an intelligent, nonmaterial entity separate from the ego or self. In the shaman's case the spirit may provide information or power that the shaman believes she cannot access alone.

Such experiences are widely recognized in both religion and psychology and may be either troublesome or beneficial. In a religious context, troublesome examples include the experience of being tormented or possessed by unfriendly spiritual entities such

as ghosts or demons. Dealing with troublesome spirits is one of the shaman's most frequent tasks. In a psychological context these same "spirits" might be interpreted as hallucinations.

Interactions with spirits may also be beneficial since the spirits may prove to be valuable sources of information, guidance, and wisdom. In a religious context some of these sources might be regarded as transcendent beings such as the shaman's "helping spirits," the Hindu's "inner guru," the Quaker's "still small voice within," the Naskapi Indian's "great man," or the Christian's Holy Spirit. On the other hand, a conventional psychological perspective might regard all such inner sources as mundane aspects of the psyche such as subpersonalities.

A transpersonal psychological interpretation might fall somewhere in between these two views. Since transpersonal psychologists acknowledge the possibility of realms and capacities of mind transcendent to our usual egoic awareness, they might interpret these inner sources of wisdom in several ways. The first would be as mundane subpersonalities, like the traditional psychological view. However, a second possibility for transpersonal psychologists would be that these spiritual sources of wisdom represent transcendent aspects of the psyche "above and beyond" the ego. Several such transcendent aspects of the psyche have been described in both Eastern and Western psychologies. Western examples include the higher Self; the transpersonal witness; the Jungian Self, which is the center of the psyche; and the inner self helper, which is a helpful and apparently transcendent personality that occurs in multiple personalities.

It is clear, then, that numerous religions and psychologies have recognized the possibility of accessing wisdom from inner sources that seem wiser than the ego or personality. Considerable effort has gone into refining ways of facilitating contact with these sources.

Religions have used a variety of rituals, prayer, supplication,

sacrifice, and altered states of consciousness. The altered states may include possession, soul travel, and quieting and calming the mind so as to be able to hear the "still small voice within."

In psychology the major techniques used for this purpose include hypnosis and guided imagery. It is apparently a relatively easy matter to create through hypnosis an experience akin to channeling. As Charles Tart puts it:

> From my studies with hypnosis I know I can set up an apparently independent existent entity whose characteristics are constructed to my specifications and the person hypnotized will experience it as if it's something outside of his own counsciousness talking. So there is no doubt that some cases of channeling can be explained in a conventional kind of way. There is nothing psychic involved.[102]

Several schools of psychology, including Jungian and Gestalt, use guided imagery or fantasy to access inner wisdom. A common technique is dialogue with the sage or inner teacher, in which the therapist asks the patient to imagine himself in a safe, pleasant environment and then meeting a person of great wisdom. The patient is encouraged to allow a dialogue with this inner sage to emerge spontaneously and to ask whatever questions seem most helpful. Such dialogues can produce surprisingly insightful information of which the patient was formerly unaware. A growing number of authors, artists, and business people commonly resort to such techniques for inspiration.[187] These methods have obvious similarities to the shaman's journeys to find a spirit teacher.

Inner teachers may also arise spontaneously and have powerful, indeed life-changing, effects. Some people who have literally changed the course of history have been directed by such inner teachers. The philosopher Socrates, the political leader Gandhi, and the psychologist Carl Jung all reported that they learned from and were directed by inner guides who arose unbidden from the depths of the psyche.

Jung provided a number of dramatic examples. One such inner teacher, whom he called Philemon, provided him with a wealth of information about the psyche. Philemon first appeared to Jung during a fantasy in which

> suddenly there appeared from the right a winged being sailing across the sky. I saw that it was an old man with the horns of a bull. He held a bunch of four keys, one of which he clutched as if he were about to open a lock. He had the wings of the kingfisher with its characteristic colors. . . . Philemon and other figures of my fantasies brought home to me the crucial insight that there are things in the psyche which I do not produce, but which produce themselves and have their own life. Philemon represented a force which was not myself. In my fantasies I held conversations with him, and he said things which I had not consciously thought. For I observed clearly that it was he who spoke, not I. . . . I understood that there is something in me which can say things that I do not know and do not intend, things which may even be directed against me.
>
> Psychologically, Philemon represented superior insight. He was a mysterious figure to me. At times he seemed to me quite real as if he were a living personality. I went walking up and down the garden with him, and to me he was what the Indians call a guru.[97]

Even a single experience of an inner guide can have life-changing effects. A dramatic example is given by a woman named Lillian who suffered chronic pelvic inflammation and pain for which no medical cause could be found. Lillian began practicing visual imagery and obtained some benefits. She started by imagining

> a stream of cool water circulating through her pelvis, and knotted ropes being untied. What felt like a cement block in her lower back was imaged as dissolving. She said she felt better; the burning was still there, but covered a smaller area.
>
> Then one night when Lillian was practicing her imagery at home, a coyote named Wildwood flashed into her mind. He advised

her to stay by his side, and watch what was about to happen, and told her that what she saw would be related to the fire in her body. She then sensed herself sitting by a campfire, in the midst of a hostile tribe of Indians who held her captive. She experienced the horror of being brutally gang-raped and murdered. "At the instant of my death . . . I woke up and was back in my body in the room, only my pain was completely gone, and hasn't returned since."[1]

What is one to make of such an experience and its dramatic outcome? Lillian attributed it to a past life. The shamanic interpretation would be that her spirit guide or power animal, the coyote Wildwood, had taken her on a journey in which she had undergone rape, death, and a healing rebirth. A psychological explanation would be that her own mind had, by a wisdom and means far beyond our present understanding, provided her an experience of profound psychosomatic healing power. Whatever the explanation, one can only feel awe for the healing power of the psyche, its images, and its inner guides.

As we have seen, both religion and psychologies have sought and found ways of accessing sources of inner wisdom that in some cases seem wiser than the ego. Clearly the wisdom they provide can be more profound than the egocentric trivia that characterizes so much channeling.

How are we to understand these inner sources of wisdom? What exactly is their nature? Or in philosophical terms, what is their ontological status? Asking the sources themselves is not particularly helpful; the answers may range from "I am part of you" to "I am Argon from the seventh plane" or "I am part of God." Clearly we're not going to get much help here, although unfortunately many people seem to believe channeled claims totally. Those of us who are skeptical of the claims of channelers are left to make our own decisions about the nature of this process and of the sources of information.

From a psychological perspective we may be able to account for spirits, inner guides, and channeling, both high and low, pro-

vided that we are willing to entertain the possibility that transpersonal aspects of the psyche above and beyond the ego do exist. The principle of dissociation, which may play a major role in the production of relatively superficial channeled works, can then be extended to the production of profound ones as well. Channeling in these latter cases would therefore involve receiving information from the transpersonal domains of mind recognized by some psychologies and many religions.

The principle of parsimony favors an explanation in terms of known mechanisms such as dissociation. However, if we are to be completely honest, we must acknowledge that even now we have not disproved the possible existence of spirits (intelligent, nonmaterial entities independent of the channel's mind) or their role in some channeling. Indeed, it is not at all clear that it is possible to disprove them.

To put the matter in more precise philosophical language, we seem to have here a case of what is called "ontological indeterminacy." This means that the fundamental nature, or ontological status, of the source of information cannot be decided definitely because the available information or observations can be interpreted in many ways and we have no absolute method by which to determine which interpretation(s) may be best.

Practically speaking, this means that people's interpretations of the phenomena will be largely determined by their personal beliefs, philosophy, and "world hypothesis." The world hypothesis consists of the fundamental beliefs about the nature of the world and reality that underlie the life and work of a community. Most people simply take the consensual assumptions of their culture or subculture unquestioningly and interpret the world accordingly.

People's decisions about the nature of spirits and channeling therefore depend in large part on their prior assumptions about the nature of reality. For example, a person who believes in philosophical materialism assumes that everything that exists is either matter or entirely dependent on matter for its existence. Such a person will obviously view "spirits" very differently from the re-

ligious practitioner or theologian who believes in a transcendent realm of pure spirit. For the philosophical materialist all sources of inner wisdom, information, advice, or visions—all perceived entities, voices, and images—are simply mental constructions, the expressions of neuronal fireworks, and probably deranged fireworks at that. From this point of view, shamans' experiences and spirits are likewise only creations of mind, and all worlds, spirits, and souls are merely mental projections. Therefore, the materialist considers shamans mistaken at best or psychotic at worst.

Things are very different for the believer in panpsychism. This is the view that everything in the universe, including plants and inanimate objects, has some kind of psychological being or awareness. Those who hold such beliefs will find no problem with the idea that at least some of the helpers, voices, and visions encountered during shamanic experiences are indeed spirits.

Of course, it must be admitted that we have no proof whatsoever that all sources of inner wisdom have the same nature. For all we know, some might be merely aspects of mind, and not terribly impressive aspects at that, while others might conceivably be some transcendent source or sources within or beyond us. At the present time we may simply not be able to decide definitively between these interpretations. Consequently, the only intellectually honest position may be an agnostic view of spirits and channels in which we confess their indeterminacy and our ignorance.

This may be honest but it may not be terribly satisfying. Indeed, it may be annoying and irksome. Yet our annoyance may be a reflection of our unwillingness to tolerate ambiguity and our attachment to our own opinions and world hypothesis. Diverse philosophies and spiritual traditions repeatedly urge us to acknowledge that we just don't know—indeed cannot know—the ultimate nature of many things. We are encouraged to recognize the "radical mystery" of existence and, in the language of Zen, to keep "don't know mind."

In light of all this, the fact that we cannot decide once and for

all about the existence of spirits, channels, and nonphysical entities is not so surprising. It simply reflects our current ignorance and perhaps even perpetual limitations on our knowing. This may not be terribly satisfying but it may be usefully humbling.

Implications and Conclusions

Given the present limitations on our knowledge, what can we conclude about the shaman's spirits and their counterparts in other countries and centuries? To begin with, it is clearly possible for many people to access inner sources of information and wisdom that may be experienced as entities separate from themselves. The information so obtained may often be trivial, nonsensical, and egotistical, but it may occasionally be meaningful, profound, and life-changing. It appears that we may have underestimated the range and depth of information available within us, the number of ways in which it can be accessed, and the frequency and impact of channeling. For channeling, through its effects on individuals, cultures, and religions, has changed the course of history.

While one can interpret the nature of this process in many ways, it clearly points to realms and capacities of the human mind that as yet are little understood. We may have underestimated ourselves and the wisdom, imagination, and creative power that lie latent within us. Shamans appear to have been the first pioneers to begin exploring and mining these resources.

PART IV

Shamanic Techniques

CHAPTER 11

Cosmic Traveling: The Shamanic Journey

We must close our eyes and invoke a new
manner of seeing . . .
a wakefulness that is the birthright of us all,
though few put it to use.
PLOTINUS

At the heart of shamanism lies the shamanic journey or soul flight. It is this that defines shamans and sets them apart from other ecstatics, healers, and mystics; it is this that makes shamans cosmic travelers. "Any ecstatic cannot be considered a shaman," said Eliade, because "the shaman specializes in a trance during which his soul is believed to leave his body and ascend to the sky or descend to the underworld."[41] Others may enter altered states, minister, or heal, but it is the shamans alone who primarily engage in soul flight.

During this cosmic traveling the shaman's soul seems to leave the body and to roam at will throughout the expanses of the upper, middle, and lower worlds. The shaman is a cosmic traveler because, according to Eliade,

> he commands the techniques of ecstasy—that is, because his soul can safely abandon his body and roam at vast distances, can penetrate the underworld and rise to the sky. Through his own ecstatic experience he knows the roads of the extraterrestrial regions. He can go below and above because he has already been there. The danger of losing his way in these forbidden regions is still great; but sanctified by his initiation and furnished with his guardian spirit, a

shaman is the only human being able to challenge the danger and venture into a mystical geography.[41]

The shaman's experiences while journeying may be dramatic and dangerous, ecstatic or horrendous, demonic or divine. He may traverse numerous worlds and discover numberless spirits. Emotions may range from terror to bliss, yet often there is "an ineffable joy in what he sees, an awe of the beautiful and mysterious worlds that open before him. His experiences are like dreams, but waking ones that feel real and in which he can control his actions and direct his adventures."[73]

The shaman journeys in order to learn, to heal, and to help. He may seek knowledge, and power either for himself or for his people. He may seek information for healing, for hunting, or to appease and petition the gods. He may also retrieve the souls of the sick or guide the souls of the dead to their eternal resting place. Hence the shaman is frequently referred to as a psychopomp, a guide of souls.

The Experience of the Shamanic Journey

The shamanic journey involves three phases: a prior period of preparation and purification, induction of an altered state of consciousness, and the actual journey.

The initial phase of preparation and purification may involve a period of isolation, fasting, and celibacy, perhaps alone in the wilderness or in a solitary hut. After this the journey is usually begun at night when the reduced illumination makes the perception of visions easier. The shaman begins the appropriate rituals and then uses techniques such as singing, dancing, drumming, or drugs to induce an altered state.

For a journey to the lower world the shaman usually visualizes an entrance into the earth. Common entrances include images

of caves, a hollow tree stump, or a water hole. The shaman sees himself entering this hole and diving deep into the earth until he eventually emerges into another world. Michael Harner describes the experiences as follows:

> Entrances into the Lower world commonly lead down into a tunnel or tube that conveys the shaman to an exit, which opens out upon bright and marvelous landscapes. From there the shaman travels wherever he desires for minutes or even hours, finally returning back up through the tube . . . to emerge at the surface, where he entered.[73]

Once in the lower world the shaman begins the next phase of his mission. This may involve anything from obtaining healing information to recovering lost souls to placating angry spirits. Rasmussen describes a classic example of this kind of placation, namely the Eskimo shaman's journey to the depths of the sea to placate the spirit Takánakapsâluk. According to Eskimo legend it is this stern goddess of fate who controls the sea animals on which the Eskimos depend for food. When she becomes angry—most often because of breeches of taboo—she withholds these animals. Then the Eskimos hunt in vain, and hunger haunts the tribe.

At this time their fate rests on the shaman. It is he alone who can journey to the bottom of the sea, the dwelling place of Takánakapsâluk, brave the barriers and beasts with which she protects herself, and beg her forgiveness. Rasmussen describes the sea spirit and the shaman's mighty journey to her as follows: "It is regarded as one of a shaman's greatest feats to visit her where she lives at the bottom of the sea, and so tame and conciliate her that human beings can live once more untroubled on earth.

"When a shaman wishes to visit Takánakapsâluk, he sits on the inner part of the sleeping place behind a curtain, and must wear nothing but his kamiks [boots] and mittens. A shaman about to make this journey is said to be nak'a': one who drops down to

the bottom of the sea. This remarkable expression is due perhaps in some degree to the fact that no one can rightly explain how the journey is made. Some assert that it is only his soul or his spirit which makes the journey; others declare that it is the shaman himself who actually, in the flesh, drops down into the underworld. . . .

"The shaman sits for a while in silence, breathing deeply, and then, after some time has elapsed, he begins to call upon his helping spirits, repeating over and over again: . . . 'the way is made ready for me; the way opens before me!'

"Whereat all present must answer in chorus: . . . 'let it be so!'

"And when the helping spirits have arrived, the earth opens under the shaman, but often only to close up again; he has to struggle for a long time with hidden forces, ere he can cry at last: 'Now the way is open.' And then all present must answer: 'Let the way be open before him; let there be way for him.'

"And now one hears, at first under the sleeping place: 'Halala—he—he—he, halala—he—he—he!' and afterwards under the passage, below the ground, the same cry: 'Halele—he!' And the sound can be distinctly heard to recede farther and farther until it is lost altogether. Then all know that he is on his way to the ruler of the sea beasts. . . .

"An ordinary shaman will, even though skillful, encounter many dangers in his flight down to the bottom of the sea; the most dreaded are three large rolling stones which he meets as soon as he has reached the sea floor. There is no way round; he has to pass between them, and take great care not to be crushed by these stones, which churn about, hardly leaving room for a human being to pass. Once he has passed beyond them, he comes to a broad, trodden path, the shamans' path; he follows a coastline resembling that which he knows from on earth, and entering a bay, finds himself on a great plain, and here lies the house of Takánakapsâluk, built of stone, with a short passage way, just like the houses of the tunit. Outside the house one can hear the animals puffing

and blowing, but he does not see them; in the passage leading to the house lies Takánakapsâluk's dog stretched across the passage taking up all the room; it lies there gnawing at a bone and snarling. It is dangerous to all who fear it, and only the courageous shaman can pass by it, stepping straight over it as it lies; the dog then knows that the bold visitor is a great shaman, and does him no harm.

"These difficulties and dangers attend the journey of an ordinary shaman. But for the very greatest, a way opens right from the house whence they invoke their helping spirits; a road down through the earth, if they are in a tent on shore, or down through the sea, if it is in a snow hut on the sea ice, and by this route the shaman is led down without encountering any obstacle. He almost glides as if falling through a tube so fitted to his body that he can check his progress by pressing against the sides, and need not actually fall down with a rush. This tube is kept open for him by all the souls of his namesakes, until he returns on his way back to earth.

"Should a great shelter wall be built outside the house of Takánakapsâluk, it means that she is very angry and implacable in her feelings towards mankind, but the shaman must fling himself upon the wall, kick it down and level it to the ground. There are some who declare that her house has no roof, and is open at the top, so that she can better watch, from her place by the lamp, the doings of mankind. All the different kinds of game: seal, bearded seal, walrus and whale, are collected in a great pool on the right of her lamp, and there they lie puffing and blowing. When the shaman enters the house, he at once sees Takánakapsâluk, who, as a sign of anger, is sitting with her back to the lamp and with her back to all the animals in the pool. Her hair hangs down loose all over one side of her face, a tangled, untidy mass hiding her eyes, so that she cannot see. It is the misdeeds and offenses committed by men which gather in dirt and impurity over her body. All the foul emanations from the sins of mankind nearly suffocate her. As the

shaman moves towards her, Isarrataitsoq, her father, tries to grasp hold of him. He thinks it is a dead person come to expiate offenses before passing on to the Land of the Dead, but the shaman must then at once cry out: 'I am flesh and blood' and then he will not be hurt. And he must now grasp Takánakapsâluk by one shoulder and turn her face towards the lamp and towards the animals, and stroke her hair, the hair she has been unable to comb out herself, because she has no fingers; and he must smooth it and comb it, and as soon as she is calmer, he must say:

"'pik'ua qilusinEq ajulErmata': 'those up above can no longer help the seals up by grasping their foreflippers.'

"Then Takánakapsâluk answers in the spirit language: 'The secret miscarriages of the women and breaches of taboo in eating boiled meat bar the way for the animals.'

"The shaman must now use all his efforts to appease her anger, and at last, when she is in a kindlier mood, she takes the animals one by one and drops them on the floor, and then it is as if a whirlpool arises in the passage, the water pours out from the pool and the animals disappear in the sea. This means rich hunting and abundance for mankind.

"It is then time for the shaman to return to his fellows up above, who are waiting for him. They can hear him coming a long way off; the rush of his passage through the tube kept open for him by the spirits comes nearer and nearer, and with a mighty 'Plu—a—he—he' he shoots up into his place behind the curtain: 'Plu-plu,' like some creature of the sea, shooting up from the deep to take breath under the pressure of mighty lungs.

"Then there is silence for a moment. No one may break this silence until the shaman says: 'I have something to say.'

"Then all present answer: 'Let us hear, let us hear.'"[147]

But the shaman does not answer immediately. Rather, he uses this dramatic moment to force the audience to confess their breaches of taboo. All must acknowledge their sins, a process that produces a powerful group confession and cohesion. Only when

this is complete does the shaman sigh with relief. Then at last "the cause of Takánakapsâluk's anger is explained, and all are filled with joy at having escaped disaster. . . . This then was what happened when shamans went down and propitiated the great Spirit of the Sea."[147]

Only the shaman can make this journey to the depths of the sea. Thus, while the ordinary human being lives as a more or less helpless pawn of the spirits, it is the shaman alone who can contact and control them.

Journeys to the middle or upper worlds have the same general features as those to the lower world. There are, however, some differences in purpose and in the types of entities likely to be encountered. The lower world is often a place of tests and challenges, but it is also a place where power animals are acquired and the shaman is guided and empowered to victory. The upper world is a place where teachers and guides may be found, and journeys here may be particularly ecstatic.[8]

The middle world is our familiar world. In their visions shamans journey over it at will, unimpeded by barriers or distance, seeing far and wide, and returning with information about hunting, weather, or warfare. Middle-world journeys are particularly common in the near-Arctic areas of North America and Siberia. Here food supplies are precarious and migrating animal herds must be located.[77]

The journey to the upper world usually begins from a raised area such as a mountain, treetop, or cliff, from which the shaman envisions himself ascending into the sky. At some stage of the journey there may be an experience of a kind of membrane that temporarily impedes the ascent. When this is pierced the shaman finds himself in the upper world, a world notably different from the middle world and perhaps populated with strange animals, plants, and people. Like the lower one, the upper world may have several levels, and the shaman can usually move between them at will, perhaps assisted by a helping spirit.

The ascent may also occur in other ways. In some variations the shaman may experience himself as transformed into a bird soaring to the upper world. At other times the experience of ascent may involve climbing the world axis, the central axis that runs between upper, middle, and lower worlds. Sometimes this axis takes the form of the world tree, which the shaman climbs, or he may ascend a mountain, rainbow, or ladder. Whatever the specifics, the common theme is an ascent from this world into a world or worlds above, where spirits abide. There the shaman can intervene with them on behalf of his earthbound tribespeople.

Spontaneous Journeys

Shamans learn, sometimes over many years, to induce and direct their journeys. Yet around the world people who have never even heard of shamanism may be surprised to find themselves having journeylike experiences. These may erupt spontaneously and entirely unsought as out-of-body experiences (OOBEs), lucid dreams, or near-death experiences (NDEs). Such experiences have presumably occurred throughout human history. As such they may have provided the inspiration for consciously induced journeys, first in shamanism, then in other religious traditions, and most recently in psychotherapy.

Out-of-Body Experiences

Spontaneous out-of-body experiences have been reported throughout history and have traditionally been referred to as "astral traveling." Perhaps the best-known travels are those of Emmanuel Swedenborg. Swedenborg was an eighteenth-century Swedish intellectual who poured forth such a wealth of scientific writings and inventions that he was regarded as one of the great geniuses of his

time. Around his fifty-fifth year he underwent a religious crisis and began to describe spontaneous personal journeys to heaven and hell and meetings with their inhabitants. He published numerous metaphysical works based on these experiences. So impactful were these that even today, some two centuries later, the Swedenborgian movement is still alive in several parts of the world.

Perhaps the best-known contemporary examples of spontaneous out-of-body experiences are those of Robert Monroe. Monroe was a conventional businessman who feared he was going crazy and sought medical treatment when he found himself having out-of-body experiences. He had never heard of such a thing and didn't believe it possible. Yet as the initial shock and fear diminished he found himself able to control, explore, and enjoy the experiences. He chronicled the explorations in his widely selling book *Journeys Out of the Body.*[122]

Persons who have out-of-body experiences may report travels similar to those of shamans. They may seem to travel at will around the world or to other worlds, meet various spirits, and feel that they have acquired all manner of valuable information. The fact that such experiences can occur spontaneously at first and later be brought under voluntary control suggests that this may be one way in which shamanic journeying was learned and relearned throughout human history.

Near-Death Experiences

A shamanic journeylike phenomenon can also occur during near-death experiences. It has long been known that those who have a brush with death may describe unusual and profound experiences. Since the publication of Raymond Moody's book *Life After Life,*[123] which has sold an astonishing total of 10 million copies, there has been a remarkable surge of interest in near-death experiences.

NDEs occur most often in people who come close to death

but are resuscitated at the last moment—after a heart attack, for example. Though there is some variability from one person to another, the experience usually progresses through a series of stages. The first stage is marked by a sense of profound peace and well-being. Next comes the shock of finding one's "self" outside the body, apparently able to hear and see everything going on in the environment, including one's own body lying unconscious. There are several reports of revived patients dumbfounding their doctors with detailed descriptions of the resuscitation procedure that occurred while they were comatose or "dead."[124]

In the next stage there is a sense of moving through a vast, dark tunnel. At the end of the tunnel is a spiritual figure or light of incomprehensible brilliance, with which the dying person merges in ecstatic love. The experience ends with a sense that death would be premature and that the person must return to the world.[124]

Near-death experiencers commonly report that the experience was the most profound, important, and life-changing moment of their lives. Almost 90 percent say they would be willing to repeat it.[150] The experience can produce dramatic and long-lasting personality changes that seem similar to those produced by other types of mystical experiences. These include a reduced fear of death; an increased belief in an afterlife; a greater sense of the preciousness of relationships, love, and life; more interest in learning and self-knowledge; and a significant shift from materialistic goals and worldly possessions toward helping and caring for others. These dramatic changes are as much as, or more than, would be expected from years of psychotherapy. Because of improved resuscitation techniques, the number of people having such experiences has increased dramatically in recent years. This combination of dramatic psychological and spiritual change among increasing numbers of people suggests that near-death experiences may eventually exert a significant impact on human culture and consciousness.[151, 152]

There are obvious similarities between near-death experiences and shamanic journeys: detachment from the body, journey

to other realms, meeting spirits. One writer has gone to the extreme of suggesting that "the shaman, then, is a master of death; he actually dies and is actually reborn. . . . The shaman is the classic investigator of the realm of death; he explores the routes of travel to and in the Beyond and thereby produces a map of the postmortem terrain."[99]

There are also significant differences between shamanic journeys and near-death experiences. For example, unlike the shaman, a person near death appears to have little if any control over the experience. As yet no single explanation—biological, psychological, or spiritual—has proved adequate to account for the near-death phenomenon.

Inasmuch as these experiences may have occurred throughout history and have had profound transformative and healing effects, they may well have served as an inspiration for shamans. Indeed, one of the traditional calls to shamanism is unexpected recovery from a near-fatal illness. If some shamans-to-be had near-death experiences, they may well have sought ways to re-create and control similar experiences for the benefit of themselves and their tribes.

Dream Travel and Lucid Dreams

A third type of cosmic traveling is one we have all experienced: the traveling or flying that occurs in dreams. Within minutes of closing our eyes we may journey to unknown worlds, meet strange inhabitants and regard them as completely real. These dream journeys may be rich sources of insight. In many religions and psychologies dreams are regarded not only as "the royal road to the unconscious," to quote Freud, but also as the royal road to wisdom and awakening. Small wonder that some native cultures and shamans regard dream experiences and journeys as no less real or valuable than waking ones.

A particularly dramatic variation is "lucid dreaming," a state

in which the dreamer knows that she is dreaming. The lucid dreamer is able to direct her dreams much as the shaman does his journeys. The dreamer can visualize traveling through this world or other worlds, meeting other beings, exploring, questioning, and learning. The technique has been developed furthest in Tibetan dream yoga. Here the yogi uses lucid dreams to study the nature of the mind or, like the shaman, to journey to other realms where he can acquire teachings.

Whatever one may think of such yogic claims, contemporary research makes clear that lucid dreaming is a real phenomenon. Training programs for cultivating them are now available. Thanks to these programs, what was once a secret technique available only in the monasteries of Tibet can now be learned in the comfort of one's own bed.[106]

It seems, then, that lucid dreaming, out-of-body, and near-death experiences have probably occurred spontaneously throughout human history. They may therefore have provided a basis for the widespread belief in a soul and soul travel and may also have provided the prototype for shamanic journeys. Since each of these experiences may be profoundly meaningful, healing, and helpful, they would doubtless have been valued and sought after. The techniques and circumstances that favored them would have been carefully noted, cultivated, and transmitted across generations. When these and other skills were collected into a coherent body of techniques and wedded to an explanatory mythology, the core elements of shamanism would be in place and the shamanic tradition would be born or reborn.

This process may provide an answer to the long-debated question of how the worldwide occurrence of shamanism is to be explained. As we noted in chapter 2, two competing suggestions have been advanced. The first is that shamanism arose spontaneously in different locations; the second is that it spread around the world by migration. If journeylike experiences occurred spontaneously throughout human history, they may have repetitively re-

inspired and reinforced similar practices and beliefs in widely separated cultures and centuries. This would favor the idea that shamanism was discovered or rediscovered in many parts of the world. It would also explain why the tradition shows such similarities across cultures and why it has been able to survive for so long.

Cosmic Traveling in Other Religious Traditions

While shamans are the cosmic travelers par excellence, they are not the only people who journey. Nowhere is cosmic traveling so central as in shamanism, yet both ancient religions and modern psychologies make use of analogous experiences.

Among religions, practitioners of Taoism, Islam, Yoga, and Tibetan Buddhism may journey to other realms. Among Taoists "visualizations were believed to help the adept ascend to paradise. In the course of the visualization he crossed the gates of the three celestial passes to enter the Yu-ching Heaven, where he undertook an excursion of paradise."[10] Some Indian Muslims practice "allowing the soul to explore the spirit world," helped on its way with hashish, which they call the "heavenly guide or poor man's heaven."[167] In contrast to shamanism, however, these traditions use journeying only occasionally; it is by no means a central practice.

Journeys in Psychotherapy

Given the potential healing power of journeys, it is not surprising that psychotherapists have sought ways to induce similar experiences. The result is a wide range of imagery techniques that have been called by many names. Carl Jung, one of the first Westerners to use them, called them active imagination. Others refer to them as visualizations, guided imagery, guided meditation, or waking

dreams. Commonly patients are asked to create images of themselves going to meet people or entities that will provide insight, understanding, and healing.

While such experiences have much in common with shamanic journeys, they usually differ in several ways. Unlike guided imagery, journeys usually occur in significantly altered states of consciousness, often involve an experience of traveling to other realms, and are believed by the shaman to be real rather than imaginary experiences.

Experiences closer to the shamanic journey can occur under hypnosis. Here subjects enter an altered state of consciousness and can experience themselves traveling through other worlds and realms, if directed to do so. While hypnotized they may believe these worlds to be real and in no way creations of their own minds. The similarity of these hypnotic journeys to the shaman's is not surprising since both occur in trance states. The difference is that the shaman is able to enter and leave the state at will and does not require another person, the hypnotist, to induce and direct the state.

Western Journeys

It is apparent, then, that several types of shamanic journeylike experiences can occur either spontaneously or through deliberate cultivation. This leads to the interesting question of whether people from nonshamanic cultures, including contemporary Western culture, can learn to journey shamanically. The answer for the large majority of people appears to be yes. With the aid of drumming, most people seem to find it surprisingly easy, and over the course of a single weekend workshop it is not unusual to see people deeply moved to joy or tears by their experiences.

Michael Harner, who has conducted literally thousands of people on shamanic journeys, reports that

> approximately nine out of ten persons have the capacity for the visualization necessary to the shamanic journey. Interestingly, among Westerners, those who tend to have the most difficulties are often professionals in the fields of law, mathematics, linguistics, and philosophy—so-called left-brain specialists heavily devoted to logic in their work.[75]

Of course, there may be wide variations in the depth of trance and in the intensity, meaningfulness, and apparent reality of journey experiences.

It is interesting to note the marked contrast between the percentage of people who are apparently capable of journeying and the number who have actually engaged in it historically. The majority of people may have had the capacity, but it was traditionally the shaman alone who engaged in cosmic travel while his compatriots remained steadfastly earthbound.

Philosophical Interpretations

It seems that the majority of people may have a latent capacity for journeying, and that shamanic journeylike experiences can occur under a variety of circumstances. The question arises as to how we are to interpret these experiences philosophically. For the shaman this is not a problem; the experiences, realms, worlds, and spirits are all real, as real as this world and perhaps even more so.[73] However, this position is hardly likely to satisfy most contemporary Westerners, who are more likely to regard the experiences as examples—dramatic examples, granted—of vivid imagery or imagination.

Philosophically speaking we have here two different ontological perspectives. The shamanic view is a realist one since it regards the phenomena found in the journey as real, objective, and independent of the shaman's mind. The shaman views the journey as,

to use the precise technical terms, truly *exosomatic* (outside the body) rather than as *imaginal* (mind-created imagery).

This perspective is consistent with the shamanic world view, which holds that other worlds and spirits exist and can be accessed directly through cosmic traveling. Since this world view may have been derived in part from shamanic journeys, this consistency is hardly surprising. Some people who have out-of-body experiences and near-death experiences interpret them similarly. They believe that the soul separates from the body and journeys through realms and meets beings that are quite separate and independent from themselves.

Certainly the idea that there is a soul and that it can leave the body to travel to other realms is an ancient and perennial one. Plato described the soul as "imprisoned in the body like an oyster in his shell." Socrates is quoted as saying that the mind only perceives absolute truths "when she takes leave of the body and has as little as possible to do with it, then she has no bodily sense or desire, but is aspiring after true being."[96]

More common today, however, is the subjective imaginal perspective that regards shamanic journeys and similar experiences as mind-created images. These images may be interpreted as either pathological or beneficial. Pathological interpretations would view them as hallucinations; positive interpretations would see them as potentially helpful and healing products of the imagination.

A more radical perspective is that of Tibetan Buddhism. Here the realms to which the yogi travels in dreams or meditation are regarded as mind creations, but so too is everything in ordinary waking experience. This world and all worlds are ultimately regarded as dreams and creations of consciousness, or Mind. Only in enlightenment is waking from all dreams, both sleeping and waking, said to occur. When asked for proof for this position, the yogi might give either a philosophical argument or the centuries-old advice, "To see if this be true, look within your own mind."

Research Studies

Research studies on shamanic states and journeys are few and far between. We have a number of good reports of shamanic experiences during journeys, but as yet almost no other research has been done. An attempt to measure electroencephalographic (brain wave) activity during a journey failed because the shaman's body movement interfered with the measurements.[1] As yet we have almost no research data on such things as the precise nature of shamanic states of consciousness or the effects of the journey on the shaman's physiology and personality.

However, there has been some meaningful research on out-of-body experiences. Charles Tart, one of the most thoughtful researchers of parapsychological phenomena, reported evidence of extrasensory perception and unusual EEG patterns in a woman who claimed to have out-of-body experiences.[178]

However, a more intensive study of extrasensory perception during OOBEs produced results that were decidedly negative.[106] In this study approximately 100 subjects were tested, all of whom believed they could readily induce OOBEs and extrasensory perception while in them. The subjects were asked to visit a specific room while in the OOBE and subsequently describe what they saw. In all but a very few cases there was almost no correspondence whatsoever between the actual room and the descriptions.

Steven LaBerge has interpreted these negative findings as supporting his hypothesis that OOBEs are actually misinterpreted partially lucid dreams.[106] This hypothesis would appear to account for a number of curious features of OOBEs and for the fact that the experiences occur most often at night. Certainly there is as yet no firm evidence that OOBEs are actually associated with consciousness separating from the body. How one could even test such a thing is unclear.

However, whatever interpretation of the shamanic journey

one adopts, and whatever future research reveals, it is clear that the experience of leaving the body and traveling to other realms is a perennial worldwide phenomenon. It may occur spontaneously or be deliberately cultivated, and techniques for inducing it are widespread among both ancient religions and contemporary psychologies. Those who experience it commonly report that it can be surprisingly helpful, healing, and insightful. It is therefore not surprising that variations on this ancient technique are now creeping into contemporary consulting rooms and that psychologists and psychiatrists are beginning to follow the footsteps and flights of humankind's earliest therapists and cosmic travelers.

CHAPTER 12

The Technology of Transcendence: Inducing Altered States

We are all prisoners of our minds. This realization is the first step on the journey to freedom.
RAM DASS

To travel the cosmos the shaman must be able to enter specific states of consciousness, and much of shamanism centers on ways of inducing these states. Of course, shamans are not the only ones who have developed means for altering consciousness. Fully 90 percent of the world's cultures have one or more institutionalized altered states of consciousness, and in traditional societies these are almost without exception sacred states. This is, to say the least, "a striking finding and suggests that we are, indeed, dealing with a matter of major importance."[21] Clearly humankind has devoted enormous energy and ingenuity to altering consciousness. It may be that the "desire to alter consciousness periodically is an innate normal drive analogous to hunger or the sexual drive."[197]

So shamans are hardly alone in seeking alternate states of consciousness. Mystics of numerous other traditions also seek them and claim that it is in these states that their deepest realizations are born. Thus mystical traditions the world over have developed families of techniques for altering consciousness in systematic ways. These techniques constitute a technology of transcendence, or the so-called technology of the sacred.

Mystical traditions serve as road maps for using this technology. From this perspective we might say that mystical traditions and religions are created and sustained by people who access transcendent states of consciousness and then provide instructions whereby others can also access them and thereby re-create the founder's insights. Ideally, mystical traditions serve to preserve and transmit these insights and instructions. The first such tradition was shamanism.

At its best the shamanic tradition transmits a body of information and techniques that allows novices to re-create the altered states, experiences, and abilities of their predecessors. Thereby each generation can perpetuate and refresh a living, continuously recreated tradition and even add to its accumulated treasure of wisdom and technique. It is this direct, personal, transformative experience of the sacred that defines the mystic and that properly allows shamanism to be called humankind's first mystical tradition.

However, transmission can fail. When this occurs a tradition no longer focuses on or even appreciates direct experience of the transcendent. Then what is left is an institution largely devoid of direct experience of the sacred, without firsthand understanding of altered states and the transcendental experiences they access. Techniques for inducing altered states then give way to mere symbolic rituals, direct experience is replaced by belief, and living doctrine fossilizes into dogma. We might call this degrading process the ritualization of religion.

Examples are tragically easy to find in any of the world's religions. In Japan shamanism itself provides an example because today "trance occurs only rarely. Capacity for this kind of dissociation, and for the visionary journey which goes with it, seems to have diminished in recent centuries."[18]

Thus the survival of mystical traditions may depend on succeeding generations being able to personally reaccess the transcendent states and experiences from which the tradition was first born. Shamanism seems to have been remarkably successful in this.

It appears to have survived, perhaps for tens of thousands of years, as a living tradition of mystics who successfully preserved and transmitted one of the world's earliest technologies, perhaps even humankind's first technology, namely a technology of transcendence, a technology for inducing specific states of consciousness.

Inducing Altered States: Contemporary Understandings

This technology can now be partly understood in psychological terms. For the first time in Western history we have some psychological understanding of altered states of consciousness, the means for inducing them, and their role in religious traditions.

This present understanding is in dramatic contrast to previous centuries of misunderstanding and dismissal. It has taken literally centuries for some now widely known states to be recognized and appreciated. Even hypnosis was once dismissed as a sham. During the nineteenth century a British physician named James Esdaile discovered that hypnosis could be used with surgery patients to reduce pain and increase survival. At a time when there was no anesthesia available even for the most devastatingly brutal operations, this was obviously a momentous discovery. Yet Esdaile's claims were dismissed as impossible and medical journals refused to publish them. He therefore put on a demonstration for the British College of Physicians and Surgeons. As Charles Tart describes:

> After hypnotizing a man with a gangrenous leg, he amputated it in front of them while the man lay there calmly smiling. The conclusion of his skeptical colleagues? Esdaile was fooling them. He had hired a hardened rogue for a gold piece to lie there and pretend that he was feeling no pain. They must have had very hard rogues in those days.[180]

This example is valuable because it demonstrates the extent to which skeptics can deny and dismiss even powerful altered states with enormous healing potentials. In our own time hypnosis is widely accepted, but similar skeptical attitudes persist toward many mystical states and the techniques that induce them. For example, many people—including even some psychiatrists and psychologists—still dismiss meditation and the states it induces, even though over one thousand research reports attest to its many psychological, physiological, and biochemical effects.[126, 163]

However, while skepticism continues, acceptance and understanding are growing and much research has been done. Recently Charles Tart, one of the field's leading researchers, put forward a theory describing the stages by which altered states are induced. This theory will be helpful in understanding the induction of shamanic states.

Tart describes three stages of induction: first destabilization of the initial state, then a repatterning stage of transition to a new state, and finally stabilization of the new state. In the first stage the usual state is disrupted by one or more destabilizing forces that disrupt the usual brain-mind function. These destabilizing forces can be of many types. They include unusual sensory input such as intense music or drumming, physiological disrupters such as hunger or sleep deprivation, and chemical disrupters such as psychedelics.

When these destabilizing forces are sufficiently intense, the usual state of consciousness is disturbed and transition to another state begins. The nature of this new state will depend largely on the nature of the patterning forces that mold it. These forces are such things as the specific beliefs, drug(s), physiological condition, and environmental setting operating on the brain-mind at the time. These tend to impose specific patterns or organizations on brain-mind function and induce corresponding specific states of consciousness. When this movement toward a new pattern or state has occurred, consciousness restabilizes into the new state during the third and final stage.[179]

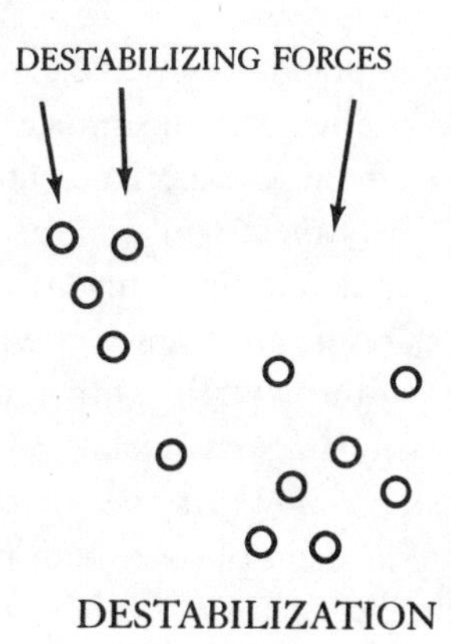

INITIAL STATE

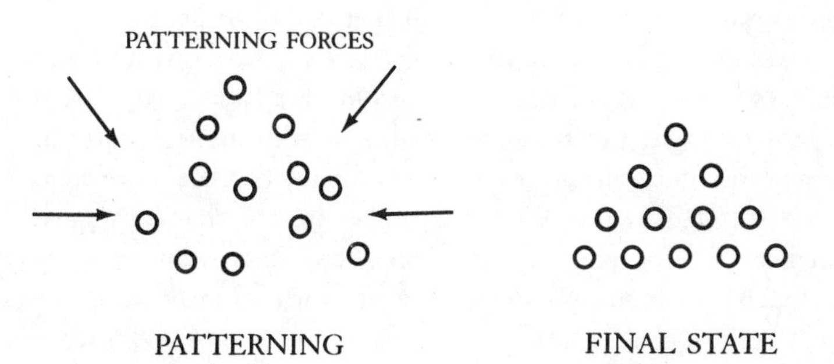

FIGURE 14. Steps in the induction of an altered state of consciousness.

Hypnosis provides a clear example. The hypnotic induction procedure destabilizes the usual waking state. The nature of the experience and state that follow vary dramatically according to the different patterning forces (instructions, expectations) that the hypnotist employs. When the new state stabilizes it may remain stable until new instructions (patterning forces) are given.

The ability to access altered states appears to be learnable. Entering a specific state for the first time may be difficult, but subsequent practice can make the process easier and easier. For example, the person who smokes marijuana for the first time may be disappointed to experience little or no effect. However, further attempts may meet with increasingly dramatic success. The result is a phenomenon, most curious and surprising to pharmacologists, known as reverse tolerance, in which the drug's effects become not less but more powerful with repeated use. The phenomenon becomes easily understandable once we realize that the ability to enter specific altered states, in this case the marijuana state, is a learned skill that improves with practice.[179]

The fact that the ability to enter alternate states can be developed and refined has several implications. The first is that practitioners may eventually be able to enter desired states rapidly and easily. This means that eventually they may no longer need prolonged preparation or external aids such as drums or drugs.

Another effect of practice is that some of the qualities and abilities of the alternate state may become available in the usual state. For example, the Buddhist meditator who masters states of extreme calm and concentration will eventually become more calm and concentrated in the usual state. Likewise the shaman's spirit vision may become more sensitive and accessible in an ordinary state. Indeed, shamanic training has as its object transforming the apprentice magician's initial and momentary ecstatic experience into a permanent condition.[41] The net result is that an altered state of consciousness becomes an altered *trait* of consciousness; and, to paraphrase Huston Smith's eloquent phrase, flashes of illumination become abiding light.

SHAMANIC TECHNIQUES

Shamanic techniques for inducing altered states include psychological, social, physiological, and pharmacological approaches. The psychological techniques comprise exercises undertaken both prior to

and during the ritual. Common preparatory techniques include periods of solitude, contemplation, and prayer and creation of the appropriate mind-set and environmental setting.

Set and setting are well recognized by contemporary psychedelic users as extremely important in determining the quality of psychedelic experience. Skillful users go to great lengths to arrange the appropriate expectation and environment in order to elicit the appropriate state and experience.

Shamans do likewise. This may include preparing the room, donning the shamanic mask and clothing, and gathering the family or tribe. The group provides support and encouragement and by its presence and dependency reinforces belief in the shamans' power and importance.

Timing is also regarded as important. Journeying is usually done at night so that the spirits and geography of the other worlds can be better seen. In psychological terms we might understand this as an example of perceptual release, the process by which subtle objects become recognized as stronger stimuli are withdrawn. For example, the fact that the house lights have been left on may only become recognizable when night falls. Likewise for shamans the subtle experiences encountered during their journeys may be more easily seen at night when bright sunlight can no longer obscure subtle images.

Physiological techniques, mostly of an ascetic kind, are also commonly used beforehand. Shamans may go for a day or more without food, sleep, sex, or even water. They may expose themselves to temperature extremes such as the icy cold of winter streams or the searing heat of the sweat lodge. During a seance shamans may subject themselves to intense rhythmic stimulation such as dancing and drumming and may ingest one or more drugs. Any or all of these techniques may disrupt normal physiological functioning sufficiently to destabilize the ordinary state of consciousness. The use of psychedelics and rhythmic stimulation are particularly powerful.

Psychedelics

At the present time it is hard to have an intelligent discussion about psychedelics, so great are the misunderstanding, misinformation, and emotion that surround them. As a culture we are remarkably ambivalent about drugs. Each year in the United States alone we consume billions of dollars worth of tranquilizers, watch over 300,000 people die from nicotine consumption, and lose almost another 100,000 to alcohol. Yet we subsidize tobacco growers while we imprison marijuana growers, and we make no distinction between socially destructive and sacred drug use.

Psychedelics have played a crucial role in religions and cultures throughout history and even today are central to the native American church and some shamans. Some of the most ancient of human writings, the Indian Vedas, which are at least 2500 years old, refer to the food of the gods, soma, which may have been the psychedelic mushroom *Amanita muscaria.*

Psychedelics also may have played a crucial role in shaping Western philosophy and culture. A reasonable though not conclusive argument has been made that Plato was a member of one of the Greek mystery schools, that these schools used psychedelics in their sacred rites, and that these experiences may have inspired parts of Plato's philosophy.[38, 196] Since Plato's thought became the foundation for Western philosophy ("Plato is philosophy and philosophy Plato," said Emerson), Western philosophy and culture may have been significantly but quite unknowingly impacted by psychedelic experiences.

There is enormous controversy over the nature and genuineness of psychedelically induced mystical states. However, at the very least they have played an important role in many religions and cultures and have been central to some, though by no means all, shamanic traditions. Their importance has often been overlooked by anthropologists, possibly because of lack of personal experience with the drugs and the states they induce. Such was the case with

Michael Harner. Only after he had ingested the psychedelic yage did he begin to appreciate its impact on the natives' view of reality:

> For several hours after drinking the brew, I found myself, although awake, in a world literally beyond my wildest dreams. . . . Transported into a trance where the supernatural seemed natural, I realized that anthropologists, including myself, had profoundly underestimated the importance of the drug in affecting native ideology.[78]

The range of drugs employed by shamans across the world is remarkable. Up to one hundred plant hallucinogens have been identified, and archaeological records suggest that shamanic drug use may extend back for more than three thousand years.[55]

It is the Siberian and Latin American shamans who have most often employed psychedelics as booster rockets to launch their cosmic travels. In Siberia the preferred substance has been the mushroom known as *Amanita muscaria* or agaric. This is perhaps the much-praised soma of early Indian religion as well as one of the drugs referred to in European legends.[177] If so, then the religious, cultural, and historical impact of this drug has been nothing short of profound.

Among the many drugs used in Latin America, two of the most powerful and popular psychedelics are peyote and yage. Peyote is an unspectacular-looking, vile-tasting cactus—so vile that many users feel nauseous and Indians describe it as "a hard road." The great American philosopher William James, who had some profoundly meaningful experiences with nitrous oxide that significantly affected his philosophical views, was sick for 24 hours after eating a single piece of the cactus. He concluded that he would take peyote visions on faith rather than personal experience. For those able to keep it down, the effects are much like those of its major active component, mescaline.

Yage, also known as ayahuasco or ayahausca, is an equally vile-tasting and nausea-producing psychedelic made from an Ama-

zonian "visionary vine" called Banisteriopsis. Yage is chemically complex, but its most important psychoactive ingredient may be harmaline.[177] Shamans, of course, attribute the effects not to chemicals but to the spirit that dwells within the plant.

Yage appears to elicit strong visual experiences. Users describe long sequences of dreamlike visions that appear in a spiritually significant progression. Yage is famous for provoking specific images, particularly jungle scenes and especially visions of dangerous creatures such as tigers, snakes, and naked women.[177] Several Westerners who have ingested the substance, including Michael Harner, have described their amazement at the power of the imagery and its consistency with native reports.[78, 177] However, much of this imagery may be due to the jungle setting in which the drug was consumed since three Western researchers whom I interviewed who had taken yage in an urban setting reported no jungle imagery whatsoever.

With regard to shamanism, yage is claimed to have healing and telepathic effects. In South America it is known as "the great medicine" that, through its intercession with the spirits, can either reveal remedies or produce healing. In contrast to Western notions of medicine, yage is believed to be curative whether the patient or the healer swallows it.[37]

Yage is also famous because of repeated claims for its clairvoyant powers. Native reports abound of yage-empowered journeys, flying, and extrasensory perception. One anthropologist reported that "on the day following one Ayahuasca party, six of nine men informed me of seeing the death of my chai, my mother's father. This occurred a few days before I was informed by radio of his death."[177] Needless to day, the validity and significance of such reports are hotly debated.

With the encroachment of civilization these traditional drugs are now being replaced in many areas by tobacco and alcohol, which are less psychedelic, less useful for spiritual and healing rituals, and far more addictive. The result is that in many places

FIGURE 15. Eskimo drawing of a shaman in flight. (Drawing by Jessie Oonark, Eskimo, 1971, Winnipeg Art Gallery.)

alcoholism is found to be largely replacing the ceremonial use of sacred drugs.[198]

Psychedelics and Mystical Experiences

One question that must be considered in any discussion of drug use for religious purposes is whether drugs can induce genuine mystical experiences.

In the West there is currently a strong tendency to dismiss the validity and religious significance of any drug experience. Consequently the fact that shamans may use drugs has caused some people to dismiss them completely. Even some firm supporters of

shamanism such as Eliade have regarded drug use as a degenerative form of the tradition.

Five major arguments have been advanced to suggest that drug experiences can never be truly mystical. (1) Some drug experiences are clearly anything but mystical and beneficial. (2) The experiences induced by drugs are actually different from those of genuine mystics. (3) Mystical rapture is a gift of God that can never be brought under merely human control. (4) Drug-induced experiences are too quick and easy and can hardly be identical to those hard won by years of contemplative discipline. (5) The aftereffects of drug-induced experiences are different, less beneficial, and less long-lasting than those of contemplatives. There are several possible answers to each of these concerns.

There is no doubt that some—in fact many—drug experiences are anything but mystical. As the religious scholar Huston Smith points out:

> There are, of course, innumerable experiences that have no religious features; they can be sensual as readily as spiritual, trivial as readily as transforming, capricious as readily as sacramental. If there is one point about which every student agrees, it is that there is no such thing as the drug experience per se. . . . This of course proves that not all drug experiences are religious; it does not prove that no drug experiences are religious.[174]

The next question concerns whether drug and natural mystical states are experientially the same. Research suggests that "descriptively drug experiences cannot be distinguished from their natural religious counterparts."[174] In philosophical terms, drug and natural mystical experiences are phenomenologically (experientially or descriptively) identical.

The most dramatic experiment affirming this was the so-called Harvard Good Friday study, also known as "the miracle of Marsh Chapel." In this study divinity students and professors were given either the psychedelic psilocybin or an inactive placebo in

Harvard University's Marsh Chapel during a Good Friday service. Researchers were unable to distinguish the reports of the psilocybin-induced "mystical experiences" from those of mystics throughout the centuries.[174]

Perhaps the people best equipped to say whether drug-induced and contemplatively induced mystical experiences can be the same are those who have had both. Such people are few and far between. However, a survey of spiritual teachers located at least one such person who concluded from personal experience that they could be.[190]

The third argument, that mystical rapture is a gift from God that can never be brought under human control, will only seem plausible to those people who hold certain specific theological beliefs. It would hardly be regarded as a valid argument by religions such as Buddhism, for example, that do not believe in an all-powerful creator God. Nor presumably would it appeal to Christians who believe more in the power of good works than of grace.

The complaint that drug experiences are too quick and easy to be genuine is readily understandable. After all, it hardly seems fair that a contemplative should labor for decades for a sip of what the drug user may effortlessly swim in for hours. However, unfair or not, if the states are experientially identical, then the fact that they arise from different causes may be irrelevant. Technically this has been called "the principal of causal indifference."[174] Simply stated, this means that if the two experiences are identical it matters not one whit how they are caused.

The final argument against the equivalence of drug and natural mystical states is that they may result in different long-term effects. Once again Huston Smith has put the case eloquently. He notes that "drugs appear to induce religious experiences: it is less evident that they can produce religious lives."[174]

This much seems clear: drug and natural mystical experiences can be similar or identical but may differ in their aftereffects. But still the debate continues over whether psychedelically induced

mystical experiences are "really genuine." Stanislav Grof concludes that "at present, after thirty years of discussion, the question whether LSD and other psychedelics can induce genuine spiritual experiences is still open."[68]

One reason the debate continues unabated is that there has been no theory of mystical states that could resolve it. What is needed is a theory accounting for the induction of similar or identical states by such different means as LSD and meditation, followed by different aftereffects. It may now be possible to create such a theory in light of current understanding of the induction of altered states of consciousness.

Charles Tart's model of consciousness is helpful here.[179] Tart suggests that any state of consciousness is the result of the function and interaction of psychological and neural processes such as perception, attention, emotions, and identity. If the functioning of any one process is changed sufficiently, the entire system or state of consciousness may shift. It therefore seems possible that a specific altered state may be reached in more than one way by altering different processes. For example, states of calm may be reached by reducing muscle tension, visualizing restful scenery, or focusing attention on the breath. In each case the brain-mind process used is different but the resulting state is similar.

The implication of this is that a similar phenomenon may occur with mystical states. Different techniques might affect different brain-mind processes yet still result in the same mystical state of consciousness. A contemplative might finally taste the bliss of mystical unity after years of cultivating qualities such as concentration, love, and compassion. Yet it is also possible that a psychedelic might affect chemical and neuronal processes so powerfully as to temporarily induce a similar state.

It seems that Tart's theory of consciousness may be extended to provide an explanation for the finding that "chemical mysticism" and natural mysticism may be experientially identical. But

what of the fact that the long-term impact of the two may be quite different? These differences may also be compatible with the theory.

Both psychological and social factors may be involved. The psychedelic user may have a dramatic experience, perhaps the most dramatic of his or her entire life. But a single experience, no matter how powerful, may be insufficient to permanently overcome mental and neural habits conditioned over decades to mundane modes of function. The contemplative, on the other hand, may spend decades deliberately working to retrain habits along more spiritual lines. Thus when the breakthrough finally occurs, it visits a mind already prepared for it. In addition the contemplative probably has in place a belief system that can make sense of the experience, a discipline that can cultivate it, a tradition and social group that support it, and an ethic that can guide its expression. One is reminded of Louis Pasteur's statement that "chance favors the prepared mind." The contemplative's mind is prepared, but there is no guarantee that the drug user's is.

In summary, these ideas suggest that some drugs can indeed induce genuine mystical experiences in some people on some occasions. However, they are more likely to do so and more likely to produce enduring benefits in prepared minds. Shamans were people whose minds were prepared, sometimes for years, and as such psychedelics may well have opened them to a variety of genuine mystical experiences.

Rhythm

Rhythmic stimulation, whether by music, singing, or dancing, has long been known to induce altered states. Such techniques have been widely used by mystics of many traditions. In the Jewish tradition the Hassidic sect placed enormous faith in the power of

song and dance. The Bible relates that the prophet Elisha said, " 'But now bring me a minstrel.' And when the minstrel played the power of the Lord came upon him."[15]

As Evelyn Underhill, author of the classic text *Mysticism*, noted:

> Dancing, music and other exaggerations of natural rhythm have been pressed into the same service by the Greek initiates of Dionysus, by the gnostics, by innumerable other mystic cults. That these proceedings do effect a remarkable change in the human consciousness is proved by experience: though how and why they do it is yet little understood.[186]

Shamans too have used these techniques. Drums and rattles have been their most widely used instruments. When a drum is played at a tempo of some 200 to 220 beats per minute, most Western novices report that they can journey successfully even on their first attempt. The remarkable ease of induction of these states and their experiences is obviously one reason for shamanism's recent popularity. This ease contrasts dramatically with the months of practice usually required by most meditative and yogic disciplines before significant altered states appear. However, the drum is sometimes used even in these more recent traditions—in Korean Zen, for example.

Drumming probably facilitates shamanic states and journeying through several mechanisms. First, it may act as a concentration device that continuously reminds the shaman of her purpose and reduces the mind's incessant tendency to wander. It also probably drowns out other distracting stimuli and enables the shaman to focus attention inward. Heightened concentration seems to be a key element in effective spiritual disciplines,[62] and shamans appear to have found one of the quickest and easiest ways to attain it.

Drumming and other loud noises may also act as destabilizing factors that disrupt the ongoing psychological process by which we continuously maintain our usual state of consciousness. Charles

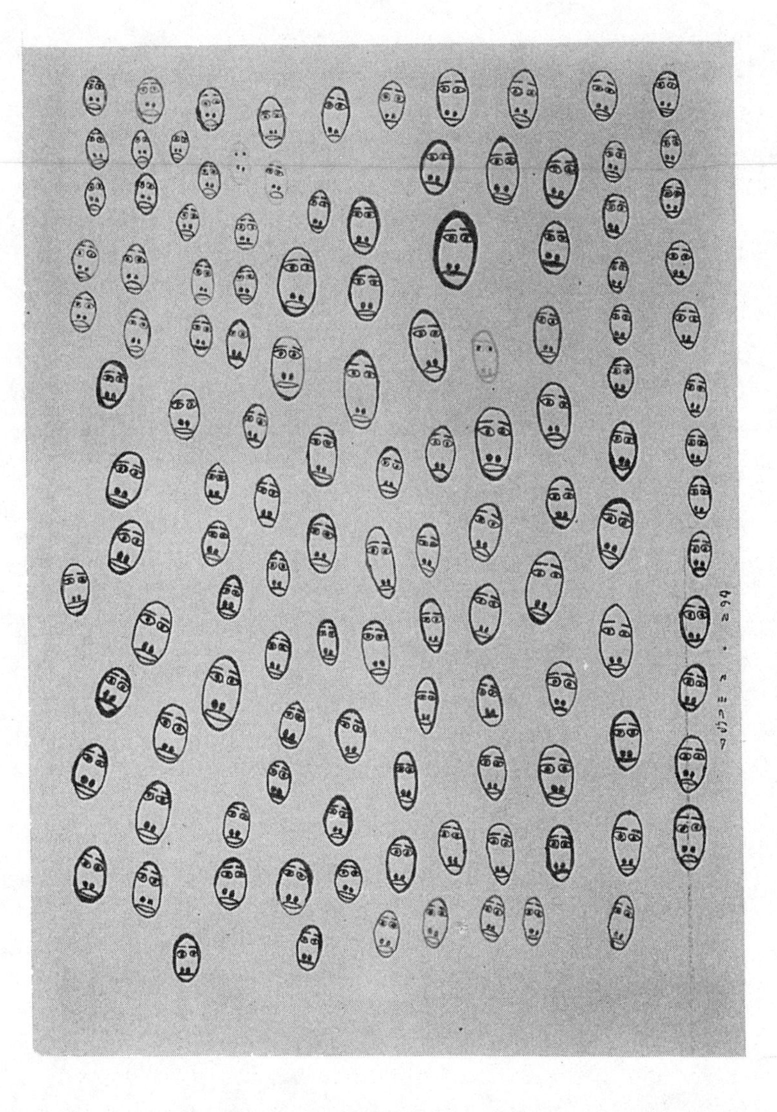

FIGURE 16. "People stunned by the drum"—an Eskimo depiction of an audience entranced by drumming. (Luke Anguhadluq, drawing, Baker Lake, Eskimo, 1972.)

Tart says that in his experience a sufficiently loud drumbeat feels as though it rapidly overwhelms stabilizing forces, making an abrupt change of state very easy. Interestingly, Zen masters appear to make use of this same principle. Numerous stories relate how they have trailed students who were at the point of breakthrough. Then when the students least expected it, the masters crept up behind them and yelled at the top of their voice. The ideal result is an instant satori, a taste of enlightenment.

Drumming is also commonly assumed to harmonize neural activity with the vibrational frequency of the sound. Two studies that appear to support this idea have been widely quoted.[127, 128] In both, electroencephalograms of subjects listening to drumming seemed to show auditory driving responses. Auditory driving occurs when a repetitive sound provokes corresponding firing frequencies in the brain. These studies have been widely quoted as proof of the neural effects of drumming, but unfortunately the studies are flawed. The measurements of brain waves were probably contaminated by the shaman's body movements, making it impossible to draw firm conclusions about brain activity.[1] Whatever the neural mechanisms may be, anyone who has been entranced by music or dancing is well aware of rhythm's powerful potential for affecting states of mind.

With greater training and expertise, shamans may become less dependent on their external aids. They may then be able to enter and remain in altered states without the aid of drumming or other techniques.[7] This would be expected if the ability to access altered states is partly a learned skill.

Overview of Shamanic Techniques

Whatever the precise neural mechanisms involved, it is clear that shamans have discovered a wide variety of psychological, physiological, and chemical aids to modify consciousness. Shamans de-

veloped a range of techniques that constituted one of humankind's earliest technologies, a technology of transcendence. The techniques were simple and were probably discovered by accident—when the tribe faced hunger, fatigue, and dehydration or ate psychedelic plants. Because of their pleasurable and valuable effects, these techniques were likely to be remembered and repeated. When collected together and set within a tradition and cosmology, shamanism would be born. Thus would be discovered and rediscovered, in different times and places, humankind's first road map to transcendent states, the first technology of transcendence, through which would pour the visions of the sacred that sustained and inspired humankind for thousands of years.

CHAPTER 13

Divination and Diagnosis

Humans respond not to events but to their meanings and can read into any event an endless variety of meanings.

JEROME FRANK

While shamans devised a variety of techniques for altering their consciousness, they also devised a variety of techniques for working in an ordinary state. Their many roles—diagnostician, counselor, healer—demanded many methods. We need not go into all of these. Some are simple physical techniques such as massage or wound cleaning; others seem to be merely superstitions. Yet some are sensitive strategies for diagnosis and treatment that foreshadow contemporary psychological techniques. Among the more interesting are the world's first projective test, the use of muscle tension to test for breaches of taboo, and group confession.

THE WORLD'S FIRST PROJECTIVE TEST

The shaman's projective test is remarkably similar to one widely used today in clinical psychology, namely the Rorschach test. With the Rorschach, also known as the inkblot test, patients look at a series of inkblots and describe what they see. Both the Rorschach test and the shaman's test rely on the mind's tendency to structure ambiguous scenes into personally meaningful images. These images tend to be particularly related to the motives and emotions operating at the time. The mind projects symbolic representations

of these motives and emotions onto the ambiguous scenes. These scenes now seem powerful or peaceful, threatening or loving, sordid or saintly, depending on the viewer's state of mind. These tests wonderfully demonstrate the wisdom of both the ancient Jews and ancient Greeks who said, respectively, "We do not see things as they are but as we are" and "Men are disturbed not by things, but by the view which they take of them." They also demonstrate the truth of a more modern saying, that of Carl Jung, who claimed that "projections change the world into the replica of one's own unknown face."

The shamanic projective test is deceptively simple. The patient with a question or problem chooses a rock and brings it to the shaman. The shaman then instructs him to hold his question in mind, to view each side of the rock and report the images he sees there. After all the sides have been examined and images reported, the shaman asks the patient to describe how each image speaks to his question or concern.

The beauty of this technique lies in its simplicity and powerful ability to reveal unconscious motives. Even in these modern times it can be a valuable tool and has been used with Westerners with good results.

The Head-Lifting Test

In a second technique an Eskimo shaman addresses a series of questions to a patient while he lifts the patient's head. Changes in the apparent weight of the head are taken to indicate positive or negative responses. Rasmussen describes the procedure as follows:

> The one who is to consult the spirits, lays a person down on the floor, or on the sleeping place, face upwards, the operator's waistbelt being often fastened around the subject's head. Various questions are now put to the qila'na: the person through whose head the

> spirits are to answer. While asking the questions, the operator endeavors to raise the person's head by means of the belt, calling upon the spirit, which is supposed to enter the scene immediately below the body of the qila'na. When the latter's head grows heavy, so heavy that the operator, despite all his efforts, cannot move it in the slightest degree, this means that the spirits are present and answer in the affirmative. If, on the other hand, the head is normal and easily moved, this constitutes a negative answer to the question put. . . . I once wrote down the proceedings in such a case. . . . The object was to ascertain the cause of a particular illness. . . .
>
> "Is the illness due to forbidden food?"
>
> The head grows lighter, the shaman lifts it with ease, and the listeners answer:
>
> "a'k'agoq": "No!"
>
> "isarajannik?": "Is the illness due to forbidden work?"
>
> The spirit answers:
>
> "Yes!" . . .
>
> Should the spirit answer yes, then it remains to investigate further, with constant pulls at the line, what breach of taboo has taken place and under what circumstances. So the questioning goes on, letting the spirit answer all the time, until the presumable cause of the sickness has been ascertained.[147]

From a psychological perspective we would interpret changes in the apparent weight of the head as due to variations in muscle tension. The technique seems wonderfully designed to allow the patient to communicate both conscious and unconscious concerns, since muscle tension is affected by both. The test probably fosters confession and expression of the patient's unconscious concerns even when such communication and confession might be consciously resisted. Confession may be good not only for the soul but also for the body, at least where psychosomatic illness is involved. Thus this type of diagnostic confession may foster both psychological and physical healing.

Group Confession

Shamans may also use group confession. An interesting example of this occurs after the Eskimo shaman has returned from the journey to placate the sea spirit Takánakapsâluk. Having interceded with her on behalf of the tribe, the shaman journeys back from the bottom of the sea to be greeted by the people's cries for information about the success or failure of the journey. But the shaman does not give the information. He hedges, saying "words will arise." Then he waits, knowing what will happen next. Rasmussen described the scene as follows:

> Then all in the house must confess any breaches of taboo they have committed.
>
> "It is my fault, perhaps," they cry, all at once, women and men together, in fear of famine and starvation, and all begin telling of the wrong things they have done. All the names of those in the house are mentioned, and all must confess, and thus much comes to light which no one had ever dreamed of; every one learns his neighbors' secrets. But despite all the sins confessed, the shaman may go on talking as one who is unhappy at having made a mistake, and again and again break out into such expressions as this:
>
> "I seek my grounds in things which have not happened; I speak as one who knows nothing."
>
> There are still secrets barring the way for full solution of the trouble, and so the women in the house begin to go through all the names, one after another; nearly all women's names; for it was always their breaches of taboo which were most dangerous. Now and again when a name is mentioned, the shaman exclaims in relief:
>
> "taina, taina!" . . . Thus at last the cause of Takánakapsâluk's anger is explained, and all are filled with joy at having escaped disaster. They are now assured that there will be abundance of game on the following day. And in the end, there may be almost a

> feeling of thankfulness towards the delinquent. This then was what took place when shamans went down and propitiated the great Spirit of the Sea.[147]

Here can be seen many of the components of contemporary group therapy. The group as a whole collaborates on a project of common concern. Individuals are confronted with their shortcomings, and this leads to confession and catharsis. The confession and sharing of intimate secrets by all members leads to a sense of mutual openness, trust, and group cohesion. Members find out that they are not, as they feared, the only sinners, and the result is a sense of relief and closeness that can be healing for all concerned. Of course, to the shaman these psychological benefits are minor concerns compared to the importance of identifying the breaches of taboo in order to appease the Great Sea Spirit. However, from a psychological perspective one can certainly see that the procedure could be therapeutic for both the individuals and the tribe. In fact, in Native American traditions this type of healing group is called a "medicine wheel."

In summary, then, it appears that shamans are able to draw on a range of psychologically skillful diagnostic and therapeutic techniques accumulated by their predecessors over centuries. Some of these techniques clearly foreshadow ones widely used today and thereby confirm the reputation of shamans as humankind's first psychotherapists.

CHAPTER 14

How Do They Heal? Psychological Principles of Shamanic Healing

I don't know what you learned from books, but the most important thing I learned from my grandfathers was that there is a part of the mind that we really don't know about, and it is that part that is most important in whether we become sick or remain well.

THOMAS LARGEWHISKERS, Navaho medicine man

Though they perform many functions, shamans are, above all, healers. For in cultures without technology, science, surgery, and medicine as we know them, it is the shaman's power that alone offers hope of healing. How do they heal? What are their techniques and how do they work? These are the questions to which we now turn.

Our perspective will continue to be primarily psychological, but this is not to say that the shamanic techniques or the means by which they work are *only* psychological. Shamans may use a variety of physical treatments such as cleaning wounds, massaging limbs, and administering herbal medications. Moreover, shamans themselves regard their healing powers as primarily spiritual.

Yet much of their effectiveness may be due to psychological factors. Like all healers they use suggestion and expectation and a variety of rituals that may elicit powerful placebo effects. Some of their practices involve what could be considered skillful psychotherapeutic techniques.

For these reasons and more, shamans have often been called humankind's first psychotherapists. This is not surprising if we consider the broad range of activities that go on in therapy. Consider, for example, the definition given by Jerome Frank, one of this century's foremost psychotherapy researchers:

> Psychotherapy is a planned, emotionally charged, confiding interaction between a trained, socially sanctioned healer and a sufferer. During this interaction the healer seeks to relieve the sufferer's distress and disability through symbolic communications, primarily words but also sometimes bodily activities. The healer may or may not involve the patient's relatives and others in the healing rituals. Psychotherapy also often includes helping the patient to accept and endure suffering as an inevitable aspect of life that can be used as an opportunity for personal growth. . . . All psychotherapeutic methods are elaborations and variations of age-old procedures of psychological healing.[50]

Certainly this definition of psychotherapy includes much of what shamans do during their healing rituals. Many of their practices—including those aimed at healing physical as well as mental symptoms—can therefore be considered as psychological or psychotherapeutic. The fact that shamans use psychological techniques for physical illness is not to say that their techniques are ineffective. Psychological treatments may be beneficial in a surprisingly wide array of illnesses.

There are several reasons for the wide-ranging effectiveness of psychological interventions. The first is that a significant number of people who present themselves complaining of physical ills are in fact suffering from psychological or psychosomatic problems. It has been estimated that approximately half the visits to Western general practitioners are motivated by psychological factors, and a similar situation may exist in other cultures. For example, a study of native healers in Taiwan found that 90 percent of their patients suffered from psychological disorders and that al-

most half of their physical complaints could be traced to psychosomatic causes.[101] Interestingly, this finding is consistent with the shamanic belief that much of their healing involves treating "soul loss," which is also described as a condition of being dispirited or disheartened.

The process can also work in the opposite (somatopsychic) direction. People with physical illness may suffer disabling anxiety or depression and this in turn may exacerbate their physical symptoms. Psychological help can therefore sometimes reduce physical suffering dramatically.

Psychological interventions may be the treatment of choice for psychological symptoms such as anxiety and guilt, which can be very strong in tribal cultures. In such societies, "the strain for survival may be intense, the structure of the society may be intricate and frustrating and the fear of the unknown may be terrifying."[153] Life is hedged in by countless taboos and the least infringement may mean sickness, suffering, and death not only for oneself but also for one's family and even the entire tribe. Small wonder that a shaman who could relieve fear and guilt through psychological strategies and spiritual interventions would be regarded as a hero of the first order.

Psychological techniques may also heal because of the placebo effect. This is the healing that results, not from the inherent effectiveness of a drug or technique, but rather from the patient's faith in the healer and the healing process. We will have more to say about this placebo effect shortly, but it will be useful first to examine the healing techniques that shamans use. The following is a survey of the most common.

Healing Techniques

The healing ritual must be preceded by careful preparation of both the shaman and the location. Equipment must be gathered, sacred

objects collected, medicines prepared. The shaman may spend time in solitude, fasting, or prayer. Both the preparation and the healing ritual itself are steeped in symbolism and ancient rituals, all of which may inspire awe and faith.

In Western medicine and psychiatry, patients are often treated in complete privacy and isolation. Shamans, on the other hand, often gather the family and even the whole tribe to participate in the ceremony. The patient is thus the center of attention and receives considerable community support.

Confession and catharsis may play major roles. All participants may be expected to confess their breaches of taboo—as, for example, in the case we have already examined of the Eskimo shaman's journey to placate the sea spirit Takánakapsâluk.

Much of the ceremony may be accompanied by music and song. The belief that music can be healing has long been common to many cultures. In ancient Greece both Plato and Aristotle ascribed curative power to certain melodies while Apollo was the god of both medicine and music. The Jewish Hassidics and American Indians also believed in the healing ability of music.[81] Today in the West music therapy is a recognized healing aid. Shamans, therefore, stand at the head of a long lineage of those who have used music for its healing power.

Music may also play a central role in the shamanic induction of altered states of consciousness. While it is well known that shamans enter altered states, it is not so widely recognized that their patients may do likewise.[207] This may occur in at least two ways: through the rhythmic stimulation of music and ritual, and through ingesting psychedelics. Both the patient and audience hear the drumming and singing that the shaman uses to enter an altered state. Therefore they too might enter trances, though perhaps less easily and deeply than the shaman who has spent years mastering this skill. If the patient receives suggestions and persuasion for healing during this trance, a (perhaps unrecognized) state of hyp-

nosis might be induced. Suggestions for healing given during hypnosis can sometimes be dramatically effective and might play a major role in some shamanic successes.

Patients may also enter altered states of consciousness through ingesting psychedelics. In Latin America either shaman or patient or both may take yage to obtain the spirit vision that will reveal the cause of illness. When this spiritual source of illness has been recognized, the shaman acts to correct it. This may mean intervening with troublesome spirits, retrieving the patient's soul, or exorcising spiritual intrusions. At the end of such an exorcism the shaman may produce, with full dramatic flourish, some unsightly object such as a spider or worm to prove the effectiveness of the treatment.

Patients may have to pay for their healing. They will almost certainly have to pay the shaman and quite possibly make offerings to the spirits as well. In addition the shaman may require them to follow rigid rituals such as a restrictive diet and carefully kept taboos. Such payments and restrictions may increase the effectiveness of treatment, or at least the patients' belief in its effectiveness; since it seems that the more people pay for something, the more they are likely to value it.

Some of these healing rituals are extremely arduous and time-consuming. There are many reports of sessions lasting throughout the night, and when psychedelics are ingested, both shamans and patients have obviously committed themselves to several extremely intense hours. Clearly, a shaman who uses these techniques may give an enormous amount of care and attention to any one patient but is likely to be able to see very few patients.

A curious paradox may therefore develop. As a shaman becomes more popular, both diagnosis and treatment may become simpler and shorter. Such was the conclusion of at least one researcher, who found that "the more popular a shaman becomes, the less time he is able to devote to any one patient. This results in

the paradoxical situation that the elaborate healing rituals described in loving detail by social anthropologists are carried out by those healers who have very few patients."[171]

The Placebo Effect

The word *placebo,* from the Latin "I shall please," refers to a powerful but little-understood healing process. The placebo effect has been defined as "a poorly understood process in which psychological factors such as belief and expectation trigger a healing response that can be as powerful as any conventional therapy—be it drugs, surgery or psychotherapy—for a wide range of medical and psychological problems."[89]

Consider, for example, the humble wart. It can be made to disappear by hypnosis, incantations, burying a rag at the crossroads under a full moon—in fact, by almost any treatment provided that the patient believes it will work. Yet no patient, physician, or researcher understands exactly how the mind and body produce this minor miracle. Many people, including some physicians, assume that since the placebo effect relies on something so ethereal as mere belief, it must be a weak effect at best. But consider the following story.

In the 1950s a man dying of advanced cancer learned of an experimental drug called krebiozen, which many people considered a miracle cure for cancer. The man desperately insisted he be given it. After a single dose his huge cancers "melted like snowballs on a hot stove" and he was able to resume normal activities.

Then disaster struck. Studies of krebiozen showed it to be ineffective, and when the man read this his cancer once again began spreading. At this stage his doctor tried an experiment. He announced that there was a new, "improved" krebiozen and the patient would now receive it. Once again the man's tumors shrank. Yet in fact the doctor had given him only water.[103]

Clearly, then, placebo effects can be extremely powerful, even life-saving. They are also widespread; approximately one-third of people who are treated with completely inactive placebos are likely to show improvement.[89] The placebo effect has probably been a major factor in most therapies through most of human history. Herbert Benson, author of the popular book *The Relaxation Response,* listed some of the many bizarre things once believed to be effective treatments:

> In the past, various useless agents were believed to be effective against disease: lizard's blood, crushed spiders, putrid meat, crocodile dung, bear fat, fox lungs, eunuch fat and moss scraped from the skull of a hanged criminal. Likewise, cupping, blistering, plastering and leeching had their day. When *both* physician and patient believed in them, these remedies could indeed have been helpful some of the time.[14]

Although the placebo effect has been perhaps the major force in healing, it has only recently been researched, and its importance is becoming better appreciated. Author Norman Cousins suggests that "an understanding of the way the placebo works may be one of the most significant developments in medicine in the twentieth century."[89]

The range of ills that the placebo effect can help is awesome. Positive responses have been found with coronary artery disease, high blood pressure, cancer, arthritis, ulcers, migraine headaches, allergies, hay fever, acne, multiple sclerosis, diabetes, parkinsonism, pain, radiation sickness, and psychiatric disorders such as depression and anxiety.[89]

Placebo effects also play a role in many, if not all, therapeutic interactions. Even a powerful and effective drug may gain part of its impact from the patients' and doctors' expectations of cure.

But expectations can also be negative. Therefore, it is not surprising that negative expectations can lead to negative placebo effects, or *nocebo* effects as they are sometimes called. Consider, for

example, the case of cancer patients who thought they were receiving a new form of chemotherapy but were actually given a placebo. One of the common complications of cancer chemotherapy is hair loss, and the patients were expecting this. A full 31 percent of those who received a placebo did in fact lose their hair.[47] Even a physician's casual comments about a patient's condition may have an awesome impact. The nocebo effect is probably also the basis for so-called voodoo sickness—even voodoo death—that can occur when a tribal person knows he has been hexed.

As yet it is unclear how the placebo works its remarkable effects. What is clear is that the process is little short of miraculous. Even the placebo healing of a simple wart is "absolutely astonishing," as Lewis Thomas, one of the best-known medical writers of our time, points out. The intelligence that directs such a healing process must combine the skills of a world-class cell biologist, immunologist, surgeon, and executive officer. This, says Thomas, points to "a kind of superintelligence that exists in each of us, infinitely smarter and possessed of technical know-how far beyond our present understanding."[182]

Certainly expectations and beliefs are key forces in the placebo response. Beliefs can harm, heal, kill, or save, and native healers may be well aware of this. A Navaho medicine man made the point about as clearly as anyone could: "If the patient really has confidence in me, then he gets cured. If he has no confidence, then that is his problem."[157] The patient's confidence and beliefs are affected by the entire context in which healing occurs. Thus the personality, status, behavior, and beliefs of the therapist as well as those of the patient all play a role. Skillful healers throughout the ages have probably recognized this and sought to bolster what Jerome Frank calls "the healing power of expectant faith" through whatever means they could. In light of this, the tricks and sleight of hand so widely used by shamans to impress their patients may actually enhance expectant faith and hence the possibility of heal-

ing. Clearly the placebo effect has been one of the most powerful forces for healing throughout human history and shamans may have been the first to harness it systematically.

HOW SUCCESSFUL ARE SHAMANIC HEALERS?

Shamans have not always been the world's most humble healers; some have claimed to be virtually infallible. The more modest among them claim that healing sometimes occurs through them but that they are mere instruments of the spirits to whom true credit is due.[73]

We have almost no actual data as to just how effective shamanic healing is. The best we can do is to make some rough assessments based on our knowledge of the shamanic procedures and the psychological principles that influence healing.

Several characteristics of shamanic healing would lead one to expect positive outcomes. These include the selection of cases, the placebo effect, the use of psychotherapeutic techniques and hypnosis, and the harmlessness of the shamans' interventions.

Shamans usually try desperately to avoid taking on hopeless cases. After all, their livelihood—and their lives—depend on success, and in some cultures the shaman who loses a patient may lose his own life.[153] Treating only those patients who are likely to recover is certainly a good way to bolster one's success rate.

Another important factor is that shamanic interventions are probably relatively harmless. This is no small claim. One of Western medicine's golden rules is "First, do no harm." This rule was unwittingly broken for centuries by physicians who often did considerable harm. Techniques such as bleeding patients or giving them mercury could hardly be called harmless, yet they were among the mainstays of medicine for hundreds of years. They stand as mute testimony to the awesome power of expectant faith

that kept patients subjecting themselves to these and other deadly treatments. The shamans' treatments, which are primarily spiritual, seem most benign by comparison.

The shamans' skillful use of the placebo effect would likely bolster success rates. Many shamanic rituals seem admirably designed to elicit it, since the effect is maximal when therapies are elaborate, detailed, expensive, time-consuming, fashionable, or esoteric.[89]

What types of success rates would general principles such as these lead us to predict? This of course will vary with the disorder being treated. With physical problems we might expect that success rates would approximate those of nineteenth-century Western physicians. For psychological problems such as mild anxiety or depression that respond well to psychological interventions and social support, success rates might well approximate those of contemporary psychotherapies. For those disorders that require, according to Western theories, intervention with such things as drugs or surgery, we would expect success rates that approximate placebo rates only.

Of course, to shamans such claims make little sense. For them the pains their patients suffer are primarily spiritual in origin, and consequently spiritual responses are in order. This raises the question of whether parapsychological factors might conceivably play a role in shamanic healing, and we will turn to this topic in the next chapter. However, at the very least it is apparent that in trying to understand the methods and mechanisms by which shamanic healing might work, we inevitably find ourselves caught in a paradigm clash. The questions of how, and how much, shamanic healing works will be answered entirely differently by shamans and Western physicians who find each other's spiritual and mechanistic world views meaningless.

Nonetheless the shaman's world view is far from meaningless to patients who share it. It is this sharing that constitutes the healing myth within which therapy can take place. In part because

of this shared healing myth, shamans have long been a source of hope and help for a wide variety of problems ranging from physical illness to spiritual crises. For the tribe the shaman is a guide, a healer, a source of social cohesion, and the keeper of the tribal myths and world view. In a world of vast and incomprehensible forces the shaman offers hope that these forces might be understood, modified, and even mastered; that humans need not be helpless, mystified victims of an uncaring universe and that illness might be healed, conflicts settled, guilt assuaged, gods mollified, evil vanquished, and even death robbed of some of its sting. What an extraordinary contribution, and what a symbol of hope, healing, and power the shaman must have been for thousands of years.

C H A P T E R 1 5

How Do They Heal? Beyond Psychology

Every transformation of man . . . has rested on a new picture of the cosmos and the nature of man.
LEWIS MUMFORD

We have seen that shamans employ a wide range of healing rituals, many of which make good psychological sense to Westerners. For shamans, however, such psychological explanations largely miss the point, for their healing myth is primarily a spiritual one. From their perspective it is spiritual problems such as spirit intrusion or therapeutic techniques such as soul retrieval that primarily account for sickness and healing.

There are, of course, two very different ways of interpreting shamanic beliefs. The first and traditionally most common is that they are classic examples of "primitive thinking" similar to the supposedly magical thinking of Western children. The other perspective is that these shamanic claims reflect, at least in part, the operation of psychic abilities.

Parapsychology is, to put it mildly, a controversial subject, one which I would like to bypass. In few areas of research is there such widespread conflict. Supporters claim that "a vast parapsychological literature exists on a host of rigorous experiments." Skeptics on the other hand report that "after 100 years of research, not a single individual has been found who can demonstrate ESP to the satisfaction of independent investigators."

Proponents point to controlled studies showing that humans are capable of both extrasensory perception (ESP) and of exerting psychokinetic (mind on matter) effects on objects and organisms

ranging from mice to electronic circuitry.[91] Of particular relevance to shamanic healing are reports of controlled studies showing psychokinetic effects on the growth of plants and fungi, on the activity of enzymes, the healing of mice, and the level of blood hemoglobin in humans.[13, 63, 104, 176] Critics dismiss such findings as either elusive, unreplicable, or due to experimental incompetence or fraud. Consensus is not a common thing in parapsychology. To complicate things further, parapsychological claims call into question some of the most fundamental and time-honored laws of physics.

Despite this, any investigation of shamanic healing, if it is to be intellectually honest and open-minded, needs to address the question of whether psi (psychic phenomena) may play some role. For, as William James said, "there is no source of deception in the investigation of nature which can compare with a fixed belief that certain kinds of phenomena are impossible."[92] We can assess the possibility of psi-induced healing in shamanism in several way. We can examine claims for psychic abilities in other religious and healing traditions as well as anecdotal reports and laboratory studies of psi in shamans. In addition we can examine similarities between shamanic healing rituals and those conditions reported to maximize psi.

Claims for psychic abilities are common among religious traditions the world over. Some practices such as yoga and Buddhist meditation contain explicit and detailed instructions on the cultivation of psychic powers. Most of these cultivation techniques involve the development of enormous powers of concentration far beyond those of normal people.[27] However, these traditions also contain strong explicit warnings about the dangers of developing psychic abilities without a corresponding development of wisdom. All power corrupts, as the old saying tells us, and psychic power is no exception, these traditions claim.

Nor are religious practitioners alone in claiming that psi may operate in their work. Several highly respected Western physicians, psychologists, and psychiatrists have made similar suggestions.

These include such notables as Freud, Jung, and Jerome Frank. Wrote Frank:

> My own hunch, which I mention with some trepidation, is that the most gifted therapists may have telepathic, clairvoyant, or other parapsychological abilities. . . . They may, in addition, possess something that is similar to the ability to speed growth . . . and that can only be termed healing power. Any researcher who attempts to study such phenomena risks his reputation as a reliable scientist, so the pursuit can be recommended only to the most intrepid. The rewards, however, might be great.[50]

Anecdotal Reports of Psychic Phenomena in Shamans

Anecdotal reports of supposedly psychic displays by shamans are common. The following examples will give the flavor of the more dramatic ones.

A French missionary claimed that he witnessed a display of clairvoyance by a New Caledonian shaman. "In the course of a great joyous feast," the missionary wrote, "he suddenly plunged himself into despair, announcing that he saw one of his illustrious relatives in Arama (a town several miles away) agonizing. A canoe was speedily sent to Arama, a three-hour trip from there. The chief had just died."[12]

An example closer to home involved a case of possible psychokinesis by a well-known Huichol Indian shaman, Don Jose, who was brought to the Esalen Institute in California by his American apprentice, Prem Dass. According to Prem Dass, at the time they arrived at Esalen the region had suffered a prolonged drought. Don Jose volunteered to perform a rainmaking ceremony, which was filmed by a visiting BBC television crew. The next day the bemused crew filmed themselves driving out of Esalen—in the rain.[143]

Are reports such as these suggestive of possible psychic abilities among shamans? Yes. Are they *proof* of psychic abilities? No.

Anecdotal reports, no matter how dramatic, can never be fully convincing for science, which requires repeated, controlled studies to remove the many sources of possible error. In addition to possible trickery, even the most sincere observer can misperceive, misunderstand, or misremember.

The same event can be interpreted in very different ways. A classic example was provided by the anthropologist Bogoras, who observed the Chukchee shamans at work. One such shaman

> made one of his "spirits" shout, talk, and whisper directly into my ear, and the illusion was so perfect that involuntarily I put my hand to my ear to catch the "spirit." After that he made the "spirit" enter the ground under me and talk right in between my legs, etc. All the time that he is conversing with the "separate voices" the shaman beats his drum without interruption in order to prove that his force and attention are otherwise occupied.
>
> I tried to make a phonographic record of the "separate voices" of the "spirits." . . . When the light was put out, the "spirits" after some "bashful" hesitation, entered in compliance with the commands of the shaman, and even began to talk into the funnel of the graphophone. The records show a very marked difference between the voice of the shaman himself, which sounds from afar, and the voices of the "spirits," who seemed to be talking directly into the funnel.[19]

Bogoras was impressed but not converted. He remained convinced that these effects were due to ventriloquism and other tricks. He wrote:

> There can be no doubt, of course that shamans, during their performances, employ deceit in various forms and that they themselves are fully cognizant of the fact. "There are many liars in our calling" Scratching Woman (a Chukchee shaman) said to me. "One will lift up the skin of the sleeping-room with his right toe and then assure

> you that it was done by spirits; another will talk into the bosom of his shirt through his sleeve, making the voice issue from a quite unusual place."[19]

Other people have been just as certain that Bogoras witnessed examples of psychic phenomena. They agree that some shamans are most definitely tricksters, but they point out that this in no way proves that all shamans are only tricksters. From their perspective the problem is that Bogoras "was never able to break through his scientific training and bias to admit that he had witnessed the miraculous. . . . He explained that everything he witnessed was no doubt due to trickery, though he never offered any hint as to how the feats could have been fraudulently performed."[154]

Another clash of interpretations centers on the practice of fire walking. Fire walking has long been demonstrated by native peoples, including shamans, and is now much in vogue in the United States—where the debate over competing explanations has become quite heated, so to speak. On the one hand are shamanic enthusiasts such as Eliade who suggest that the ability, at least among shamans, is due to special skills and training. On the other hand are interpreters who explain the ability to walk on hot coals in purely physical terms. They emphasize such factors as the low conductivity of coal, the brief time the foot is actually in contact with the coals, and the so-called Leidenfrost effect, which suggests that evaporation of sweat on the soles of the feet may provide a microlayer of insulating water and steam. Somewhere in between are people like Charles Tart, who suggests that physical mechanisms operate but may be supplemented by the protective effects of trance states, which at the very least may reduce blistering.[181]

These conflicting interpretations epitomize much of the debate over parapsychology. Most people tend to decide the issue according to their prior beliefs. For some, shamans are "psi masters . . . veritable early warning systems for their peoples";[199] for others psi is clearly impossible and shamans must therefore be charlatans. Opinions run very strong in this area.

Theoretical and Experimental Data

Let us therefore turn from opinions to data and ask what, if any, evidence beyond anecdotal reports we have of psychic abilities in shamans. Two types of support are available: theoretical and experimental. The theoretical support comes from a reevaluation of traditional interpretations of tribal and shamanic "magic." Most tribal cultures assume the validity of magic powers and possess specialists who claim to master them. Anthropologists have traditionally dismissed these claims as reflections of various psychological and social factors, such as the need to explain and control the universe.

Michael Winkelman of the University of Arizona has suggested an alternative, and of course controversial, interpretation. Winkelman investigated the conditions that native practitioners use in their magic rituals. These conditions—such as certain altered states of consciousness, visualizations, and positive expectations—parallel those which modern parapsychological researchers believe facilitate psi.[206] Conceivably, then, trial and error could have led tribal peoples to adopt rituals, magical practices, and "superstitions" that favored the occurrence of psi.

If psi does occur in shamanic practices, it could be of two kinds. It could be an extrasensory ability to pick up information about the nature, cause, and treatment of a patient's illness; or it could be a psychokinetic effect (PK) such as accelerated healing.

Psychokinetic Effects

Although there have been two reports of PK effects in healers whom the researchers loosely called "shamans,"[57, 156] I have been unable to locate any studies of psychokinesis in true shamans as they are defined in this book. So the question of whether shamans are ever successful in using PK to enhance healing cannot be answered at this time. The best we can do is to examine research

on other types of healers. If they turn out to demonstrate any signs of PK-enhanced healing, this would suggest that shamans might also be able to do so. It is obviously impossible to review the entire field of psi and healing here, so we will focus on some key studies.

One classic study involved not shamans but a European healer, and as patients not humans but mice. These studies were performed by Bernard Grad, a respected cancer researcher at McGill University in Montreal.[63]

The healer was a Hungarian man who used laying on of hands as his primary healing procedure. The subjects were mice with skin wounds of equal size. For the "treatment" an assistant would place a mouse from the experimental group in a paper bag, close the bag, and take it to the healer in another room. The healer held the bag in his open hands for a few minutes while focusing on healing the mouse. The bag was employed in order to minimize the effects of simple touch on the mouse. Control mice were similarly bagged and then held by people who had no known psychic abilities, in this case medical students. The size of the skin wounds was measured regularly by an assistant who did not know which mice were experimental subjects and which were controls.

The results were dramatic. The skin wounds of the experimental mice healed significantly faster than those of the controls—often at double the rate.

In a further study the mice were subjected to near-freezing temperatures. Only 14 percent of the control mice survived, as opposed to a full 60 percent of the treated ones.

In a third study mice were put on iodine-deficient diets capable of producing thyroid tumors. The measure of healing effect was the weight of the thyroid, which was expected to be less if treatment was effective. At the end of the study the treated mice did in fact have significantly lighter thyroids.

These findings are certainly dramatic. However, as Charles Tart points out, there are several possible explanations other than psychic healing. For example, the healer might have had warmer

hands or handled the bags differently than did the medical students with the control mice.[181] Exploring these alternatives is important because it is crucial that other possibilities are ruled out before parapsychological explanations are accepted.

Needless to say, these studies, like most others in parapsychology, have been the subject of considerable debate. Critics point out that the healer was also employed as a laboratory assistant and could therefore have interfered with the mice.[170] Supporters counter that the healer was kept unaware of which animals were treated and which were controls, so he could not have manipulated the data.[206]

It is possible to design experiments that would ensure that the healer has no unauthorized access to the animals and that would control for factors like hand warmth and type of handling. Given the dramatic nature of the findings, such studies are highly desirable.

In summary, then, we can say that a few carefully designed studies suggest that some healers may be able to speed healing through mechanisms that are as yet uncertain. We cannot say that these necessarily involve psi, but we also cannot say that they do not. Much research remains to be done. As regards shamanic healing, all that can be said is that some studies may support shamanic claims that healing can be facilitated by means as yet unrecognized by Western science.*

*Two dramatic studies of possible PK effects came to light after this book was completed. The findings are so extraordinary that the first response may be to dismiss them as ridiculous. Yet both studies appear to have been carefully designed and controlled and were published in respected journals. In the first, cardiac patients who were prayed for by Christians standing outside their hospital recovered better than patients who were not prayed for. In the second, the intensity and fatality of the war in Lebanon decreased in proportion to the number of people practicing TM meditation in the area.

Needless to say, both these studies need to be *very* carefully replicated, preferably several times, and all possible sources of error need to be checked before the findings can be accepted. If they are replicated, then the implications—for everything from psychology to medicine to peace to physics—will be remarkable.[211, 212]

ESP in Shamanic Healing

The other major form of parapsychological ability that might possibly be involved in shamanic healing is extrasensory perception, or ESP. Certainly shamans claim to be able to perceive things unseen by ordinary people. The development of spirit vision, as we have seen in an earlier chapter, is a central part of shamanic training. This vision is essential for diagnostic and healing work, much of which involves removing or restoring misplaced "spiritual energy."

Despite the importance of spirit vision or ESP to shamans, I have been able to find only two experimental studies of it, conducted on Afro-Brazilian "shamans."[58, 59] The subjects, however, seem to have been mediums rather than shamans since they became possessed by spirits but did not usually engage in soul flight. The subjects were tested on a remote viewing task in which they were asked to identify unseen objects located some distance away. They showed no evidence of ESP, and in one study they scored significantly worse than did controls.[57]

The negative findings are not particularly surprising since the subjects performed in an ordinary state of consciousness. Yet mediums and shamans usually claim that their psi abilities are, if not strictly limited to, then at least enhanced in, nonordinary states of consciousness. So these studies do not rule out the possibility that true shamans may sometimes display psi abilities in altered states. An experimental test of this possibility is much to be desired.

Since shamans claim that psychic ability is greater in altered states of consciousness, it is not surprising that they also claim psychedelics may enhance this ability. For this reason psychedelics are sometimes used as diagnostic aids, particularly in Latin America. Yage is regarded as a particularly potent booster of psychic powers, and shamans regularly use it to assist with diagnosis and journeys.[37] For this reason the plant from which yage is produced has been called "the visionary vine." Several anthropologists have reported observations of possible yage induced psi, and one of

the earliest chemicals extracted from the plant was called telepathine.[177]

Despite such tantalizing stories, no experimental research has been done on shamans' psychic abilities after taking yage—or any other psychedelic, for that matter. To learn more we must therefore turn to clinical and research observations in the West. Stanislav Grof states, "In my own clinical experience, various phenomena suggesting extrasensory perception are relatively frequent in LSD psychotherapy particularly in advanced sessions. . . . Every LSD therapist with sufficient clinical experience has collected enough challenging observations to take this problem seriously."[68]

However, as Grof is the first to point out, there are major difficulties in verifying such clinical observations. He warns, "Unless these instances are reported and clearly documented during the actual psychedelic sessions there is a great danger of contamination of the data. Loose interpretation of events, distortions of memory, and the possibility of deja vu phenomena during the perception of later occurrences are a few of the major pitfalls involved."[68]

For these reasons controlled laboratory studies are desirable, and several have been done. The results have been largely negative and failed to demonstrate a predictable, constant psychedelic increase in extrasensory perception. While occasional subjects did well, on average there was usually no detectable effect.[68] It is possible that these negative findings may be due to the uninteresting nature of the experiment and the difficulties subjects had in concentrating. At the height of the psychedelic experience, subjects are bombarded with a cavalcade of images, some of them dramatic and powerful beyond belief. It is not surprising that subjects report great difficulty and little interest in focusing on an experiment that by comparison may seem infinitely boring and insignificant.

There is, therefore, a major discrepancy between native reports and clinical observations of psychedelically enhanced psi on the one hand and experimental findings on the other. This suggests

that psychedelic enhancement of psi abilities is, at the very least, not something that occurs regularly in laboratory situations. Whether it occurs at all and whether it can be directed and harnessed remain to be seen.

Conclusions

What can we conclude from these reports and studies? At the present time all that can be said is that shamans claim to have parapsychological abilities and that there are indeed some remarkable anecdotal reports of psi in shamans and other native healers. Moreover, the conditions often used in tribal magic rituals seem to correspond to conditions reported to facilitate psi in the laboratory. As yet we have no firm experimental evidence of psi in shamans, but since shamans have not been adequately tested, the possibility of psi has not been ruled out.

C H A P T E R 1 6

How Do They Heal Themselves? Healing the Healer

Finding the center of strength within ourselves is in the long run the best contribution we can make to our fellow men.

ROLLO MAY

Healing in relationships is not a one-way street. The healer may be healed, the helper helped. The same relationships, rituals, and states of consciousness that heal the patient may also heal the therapist. As we will see, even the desire to help and heal another may benefit both people. This process of mutual healing may be especially important for shamans, for shamans were the original "wounded healers," healers who had themselves once been hurt in some way. Both clinical observations and the world's myths relate that those who have themselves suffered may sometimes be best able to relieve the suffering of others. As Carl Jung said, "The sufferer takes away suffering."

Shamans are often people who have suffered greatly. This suffering may have burst on them unsought in the initiation crisis, or it may have been sought deliberately during periods of isolation and asceticism. In many cases shamans have been rescued from their initial crises by learning to shamanize and help others. In other cases "the shaman must first cure himself and his initiatory sickness and only afterwards can cure the other members of the community."[84]

Whether the shaman cures himself by helping others or first cures himself and then helps others, it may be essential that he continue shamanizing and helping in order to avoid a relapse. According to the Chukchee, "While the shaman is in possession of the inspiration, he must practice, and cannot hide his power. Otherwise it will manifest itself in the form of bloody sweat or in a fit of madness similar to epilepsy."[19]

If shamanic practices are self-healing, how might such healing occur? In shamanic cultures the cure is seen as largely due to the shaman's relationship with spirits, but it is also possible to view this self-healing in terms of psychological processes. According to one's belief system these psychological processes can be viewed as either complementing the spiritual factors, mediating them, or accounting for them entirely.

What then are the psychological factors that might account, at least in part, for the shaman's dramatic reversal from patient to physician, from victim to helper, from psychologically disturbed to psychotherapist? What might account for the fact that shamans may end up as some of the healthiest people in the community? The processes include a shift in the shamans' interpretation of their symptoms, the effects of the shamanic work and role, effects of altered states of consciousness, the psychological changes that occur during shamanic journeys, and the effects of altruism and service.

Reinterpreting Symptoms of the Initiation Crises

The shamanic initiation crisis begins as a dramatic, even life-shattering, disturbance. In our own culture a person going through such a disturbance would probably be diagnosed as psychologically ill, as we have previously discussed, and the symptoms would likely be suppressed with medication. The result is that the patient is seen, and sees himself, as sick and disturbed.

In tribal cultures similar symptoms might be viewed very differently. The patient would be regarded as a shaman-to-be, and the symptoms would be regarded not as evidence of pathology but as evidence of a calling, not as an emergency to be suppressed but as an emergence to be guided. Here we have an example of what Western psychologists call reattribution or reframing. This is a powerful technique by which psychological symptoms are reinterpreted from a more helpful and healthful perspective. This encourages the patient to accept and work with the symptoms, even to value them as part of an important developmental learning process.

The shaman-to-be does not languish or wallow in these experiences. Rather he or she is encouraged to learn and practice healing rituals and eventually to help others. This may encourage novices to believe that the symptoms are treatable and that they themselves have the power to heal them. This could foster a sense of greater power and self-confidence, which would also be fostered by the shaman's work and role.

The net result of these processes would be a radical shift in the shamans' beliefs and expectations about themselves. The negative stigma of illness would be removed, and the shamans would likely be left with a set of positive expectations about themselves, their capacities, and their role. Since beliefs and expectations tend to function as self-fulfilling prophecies, the effects of these shifts could be powerful and healthful.

The Shaman's Work and Role

To love and to work; these were the hallmarks of psychological health for Sigmund Freud. Of the shaman's ability to love we know very little, but of his ability to engage in meaningful, helpful work we are certain. For the tribe the shaman's work is valuable, even crucial. Consequently the shaman's role confers significant

status, power, and other benefits, possibly rescuing the shaman from an otherwise obscure fate and enhancing his self-confidence and self-esteem.

Altered States of Consciousness

Shamans are able to enter altered states of consciousness at will, a skill that is one of their defining characteristics. Some altered states may be both psychologically and psychosomatically healing. Perhaps the simplest and best known such healing state is relaxation, which is an effective antidote to psychological stress as well as a variety of stress-based somatic disorders.

Trance states may also be healing. As we have seen, shamans enter trance states, which can easily slip into self-hypnosis. Considerable data support the idea that self-hypnosis can be a powerful means for self-healing. Since the shaman enters altered states with the expectation of receiving help and healing and since such expectations can act as self-fulfilling prophecies, these expectations alone might produce significant healing. When the power of trance and hypnosis is added to the power of expectation, it seems reasonable to expect that significant self-healing might occur in shamanic states. In addition, much shamanic work is done to the accompaniment of song and music, which many ancient traditions and some modern therapies regard as healing.

The Shamanic Journey

In addition to the healing state of the shamanic journey, the specific experiences that occur during the journey may also be beneficial. For example, fear may be significantly reduced during journeys when shamans confront fearful scenes and spirits. Visions of death and destruction, malevolent spirits, and supernatural

forces may arise to threaten the shaman's life and soul. Yet the shaman's task is to confront, not flee, whatever horrors arise and to overcome all that stands in the way of bringing information and healing to the community.

Contemporary research shows that consciously confronting fears may extinguish them. In fact, one major therapeutic strategy called implosion can be similar to the shamanic experience. The basic principle of implosive therapy is to have patients create and confront intense images of whatever they fear for as long as it takes them to become less reactive to these images. The result is a desensitization in which the images, as well as the actual feared objects, events, or people that the images symbolize, lose their fearful impact.

The similarities of this process to the shamanic journey experience are obvious. Shamans themselves recognize this desensitizing process and say that "you may see dead persons walking towards you, and you will hear their bones rattle. If you hear and see these things without fear, you will never be frightened of anything."[42]

One difference between the shamanic journey and implosion is that in the journey fearful images arise, not by deliberate choice as in implosion, but spontaneously. Spontaneous fearful images may symbolize the shadow, those aspects of self and psyche that have been disowned and repressed because we judge them as bad, evil, and fearful. When these shadow aspects of ourselves are recognized and confronted, they lose their compulsive terror.

This confrontation with the shadow is regarded in Jungian psychology as an essential stage on the road to individuation, the process of becoming who and what we truly are. It is interesting that Jung himself regarded shamanic imagery as indicating that the shaman was going through a process of individuation.[132]

One other healing process that occurs in journeys is the identification with spirits or power animals. As we have discussed, contemporary therapists find similar types of identification to be

powerful psychotherapeutic tools. This process may well have helped heal shamans for thousands of years.

ALTRUISM AND SERVICE

Shamans serve their communities. Such service is the final stage of the hero's journey and the end result of all the shaman's trials, initiations, and training. As Michael Harner points out, shamanism at its best

> goes far beyond a self-concerned transcendence of ordinary reality. It is transcendence for a broader purpose, the helping of humankind. The enlightenment of shamanism is the ability to light up what others perceive as darkness and thereby to *see* and to journey on behalf of . . . humanity.[73]

Of course shamans are not alone in this. A variety of ancient religious traditions and modern psychologies see service as the natural expression of successful development. Over a thousand years ago the Third Zen Patriarch exclaimed that "for the unified mind in accord with the Way all self centered striving ceases."[161]

Today several schools of psychology see altruism and service as hallmarks of health. According to Abraham Maslow, "self actualizing people are, without one single exception, involved in a cause outside their own skin."[117]

Service can be neurotically motivated, but in general there seems to be a clear correlation between people's psychological well-being and the amount of service they do. In short, greater psychological health tends to result in greater service.[193]

It has only recently been recognized that the reverse also holds true. Not only does health result in service, but service may result in health. Research suggests that there may be both psychological and physical benefits from service. Those who help others

may experience what has come to be known as "helper's high," a generalized sense of well-being, satisfaction, and self-esteem that may bathe helpers after their good works.

Helper's high may also translate into physical benefits. Headaches, high blood pressure, and other stress-related conditions may be relieved and the functioning of the immune system be enhanced.[90] Thus helping others and helping oneself can fuse into a single process. Maslow, one of the first people to recognize this, wrote: "The best way to become a better 'helper' is to become a better person. But one necessary aspect of becoming a better person is *via* helping other people. So I must and can do both simultaneously."[117]

This is remarkably similar to Michael Harner's observation that "in shamanism there is ultimately no distinction between helping others and helping yourself. By helping others shamanically, one becomes more powerful, self-fulfilled and joyous."[73]

Shamans may have been among the earliest humans to discover the truth of Albert Schweitzer's statement that "the only ones among you who will be truly happy are those who have sought and found how to serve." Indeed shamans may not only have made themselves happy but also healthy.

PART V

Shamanic States of Mind

CHAPTER 17

Mapping Shamanic States

The mind is its own place, and in itself
Can make a Heaven of Hell, a Hell of Heaven.
JOHN MILTON, Paradise Lost

Shamans were the world's first mystics, heroes, and Master Game players because of one simple fact: they were able to voluntarily and systematically alter their state of consciousness. They were the first to make systematic use of discoveries that stress, fatigue, hunger, and rhythm could produce profound and mysterious changes in one's experience. These initially haphazard discoveries were presumably remembered, tested, organized, and eventually transmitted across generations as the tradition now known as shamanism. The tradition that was transmitted included a technology for inducing, using, and exploring altered states of consciousness (ASCs).

We now know that there are many varieties of altered states. There are the ones we are all familiar with such as dreams, fatigue, and hypnosis, and there are pathological ones such as those of panic, paranoia, and schizophrenia.

In addition there are alternate states induced by various religious and mystical practices. When research on these began in the 1960s, it was assumed that these were all the same or at least very similar. It was commonly said that different meditation practices were just different roads up the same mountain. Neat and simple as this idea was, it was also wrong. Careful study has revealed literally dozens of meditative and yogic states.[62]

What types of altered states occur in shamanism, and how do they compare with other states such as pathological or meditative

ones? To begin with, it is important to recognize that, contrary to much popular writing, there seems to be no reason to assume that there is only a single shamanic state. Shamans employ a wide variety of techniques and each may induce its own unique state, although of course there may be significant overlap between these states.

Here we will focus on states occurring during the shamanic journey. These warrant careful description and mapping for several reasons: (1) because the journey is one of the defining characteristics of shamanism; (2) because we have many detailed descriptions of it from both tribal and Western people; and (3) because the journey state has long been confused with pathological states and is now being confused with meditative-yogic states. Witness, for example, recent claims that "shamans, yogis and Buddhists alike are accessing the same state of consciousness"[39] and that the shaman "experiences existential unity—the *samadhi* of the Hindus or what Western spiritualists and mystics call enlightenment, illumination, unio mystica."[99] These claims seem to be based on relatively superficial similarities. When more subtle comparisons are made, differences leap into view and each tradition is found to foster its own unique family of states.

Even to say that there is only a single state of consciousness associated with the shamanic journey may be an oversimplification. As anyone who has done several journeys knows, one's state can vary perceptibly from one experience to another: sometimes deep, sometimes shallow; sometimes murky, sometimes clear. There may also be differences from one shaman to another.

This is not to deny that these many states and experiences may have much in common. It is to point out that considerable variation can occur and that even the concept of "a state of consciousness" is a static crystallization of what is in real life a dynamic flow of experience. However, for the sake of simplicity it is often convenient to refer to a single characteristic shamanic journey state. In any event, we can describe journey states precisely enough so as to be able to map out their key characteristics.

Having done so, we will then compare them to pathological and meditative-yogic states.

How are we to describe and map shamanic journey states? We cannot use physiological or biochemical measurements for the simple reason that we don't have any. We can, however, use the many descriptions of these experiences given by shamans.

This type of careful description and analysis of raw experiences is known in the West as phenomenology or phenomenological mapping. In the East, traditions such as Buddhism and yoga have used phenomenological approaches to classify states of consciousness with extraordinary precision for over two thousand years. Using a similar phenomenological approach will allow us to classify shamanic states and compare them to others more precisely than has been done in the past. With this precision we can identify differences—for example, between shamanic and yogic ASCs—that other researchers have missed. All too often these diverse religious states have simply been lumped together as "trances." Therefore we first need to determine what is meant by this term.

Trance States

The states of consciousness during shamanic journeys are often spoken of as trance states. The term *trance* seems to be widely used but imprecisely defined in anthropology. It is usually so imprecisely defined that some researchers try to avoid using it at all.[180] It seems to have been used broadly to cover all waking ASCs and more narrowly to indicate an ASC marked by focused attention.[141]

I would suggest that the key defining characteristics of a trance state are a focusing of attention accompanied by reduced awareness of surroundings outside this focus. The shamanic journey state, with its inner focus and reduced awareness of the environment, seems clearly to fit this definition.

We can go further and ask, what type of trance? In other words, to what extent can we differentiate and map trance states?

To answer these questions we need to consider the key dimensions of experience that characterize trance states. These dimensions can be outlined as follows.

Key Dimensions for Mapping Trance States

1. Degree of control. There are two important types of control:
    - the ability to enter and leave the ASC at will; and
    - the ability to control experiences while in the ASC.
2. Degree of reduced awareness of the environment.
3. Ability to communicate. To what extent is the subject able to communicate with other people while in the trance?
4. Concentration. Important factors here include:
    - the *degree* or *intensity* of concentration; and
    - whether attention is *fixed* immovably on a single object (as in certain yogic samadhi states), or *momentary* or fluid, allowed to shift between selected objects (as in shamanic journeys).
5. Degree of energy or arousal.
6. Degree of calm. This refers to more than simply low arousal; calm also implies low levels of agitation and distractibility.
7. Emotion, especially whether the experience is pleasurable or painful.
8. The sense of identity, which may vary widely. In addition to the usual self sense, it may include such experiences as a sense of being a soul detached from the body, or a sense of unity with all things.

9. Out-of-body experience (OOBE). Does the subject experience perceiving from a point apparently outside the body?

10. Content of inner experiences. Here several further distinctions can be made, such as:
    - Degree of organization. Do the experiences consist of a random array of thoughts and images, or are they organized into coherent meaningful sequences?
    - Sensory modality. Are the experiences primarily auditory, visual, or somatic?
    - Intensity of the objects. Are they subtle, faint, and barely perceptible (as in some meditations) or intense and overwhelming (as in schizophrenic states)?

Mapping Shamanic Journey States

Using these major dimensions of trance experience, we can begin to map specific trance states. Shamanic journey states can be mapped as follows.

Control

One of the defining characteristics of shamans is their ability to control their states of consciousness. The master shaman is able to enter and leave the journey state at will or at least with the assistance of appropriate aids such as drumming and rituals.

In addition, the shaman has some ability to control the type of images and experiences that occur. This control is not complete since there is some degree of spontaneity to the images, spirits, and worlds that arise. Thus the shaman may decide to journey to the lower world and voluntarily control the descent, but the world that arises to greet her may be quite unexpected, unfamiliar, and un-

known. The shaman may choose how to respond to these strange worlds and spirits, but how they respond to her may seem quite outside her control.

Perhaps the closest experience to this that most of us have had is lucid dreaming. These are dreams in which we know that we are dreaming. Here too there is partial control of the state and experience. Strange worlds and scenes seem to arise spontaneously, but we are usually able to control our responses to them and, if we wish, to awaken from the dream at any time.[106] The shaman's control during journeys is similar, and lucid dreams may well have provided inspiration for early shamanic journeys.

Awareness of the Environment and Ability to Communicate

During journeys awareness of the environment is significantly reduced. This is hardly surprising since the shaman is preoccupied with life-and-death dramas in other worlds. In spite of these other-world adventures, the shaman may be able to split her awareness between those worlds and this one sufficiently to communicate with her audience. In such cases the listeners may be treated to a blow-by-blow account of the worlds, spirits, and battles encountered by the shaman.

Table 1. Experiential Mapping of the Shamanic Journey State

Dimension		*Shamanic Journey State*
Control	ability to enter and leave ASC at will	Yes: good control
	ability to control the content of experience	Partial control
Awareness of Environment		↓ Decreased
Ability to Communicate		Sometimes
Concentration		↑ Increased, fluid attention

Dimension	*Shamanic Journey State*
Mental Energy/Arousal	↑ Increased
Calm	↓ Decreased
Emotion	Can be either pleasurable and positive (+) or painful and negative (−)
Identity or Self Sense	Separate self sense, may be a nonphysical "soul" or "spirit"
Out-of-Body Experience	Yes, controlled ecstasy
Content of Experience	Organized, coherent imagery determined by shamanic cosmology and purpose of journey

Concentration

Shamans are known for their good concentration.[41] During a journey they must focus for long periods without distraction, but their attention is not fixed immovably on a single object as is the yogi's. Rather their attention is fluid, moving freely at will from one thing to another as their journeys unfold.

Energy/Arousal, Calm, and Emotion

Since they are roaming between worlds, battling spirits and interceding with gods, it is small wonder that shamans may feel aroused during their exploits. *Calm* is not a word that would be applied to many shamanic journeys. The emotions during the journey vary with the type of adventure and may range from dread and despair to pleasure and excitement.

Sense of Identity and Out-of-Body Experience

One of the defining characteristics of the shamanic journey is an out-of-body experience. It is partly for this reason that the journey state is sometimes described as ecstatic. During the journey shamans experience themselves as disembodied spirits, no longer limited to or constricted by the body, able to roam vast distances at great speeds. Their earthbound tribespeople experience themselves as tethered to, confined within, and identified with a body. It is the shamans alone who are able to escape this constricting identity and experience themselves as free spirits.

Content of the Trance Experience

The shaman's experiences are remarkably rich and highly organized. They involve several senses, including auditory, visual, and body sensations. These experiences are neither the chaotic patterns of random neural fireworks nor the incoherent images of schizophrenic disturbances. They are coherent and purposeful, reflecting both the shamanic cosmology as well as the purpose for which the journey is undertaken.

In the next chapter we will use the same phenomenological map to compare the shamanic journey state with those of schizophrenia on the one hand and meditation and yoga on the other.

CHAPTER 18

Comparing States: Shamanism, Schizophrenia, Buddhism, and Yoga

If mind is comprehended
all things are comprehended.
BUDDHISM'S RATNAMEGHA SUTRA

Until now, comparisons between different states of consciousness, such as between the states of shamanism and schizophrenia, have been rather superficial. All too often people have simply concluded, on the basis of very little evidence, that these states were identical or that they were different. However, experiential or phenomenological mapping allows us to move deeper and compare several dimensions of experience. This approach allows us to move from unidimensional comparisons to multidimensional comparisons and to distinguish between states with greater sensitivity.

We can now use this approach to compare shamanic states with those that occur in other conditions. Since it has been claimed that shamanic states are the same as those of schizophrenia, Buddhism, and yoga, let us map these states according to the dimensions of experience outlined in the preceding chapter.

Shamanic and Schizophrenic States

Many people who claim that shamans are schizophrenic and that shamanic and schizophrenic states are equivalent seem to assume that there is only one shamanic altered state and one schizophrenic state. Yet we have already seen that there are probably multiple shamanic states, and the same is certainly true of schizophrenia.[4] To simplify things we will focus here on the state that occurs in an acute schizophrenic episode. This is one of the most devastating experiences any human being can undergo. Psychological disorganization is extreme, disrupting emotions, thought, perception, and identity. Victims can be completely overwhelmed, plunged into a nightmare of terror and confusion, haunted by hallucinations, swept from their usual sense of reality and identity, and lost in a private autistic world.

In terms of our experiential dimensions we can map the acute schizophrenic episode and compare it to the shamanic state as follows.

Control is almost entirely lost. The victim of an acute schizophrenic episode has little ability to halt the process or to control experiences. Awareness of the environment may be reduced when the person is preoccupied with hallucinations, and thinking may be so fragmented that the person can hardly communicate. Concentration is drastically reduced, and the patient is usually highly aroused and agitated. The experience is usually extremely unpleasant; emotional responses are often distorted and bizarre.

So destructive is the process that the schizophrenic's experience is usually highly disorganized and incoherent. This disorganization extends even to the sense of identity, and the schizophrenic may consequently feel that he is disintegrating, dying, and losing the ability to discriminate what is himself and what is not. This may occasionally result in a sense of being outside the body, but the experience is brief and uncontrolled. The whole experience is an incoherent, fragmented nightmare.

Table 2. Comparison of the Shamanic Journey State with an Acute Schizophrenic Episode

Dimension		*Shamanism*	*Schizophrenia*
Control	ability to enter and leave ASC at will	Yes: good control	↓ ↓ Dramatic reduction of control: inability to halt the process or to control the experience
	ability to control the content of experience	Partial control	
Awareness of Environment		↓ Decreased	↓ Awareness often decreased and distorted
Ability to Communicate		Sometimes	↓ Decreased; communication usually distorted
Concentration		↑ Increased	↓ ↓ Great reduction of concentration
Mental Energy/ Arousal		↑ Increased	↑ ↑ Increased; agitation may be extreme
Calm		↓ Decreased	↓ Decreased
Emotion		+ or − Positive or Negative	− − Usually very negative, though rarely positive; often distorted and inappropriate

Table 2. Comparison of the Shamanic Journey State with an Acute Schizophrenic Episode (continued)

Dimension	*Shamanism*	*Schizophrenia*
Identity or Self Sense	Separate self sense, may be a nonphysical "soul"	Disintegrated, loss of ego boundaries; inability to distinguish self from others
Out-of-Body Experience	Yes, controlled ecstasy	Rarely, uncontrolled
Content of Experience	Organized, coherent imagery determined by shamanic cosmology and purpose of journey	Often disorganized and fragmented

This schizophrenic experience is very different from the shamanic journey. The shaman's experience is coherent, meaningful, and consistent with the purpose of the journey. In addition the shaman has good control of his experience, heightened concentration, and a clear, coherent sense of identity. The shaman experiences leaving her body and roaming at will. By comparison with the almost invariable terror of the schizophrenic, the shaman's experience may be a source of wonder and delight.

To these experiential differences can be added the differences in social functioning of schizophrenics and shamans. Shamans are often outstanding members of the community and may display considerable intellectual, artistic, and leadership skills and make significant contributions to their community. Such skills and contributions are very rare among schizophrenics.

Although it is understandable that early researchers sometimes labeled shamans as schizophrenic, it is clear that shamanism and schizophrenia are quite different phenomena.

Comparisons with Other Traditions

Recently there has been a growing tendency to equate shamans with masters of various spiritual traditions, especially Buddhism and yoga, and to assume that shamanic states of consciousness are identical to those of these traditions. Such claims seem to be rather superficial, for the fact is that there is no one yogic or Buddhist state any more than there is one shamanic state. When shamanic, Buddhist, and yogic states are compared carefully, significant differences leap into view.

As we have already seen, there are probably multiple shamanic states, including journey, mediumship, and drug states. In Buddhism and yoga the situation is even more complex. There are literally dozens of meditation practices, and the states they induce can differ dramatically. Moreover, each meditation practice may evolve through several distinct stages and states. The result is that a practitioner in a tradition such as Buddhism may access dozens of altered states during the course of training.[62]

Comparing the states accessed in shamanism and other traditions is therefore a complex business. Those who wish to claim that shamans and masters of other traditions are equivalent and that they access identical states of consciousness will need to make multiple comparisons between multiple states on multiple dimensions. This has simply not been done. In fact, when we make direct comparisons we find major differences. Let us therefore briefly outline some yogic and Buddhist meditation practices and then compare some of the advanced states that occur in them with the shamanic journey state.

Classical yoga is a concentration practice in which the mind is stilled until it can be fixed with unwavering attention on inner experience such as the breath, an image, or a mantra. To do this the yogi withdraws attention from the body and outer world to focus inward "like a tortoise withdrawing his limbs into his shell." As a result awareness of the body and outer world is largely lost

and the yogi can now focus undistractedly on ever more subtle internal objects. Finally all objects drop away and the yogi experiences samadhi, or ecstatic mystical union with the divine Self.[46]

Whereas classical yoga is a concentration practice, Buddhist insight meditation is an awareness practice. Whereas yoga emphasizes the development of unwavering attention on inner objects, insight meditation emphasizes fluid attention to all objects, both inner and outer. Here all stimuli are observed and examined as precisely and minutely as awareness will allow. The aim is to examine and understand the workings of body and mind as fully as possible and thereby to cut through the distortions and misunderstandings that usually cloud awareness. "To see things as they are" is the motto of this practice, and this seeing can become very sensitive indeed.

How do the states of consciousness achieved in classical yoga and in Buddhist insight meditation compare with the shamanic states? In contrast to schizophrenia, where control is drastically reduced, all three of these disciplines enhance self-control. Practitioners are able to enter and leave their respective states at will, although some shamans may require external assistance such as drugs or drumming. Both shamans and insight meditators exert partial control over their experiences in the ASC, while yogis in samadhi have almost complete control over thought and other mental processes. Indeed, the second line of the classic yoga text states that "yoga is the control of thought-waves in the mind."[142]

Perceptual sensitivity to the environment shows dramatic differences among the three states. Both ancient and modern descriptions as well as recent psychological tests suggest that Buddhist insight meditators may show dramatic increases in perceptual sensitivity to the environment.[25, 26] By contrast, awareness of the environment is usually somewhat reduced in the shamanic journey and is drastically reduced, even to the point of nonawareness, in advanced yogic states. Eliade defined samadhi as "an invulnerable state in which perception of the external world is absent."[40]

These differences in environmental awareness are reflected in differences in communication. Shamans may communicate with spectators during their journeys.[140] For the yogi, on the other hand, even attempting to speak may be sufficient to break the fierce one-pointed concentration.

Concentration training appears to be widespread among authentic spiritual practices, including shamanism, Buddhism, and yoga, but the type and depth of concentration can differ dramatically. In both shamanism and Buddhist insight meditation, attention moves fluidly from one object to another. This is in marked contrast to advanced yogic practice, where attention is fixed immovably on a single object.

There are also significant differences in arousal or energy levels. Shamans are usually aroused during their journey and may dance or become highly agitated. Buddhist insight meditators, on the other hand, gradually develop greater calm. In yogic samadhi, calm may become so profound that many mental processes cease temporarily.[23]

The sense of identity differs drastically among the three practices. The shaman usually retains a sense of being a separate individual, though perhaps identified as a soul or spirit rather than as a body. The Buddhist meditator's microscopic awareness becomes so sensitive that it is able to dissect the sense of self into its component stimuli. Thus the meditator perceives not a solid unchanging ego or self sense, but rather a ceaseless flux of thoughts and images of which that ego is composed. This is the experience of "no self" in which the sense of a permanent egoic self is recognized as an illusion. This illusion of a continuous self or ego is a product of imprecise awareness that arises in much the same way as an apparently continuous movie arises from a series of still frames.[61] The meditator's precise awareness sees through this egoic illusion and hence frees the meditator from egocentric ways of thinking and acting.

The yogi's experience is different yet again. In the highest

Table 3. Comparison of the Shamanic Journey State with Advanced Yogic and Buddhist Meditative States

Dimension		*Shamanism*	*Buddhist (Vipassana) Insight Meditation*	*Patanjali's Yoga*
Control	ability to enter and leave ASC at will	Yes	Yes	Yes
	ability to control the content of experience	↑ Partial	↑ Partial	↑ Extreme control in some samadhis
Awareness of Environment		↓ Decreased	↑ Increased	↓ ↓ Greatly reduced sensory and body awareness
Ability to Communicate		Sometimes	Usually	None
Concentration		↑ Increased; fluid	↑ Increased; fluid	↑ ↑ Greatly increased; fixed
Mental Energy/Arousal		↑ Increased	↓ Usually decreased	↓ ↓ Greatly decreased
Calm		↓ Decreased	↑ Usually increased	↑ ↑ Greatly increased; extreme peace
Affect		+ or − Positive or negative	+ or − Positive or negative (positive tends to increase as practice deepens)	+ + Highly positive; Ineffable bliss
Identity or Self Sense		Separate self sense, may be a nonphysical "soul"	Self sense is deconstructed into a changing flux: "no self"	Unchanging transcendent Self, or *purusha*
Out-of-Body Experience		Yes, controlled ecstasy ("ecstasis")	No	No; loss of body awareness ("enstasis")
Content of Experience		Organized, coherent imagery determined by shamanic cosmology and purpose of journey	Deconstruction of complex experiences into their constituent stimuli. Stimuli are further deconstructed into a continuous flux.	Single object ("samadhi with support") or pure consciousness ("samadhi without support")

reaches of meditation, attention is fixed immovably on consciousness. Nothing remains in awareness but consciousness itself, and consequently this is what the yogi now experiences him- or herself to be—pure consciousness, ineffable, blissful, beyond time, space, or any limitation. This is samadhi, the highest reach of yoga. It is this experience—the union of self and Self—that gives yoga, which means union, its name. This blissful union contrasts dramatically with the sometimes pleasant, sometimes painful experiences of both the shaman and the Buddhist meditator.

The yogi's experience of pure consciousness also contrasts dramatically with the complex images of the journey that fill the shaman's awareness. The Buddhist meditator has yet a third type of experience. Here awareness becomes so sensitive that all experiences are eventually broken down into their components, and the meditator perceives a ceaseless flux of microscopic images that arise and pass away with extreme rapidity.[62]

One of the defining characteristics of shamanism is soul flight, which is a form of out-of-body experience (OOBE) or ecstasy or "ecstasis." Neither the yogi nor the Buddhist meditator experiences this. The yogi may become so inwardly concentrated, in fact, as to lose all awareness of the body and become absorbed in the inner bliss of samadhi, a condition sometimes called "enstasis." Eliade, whose theoretical knowledge of both shamanism and yoga was probably as extensive as anyone's, was very clear on the difference between the two. In his classic book *Yoga* he stated emphatically:

> Yoga cannot possibly be confused with shamanism or classed among the techniques of ecstasy. The goal of classic yoga remains perfect *autonomy,* enstasis, while shamanism is characterized by its desperate effort to attain the "condition of a spirit," to accomplish ecstatic flight."[40]

In summary, claims that shamanic states are identical to those of schizophrenia, Buddhism, or yoga appear to have been based on

imprecise comparisons, and both theory and data suggest that these states are quite distinct. More precise, though still preliminary, multidimensional mapping and comparisons of altered states are now possible. The maps and comparisons presented here are obviously only initial steps, but even at this stage they suggest that shamanic, schizophrenic, Buddhist, and yogic states differ on several important dimensions of experience and are clearly distinguishable.

CHAPTER 19

Mapping Levels of Consciousness

The exploration of the higher reaches of human nature and of its ultimate possibilities and aspirations . . . has involved for me the continuous destruction of cherished axioms, the perpetual coping with seeming paradoxes, contradictions and vagueness and the occasional collapse around my ears of long established, firmly believed in and seemingly unassailable laws of psychology.

ABRAHAM MASLOW

We have seen that it is possible to map states of consciousness on various dimensions of experience. This type of mapping allows us to distinguish between different states that in the past have mistakenly been regarded as the same.

However, the mapping that we have done so far has not taken one crucial dimension into account: that of development. We know from studies of both child and adult development that certain stages and capacities tend to develop later than others and to emerge in a fixed sequence. Abstract reasoning, for example, invariably appears later in life than less sophisticated forms of thinking.

It seems that similar stages and sequences may occur with the development of states of consciousness. Unvarying sequences of states are described in several traditions, such as the samadhis of yoga and the stages of insight meditation in Buddhism. These and other traditions claim that their practices induce a constellation of states that emerge in a fixed order, with later states being regarded as more profound, more developed, and more valuable than earlier ones.

How then are we to map the states that emerge at different stages of development? In general, we can apply three criteria.[204]

The first is the sequence of emergence; in general, more developed states tend to emerge later than less developed ones. The second criterion is access to other states. A state can be said to be more developed than others if a person who can enter it can also access those other states but not vice versa. Third, later developmental states may have additional capacities not available in earlier states.

Thus, in addition to comparing states experientially or phenomenologically, we may also be able to compare them according to their developmental level. Metaphorically speaking we can now add a vertical dimension of assessment to the horizontal dimensions we have been using up to now, just as in chapter 3 we added a vertical dimension to Campbell's account of the hero's journey.

That we can map states occurring in a particular tradition or practice on a vertical developmental dimension seems clear. It is not so clear whether we can hope to make developmental comparisons of states occurring in different traditions or practices. After all, different practices induce very different types of experiences.

Yet some underlying commonalities can be found. To give some obvious examples, the Christian contemplative and the journeying shaman who see visions of angels and spirits, respectively, are both seeing spiritual figures. The Buddhist and Hindu meditators who attain nirvana and *nirvikalpa samadhi*, respectively, are both in states in which no thoughts, images, or sensations arise to awareness; there is only awareness and nothing else. It is also clear that there are radical differences between the first pair and second pair of experiences. Consequently we can see that it may be possible to group experiences from different practices and traditions into clusters.

Deep Structures of Transpersonal States

Ken Wilber has suggested that we may be able to cluster states and stages of transpersonal development according to the underlying

deep structures of the experiences.[204] The deep structure of a family of experiences is the common form that underlies and molds them. By way of analogy, consider human faces. They vary so dramatically that we can distinguish almost every person on the planet from almost everyone else. Yet underlying these almost infinite differences in appearance lies what Wilber would call the same deep structure, comprised of two eyes, a nose, a mouth, and two ears. This single deep structure can produce literally billions of different appearances.

On the basis of a remarkably wide-ranging review of the world's spiritual traditions and experiences, Wilber has suggested that underlying the vast array of such experiences lies a finite number of recognizable deep structures. For example, Wilber suggests that the Buddhist nirvana, Hindu *nirvikalpa samadhi*, and Christian gnostic abyss all spring from the same deep structure—a condition of formless, objectless awareness.

Wilber's approach is an exciting one, for he is suggesting that it may be possible to make sense of the extravagant profusion of experiences found in the world's spiritual traditions. Hidden behind different experiences, names, and interpretations may be common characteristics and clusters. If further research supports this claim, it will be a major advance in our understanding of transpersonal states of consciousness.

This would be a significant contribution by itself, but Wilber goes further. He suggests that deep structures emerge in a set sequence during spiritual practice and that this same sequence is found across different traditions and practices. There may be, he suggests, a widespread, perhaps universal, sequence of development or emergence of transpersonal states. In other words, no matter what the practice being used, certain deep structures and their corresponding types of experience will tend to emerge before others.[200, 204]

It must be remembered that this idea, exciting as it is, is still only a theory and awaits further research before it can be fully accepted.[154] The theory will doubtless be refined and expanded,

and Wilber is the first to admit this. Consequently the following map should be regarded as tentative.

Wilber suggests that transpersonal states seem to fall into three major groups. These he calls, in order of their emergence, subtle, causal, and absolute or ultimate.

Subtle Experiences

Subtle experiences comprise those faint images and sensations that tend to emerge when the more raucous mental contents are stilled; as, for example, in meditation. The experiences that arise may be with or without form. Formless experiences comprise pure light or sound. Experiences with form may comprise all manner of images, including vast scenes of worlds of extraordinary richness and complexity. Archetypal figures symbolizing transpersonal and spiritual qualities may arise, such as images of sages, angels, or Buddhas. Such experiences may be stably accessed; for example, in *shabd* yoga, Buddhism's *jhanas*, or Hinduism's *savikalpa samadhi*.

Causal Experiences

Beyond the subtle stage lies the causal. In this stage there are no longer any objects or things in the field of awareness. Only awareness itself remains, but that awareness is not an awareness of any thing; it is just awareness itself, pure and simple. This is the unmanifest realm or void in which no phenomena whatsoever appear. This realm is realized in states such as Buddhism's nirvana and Hinduism's *nirvikalpa samadhi*.

Absolute Experience

Profound and rare as this causal realization is, it is not the final realization. According to some traditions there lies beyond this a

further stage, which Wilber calls the absolute or ultimate. Actually this is not so much a stage as the ground out of which all previous stages and phenomena emerge. Here phenomena once again appear but are now instantly recognized as creations and modifications of consciousness, Spirit, or Mind. Consciousness or Spirit alone is now seen to manifest and express itself in and as all the levels and worlds and beings of the universe. This is the realization of zen's "One Mind" or Hinduism's *turiya* or *sahaj samadhi*. Consciousness, Spirit, or Mind has rediscovered its true nature, returned to its Self as its Self, and recognizes its Self in all things. This is said, by several traditions, to be the final realization.[204]

If these experiences seem difficult to comprehend, it is hardly surprising. They and the states in which they occur are so unlike our usual waking experiences that we have almost no basis for comparison and understanding. Spiritual masters repeatedly warn us that it is almost impossible to truly comprehend these states without direct experience of them. Indeed, the Buddha forbade his monks to speak about advanced meditative experiences to laypeople because he felt the experiences would almost inevitably be misunderstood. But while the upper scales of spiritual attainment may be only partly comprehensible to the many of us who remain earthbound, we can at least gain enough of a sense of them to begin to appreciate the differences between the subtle, causal, and absolute conditions.

Mapping Shamanic States

Where do shamanic states of consciousness fit into this scheme? Their major, indeed defining, state is that in which the shamanic journey occurs. From the many descriptions available to us we know that the journey is usually done at night because the images may be faint; that complex worlds, lights, sounds, and other images occur; and that encounters with archetypal spirit figures are common. These are clearly consistent with subtle level experiences and

Wilber has proposed that the shamans were the first to systematically access this level.[201]

A skeptic might argue that these experiences are simple fantasies or even hallucinations and there is no reason to invoke any transpersonal or spiritual state. Such criticism is understandable and points to the primitive nature of current mapping skills with regard to states of consciousness. Many questions remain unanswered. For example, what exactly constitutes subtle experiences? How, if at all, are these experiences to be differentiated from ordinary fantasy—by intensity or by the type or meaning or religious significance of the objects encountered?

At the present time these questions cannot be answered definitively. My own estimation, which must remain very tentative at this stage, is that ordinary fantasy and subtle-level experiences are part of a continuum. Both are mind creations but they differ in certain ways. Subtle-level experiences occur in altered states characterized by increased sensitivity to inner experience. The objects of awareness are indeed subtle and hence can be recognized only in sensitive states and supportive environments, whereas ordinary fantasy is relatively intense and easily recognized. The apparent scale of subtle experiences may be much larger than that of ordinary fantasies. Whole worlds—even universes—may seem to arise in which the Earth seems a mere speck. In subtle states there also seems to be a greater likelihood of encountering spiritually significant images and themes and archetypal figures such as sages, spirits, or angels. By contrast, our usual waking fantasies tend to focus on more mundane topics.

No one of these characteristics by itself would necessarily distinguish ordinary fantasy from subtle-level experiences. Taken together however, they point to differences that, at least to the person having them, may be vast in scope, subtlety, and significance.

Shamans were perhaps the earliest masters of this subtle realm. Their specialty was "soul travel" in which they experienced themselves unshackled from the body. As free souls they journeyed

through these subtle realms, mastering and placating their inhabitants, and bringing back information and power from this realm to their earthbound compatriots.

Mystical Union

The description of the subtle-level experiences given above is a simplified one; there are other possibilities at this level. For example, although shamans usually experience themselves as free souls, separate from other beings and worlds, they may sometimes unite with other spirits. In other religious traditions the sense of being a separate individual may give way to an experience of union not only with other individuals or spirits but with the entire universe or God. Thus, in the upper reaches of the subtle realms there may occur forms of the *unio mystica*, the mystical union so celebrated and sought after by the world's mystics.

Do shamans ever experience this mystical union? I have found no reference to it in the literature; nor, apparently, have others. One authority categorically states that "we never find the mystical union with the divinity so typical for the ecstatic experiences in the 'higher' forms of religious mysticism,"[87] Consequently he concludes that shamanism can be considered a form of mysticism only "if mysticism is not restricted to mean just the *unio mystica*."[86]

Three lines of evidence suggest that this conclusion might be incorrect: the facts that shamanism is an oral tradition, that powerful psychedelics may be used, and that some Westerners report such experiences.

Because shamanism is an oral tradition, such experiences of mystical union may have occurred at least occasionally but been lost to subsequent generations—and, of course, to anthropologists. Without writing there may be no way to adequately preserve a record of the highest and rarest flowerings of a tradition.

Although not an essential part of shamanism, the use of psychedelics is common in some areas. Peyote and ayahuasca, for example, are powerful substances capable of inducing experiences that some authorities regard as genuine mystical ones.

Finally, Westerners trained in shamanic practices may report unitive experiences and I have personally heard two such accounts. These seemed to be experiences of union with the universe rather than with a deity. This points to the fact that there are actually different types of mystical union, and the experience of union with the universe is an example of so-called nature mysticism rather than theistic mysticism (union with God). Though unitive experiences may not be the aim of shamanic journeys that focus on soul travel, they may occur. In light of this and the other lines of evidence considered above, it seems that shamanism deserves to be considered a potentially mystical tradition.

Higher States

So shamans have probably gone beyond the goals of their own tradition on occasion. This then raises the question of whether shamans may have gone beyond subtle states altogether and accessed either causal or absolute realms. Here we are on shakier ground and it seems impossible to make definitive statements. However, three lines of evidence suggest the possibility that shamans may occasionally have done this. First, in any tradition one may find a few practitioners who leap into realms of consciousness outside those aimed for by the tradition.[201]

Second, psychedelics appear to occasionally elicit causal or absolute experiences.[65, 190]

The third line of evidence comes from the unusual psychological-test pattern of an outstanding Apache shaman whose Rorschach test showed marked similarities to that of an advanced Buddhist meditation master.[24] Since this Buddhist practitioner had

achieved causal-level realization, it is possible that the Rorschach similarities indicate that the Apache shaman may have also accessed this state. On the other hand, it could simply be that spiritual mastery in any tradition results in similar personality changes and consequently similar Rorschach responses.

Taken together, these lines of evidence suggest that, although shamans traditionally have aimed for the experience of soul travel in the subtle realms, a few of them may also have explored the causal and absolute. But no matter how many or how few explored these realms it seems that shamans may have been humankind's first transpersonal heroes—the first to systematically break their identification with the body and the world; the first to systematically enter transpersonal domains; and the earliest explorers and masters of the subtle realms.

CHAPTER 20

The Evolution of Consciousness

In the history of the collective as in the history of the individual, everything depends on the development of consciousness.

CARL JUNG

If it is true that shamans were the first humans to systematically access transpersonal states and experiences, their states and journeys may represent a major leap for humankind, a leap in the evolution of consciousness. For if the capacity to access subtle-level states lies latent within all of us, the question arises as to whether shamans may be evolutionary forerunners. The answer depends on one's view of evolution. Therefore, before we can decide on the shaman's place in evolution we need to consider the various theories of evolution of consciousness.

THEORIES OF EVOLUTION OF CONSCIOUSNESS

In general these take three main forms. The first is mainly a downhill view that things are getting worse, that consciousness is not evolving but devolving. The second is a no-change view; namely that consciousness, at least religious consciousness, has not evolved significantly since prehistoric times. The third is an upward view, the idea that human consciousness has evolved significantly since earlier times.

Degeneration

The idea that the human condition and consciousness have degenerated is found most often in world mythology. The story of a prehistoric golden age is common in myths, as is the story of a subsequent fall from grace. In Christianity it is the garden of Eden and our subsequent eviction; in China it is the age of virtue and subsequent decline. In Hinduism it is the fall from the Satya-yuga, the golden age of wisdom and virtue, into the Kali-yuga, a time of viciousness and ignorance. Among contemporary scholars these ideas are usually considered purely mythological, although a few respected thinkers have at least considered the general idea of decline as a possibility.[175]

The No-Change View

The second theory holds that there has been no significant change for better or worse in human consciousness, or at least in religious consciousness. From this perspective the earliest spiritual practitioners were on a par with the latest; prehistoric realizations were as deep as contemporary ones; and early shamans accessed the same experiences, states, and realms as recent mystics. Such ideas are at least implied, although not forcefully argued, by such notable scholars as Mircea Eliade, Joseph Campbell, and Carl Jung. Eliade, for example, notes that

> more than once we have discerned in the shamanic experience a "nostalgia for paradise" that suggests one of the oldest types of Christian mystical experience. As for the "inner light," which plays a part of the first importance in Indian mysticism and metaphysics as well as in Christian mystical theology, it is, as we have seen, already documented in Eskimo shamanism.[41]

This theme is being echoed more forcefully by some of the new popularizers of shamanism. To these people shamanic experiences, stages, and insights are on a par with, or even greater than, those of the mystics of later traditions. This represents an example of a current popular but questionable view that all spiritual practices lead to the same mystical end point; they are all just different roads up the same mountain.

Some of the more sophisticated popularizers of this idea use the language of states of consciousness to claim equivalence of shamanic and other states. We have already noted claims that shamans, yogis, and Buddhists alike access the same state of consciousness and that the shaman "experiences existential unity—the *samadhi* of the Hindus or what Western spiritualists and mystics call enlightenment, illumination, unio mystica."[99]

However, we have also seen that when the states of shamans, yogis, and Buddhists are carefully compared they appear quite different. Of course, these experiential differences do not necessarily prove that the states are at different developmental levels. In order to compare the developmental level of these states we need a developmental scale by which to assess the level; such scales are nowhere to be found among the people claiming the equivalence of these states. For that we must turn elsewhere, and we find it in the work of some of those who hold the third view—namely that consciousness has evolved, and may still be evolving, upward.

Evolution

For most of human history time was regarded not so much as a march of progress but rather as cycles of day and night, winter and summer, birth and death. The idea that time is going somewhere, that there is an ongoing evolutionary process, is a surprisingly recent idea but one that is now firmly entrenched in the Western

mind. Consequently it is not surprising that consciousness itself is also seen as evolving. This idea has been advanced by such luminaries as Teilhard de Chardin, Jean Gebser, Ken Wilber, and the Indian intellectual and spiritual genius Aurobindo. Since Wilber integrates the ideas of these previous thinkers, we can focus on his work as representative of this evolutionary view. In addition, as we saw in the last chapter, Wilber provides a useful scheme for locating transpersonal states of consciousness along a developmental continuum.

Wilber suggests that, just as the subtle, causal, and absolute states emerge sequentially in today's contemplatives, they emerged sequentially in human history. He therefore offers the idea that the subtle states were the first transpersonal states that humankind realized. This realization was followed thousands of years later by the causal, and hundreds of years later still by the discovery of the absolute.

The subtle states, he suggests, emerged in the dawn of prehistory with the shaman. The causal he locates some 2000 to 2500 years ago with such great sages as the authors of the Upanishads, the Buddha, the early Taoists, and Jesus. The absolute he places around the sixth century A.D. It is associated with sages like Bodhidharma in China and Padmasambhava in Tibet.

Where do shamans fit in this evolutionary ascent of consciousness? Wilber places them at the beginning of this vast process and regards them as the first spiritual heroes, the first humans to develop a systematic technology of transcendence, and the first to systematically access subtle states. Though they may have occasionally broken through into the causal realm, their focus was clearly on certain subtle states and experiences. Their mythology and technology were directed toward assisting people to attain these states.

For thousands of years shamans may have constituted humankind's only organized link to transcendence. It was not until cen-

turies, millennia, or even tens of thousands of years after the first shamans that technologies were developed to systematically access the causal and absolute realms.

Technologies for Transcendence

The technologies of spiritual traditions that produce causal and absolute realization seem to contain four common elements of practice: a rigorous system of ethics, emotional transformation, training of attention and concentration, and the cultivation of wisdom. Different paths focus on some of these elements more than others, but all four seem to be found in varying degrees among authentic causal and absolute traditions.

Ethical training is widely regarded as an essential preliminary to any significant realization. This is not an ethics of conventional fear and guilt-based morality, of "do this or God will get you." Rather it is a precise discipline of mind training based on the understanding that unethical behavior both springs from and further reinforces such destructive mind states as greed, hatred, judgment, and jealousy. Ethical behavior, on the other hand, tends to weaken these disruptive influences and to reinforce more healthful and helpful states—such as generosity, calm, and compassion—that foster transcendence.[61] Interestingly, ethical behavior seems to have significant psychological benefits in addition to spiritual ones, a fact that was appreciated in classical times but is only now being rediscovered by contemporary therapists.[5]

Transforming emotions is part of ethical training and reinforces it. Almost universally, the great spiritual traditions emphasize the importance of working to reduce disrupting emotions such as fear and anger while simultaneously cultivating more personally and socially beneficial states such as love, joy, and compassion.

As destructive emotions are relinquished, their disruptive influence on the mind diminishes. With the mind no longer caught

between the pull of greed and the push of fear, it becomes easier to concentrate and to hold attention on whatever the practitioner wishes. This allows further development since the mind can now be consciously directed toward, and thereby cultivate, desired states.

These traditions claim that attention can and must be trained. However, Western psychologists have largely agreed with William James that "voluntary attention cannot be continuously sustained."[93] There is thus a dramatic contrast between the ideas of mainstream Western psychology (attention cannot be trained) and the spiritual traditions (attention must be trained). It is therefore understandable that "no subject occupies a more central place in all traditional teaching; no subject suffers more neglect, misunderstanding and distortion in the thinking of the modern world."[159]

While James recognized the limits of our untrained attention, he also realized the importance of training it:

> The faculty of voluntarily bringing back a wandering attention over and over again is the very root of judgement, character and will. No one is *compus sui* if he have it not. An education which would improve this faculty would be education par excellence.[94]

Meditative traditions such as classical yoga and Buddhism claim to provide this education par excellence.

The final strand of this four-part training program is the cultivation of wisdom. This is not ordinary knowledge or even wordly wisdom. Rather, it is a transcendental wisdom, known as gnosis in the West or jnana in the East, based primarily on direct experience and intuitive insight into one's own mind and nature.

Different traditions have focused on some of these four components more than others, but all authentic paths seem to use all four to some extent. Ethical training may be universal. Training attention to the point of unshakable stability has been the focus of classical yoga. Emotional transformation and the cultivation of love

have been the emphasis of bhakti yoga and Christianity, while Tibetan Buddhism has emphasized compassion. Wisdom has been the focus of jnana yoga and some schools of Buddhism.

The precursors of these ethical, emotional, attentional, and wisdom trainings can be found in shamanism. The best of shamanism has long been based on an ethic of compassion and service. Some degree of emotional transformation, especially the reduction of fear, is an essential component of its training. For example, Australian aboriginal shamans would be warned of the terrifying visions they would confront during their training and were told that they must not yield to fear. "You see your camp burning and bloodwaters rising, and thunder, lightning and rain, the earth rocking, the hills moving, the waters whirling, and the trees which stand swaying about. Do not be frightened. . . . If you hear and see these things without fear you will never be frightened of anything."[42]

Shamans have often been described as having superior powers of concentration.[41] Although they do not aim for extraordinary degrees of unshakable attention cultivated by later yogis, it is clear that arduous attentional training was sometimes part of shamanic training. For example, the Eskimo shaman Igjugarjuk, whose initiation we discussed in chapter 5, was left for thirty days in a tiny snow hut. He was given only the smallest amounts of food and water and "was exhorted to think only of the Great Spirit and of the helping spirit that should presently appear—and so he was left to himself and his meditations."[146]

Thus it seems that there has been a significant evolution of the technology of transcendence since some early human discovered that if a stretched skin was hit it emitted a resonant sound and that if it was hit repeatedly, curious and pleasurable experiences ensued. Shamans remembered and re-created such chance discoveries and welded them into an effective collection of techniques and wisdom that could be transmitted across generations. Millennia later, early sages refined aspects of the shamanic technol-

ogy and added to them techniques of their own, thus enabling humankind to discover causal and absolute realization.

The Relative Difficulties of Different Realizations

This seems an appropriate time to comment on the relative difficulties of accessing experiences at the subtle, causal, and absolute levels. The crucial question is what percentage of practitioners actually attain the realizations aimed for by different traditions? We have some hints but very little firm data. These hints suggest that it may be significantly easier to attain some degree of shamanic realization than to realize the goals of later traditions.

For example, Michael Harner implies that in his experience some 90 percent of shamanic workshop participants are able to begin shamanic journeys.[75] On the other hand, when we come to later traditions, the general sense is that among (for example) Christian contemplatives, Indian yogis, Buddhist meditators, and Neo-Confucians, relatively few actually experience significant realization and those usually only after years of arduous training. It is said, for example that only one in approximately 100,000 Buddhist meditators is likely to master advanced concentration practices.[27]

This suggests that there is a relationship between the developmental stage and its time, frequency, and ease of discovery. In general, the higher the developmental stage, the later it may emerge both in individual practitioners and in history and the smaller the percentage of practitioners who actually realize it. Consistent with this is the fact that shamanism was the earliest tradition to emerge and even today allows people relatively easy access to altered states and their attendant insights.

This relative ease may be one of the major reasons for shamanism's current popularity in the West. Shamanism continues to offer today what it has offered for hundreds of thousands of yesterdays: namely, a relatively easy means—and for most of human

history perhaps the only means—of controlled transcendence. Shamans, therefore, might be considered forerunners of the countless sages of other traditions and the original founders of "the great tradition": the sum total of humankind's religious-spiritual wisdom.[51]

PART VI

Ancient Tradition in a Modern World

C H A P T E R 2 1

Shamanism in a World at Risk

This we know: All things are connected
like the blood which unites one family.
All things are connected.
Whatever befalls the earth
befall the sons of the earth.
Man did not weave the web of life.
He is merely a strand in it.
Whatever he does to the web
He does to himself.
Chief Seattle, upon surrendering his tribal lands in 1856

Our Endangered Planet

It is no secret that ours is a time of enormous opportunity and enormous risk. Though we have the resources to create a veritable heaven on earth, we seem just as likely to create a veritable hell.

The figures are familiar yet staggering. Our population is exploding, in fact doubling every forty years. Our environment is being destroyed by the chemical leprosies of urban smog, acid rain, ozone depletion, carbon dioxide, and toxic pollution. Our forests are disappearing and our deserts expanding. Some 20 million of us die slowly, painfully, and needlessly of starvation each year and another 700 million go malnourished.

Yet overshadowing all these is the nuclear threat that places the survival, not just of individuals and of cultures, but of our entire civilization and species at risk. The world's nuclear warheads now carry an explosive power equivalent to *20 billion* tons of TNT, enough to fill a freight train stretching for approximately

4 million miles. Such a train could circle the earth 160 times or reach to the moon and back eight times.[191]

Even if these weapons remain unused they still cause untold death and suffering. Each year the world spends over $1 trillion on arms. Yet the Presidential Commission on World Hunger estimated that it would cost only $6 billion per year to eradicate starvation and malnutrition, an amount equivalent to less than three days' arms expenditure.[144] Small wonder that Pope Paul IV anguished that the arms race kills whether the weapons are used or not.

We stand therefore at a turning point in human history with boundless possibilities on the one hand and boundless suffering on the other. Never in the course of human history have the opportunities and risks been greater.

What is remarkable about this era is not only the awesome scope and urgency of our problems. It is that for the first time in millions of years of evolution, all the major threats to our survival are human-caused. Problems such as starvation, pollution, and nuclear weapons stem directly from our own behavior and the hopes and fears, phobias and fantasies, desires and delusions that power this behavior. The state of the world, in other words, reflects the state of our minds. The conflicts outside us reflect the conflicts inside us; the insanity without mirrors the insanity within.

What this means is that the current threats to human survival and well-being are actually symptoms of our individual and collective state of mind. If we are to understand and correct the state of the world, we must better understand the source of both our problems and their solutions: ourselves. For, as Senator William Fulbright said, "Only on the basis of an understanding of our behavior can we hope to control it in such a way as to ensure the survival of the human race."[54] None of this is to deny the importance of social, military, and economic forces. It is rather to emphasize the much-neglected psychological roots that underlie them.

These psychological roots are becoming better understood, and work is under way to create a psychology of human survival.[191]

Many psychological factors have been identified, and some of them relate directly to shamanism and its view of the world. These include our relationship to one another, to the earth, and to all life on it.

In the West the prevailing view has been, at least implicitly, that the world and everything in it exist for our benefit. The earth has been widely regarded as inanimate real estate available for our plunder. As to life on it, it is usually assumed that, as the book of Genesis says, we "have dominion over the fishes of the sea and over the birds of the air and over every living thing that moves upon the earth." In short, we see ourselves as separate from and superior to everything on and in the earth, and we have misused this perspective to justify destruction of whatever stands in the way of our desires.

We also see ourselves as separate from each other. While we may communicate with, relate to, and even love, others, ultimately we live and die alone. We emphasize our separateness more than our connectedness and our independence more than our interdependence. This perspective places few checks on our aggression.

Yet throughout history many people have viewed this sense of separation as the cause of human fear and suffering. "Wherever there is other there is fear," claim the ancient Indian Upanishads, while in our own time the French existentialist Jean-Paul Sartre summarized a similar view by saying that "hell is others."

How different the shamanic world view is. For the shaman all is sacred and alive, everything is interconnected and interdependent, all creatures are part of one great web of life that holds all things in harmony. For the shaman, as for Chief Seattle, "all things are connected like the blood which unites one family." This holistic sacred world view seems to be fostered by shamanic experiences. Michael Harner states:

> The experiences that come from shamanism tend to foster a great respect for the universe, based on a feeling of oneness with all forms of life. By getting into harmony one has much more power available

to help others, because harmony with the universe is where the true power comes from. Then one is much more likely to lead a life that emphasizes love rather than hatred, and which promotes understanding and optimism.[76]

Emerging World Views

This view of life, the world, and the universe as alive, interconnected, and interdependent has much in common with several holistic world views now appearing in the West. These include perspectives emerging from contemporary physics, earth sciences, ecology, feminism, animal rights, and the appreciation of our common humanity.

From physics comes the appreciation that "we are the univere," or at least inextricably linked with it, and that together we constitute an undivided whole. Two of the cutting-edge theories in physics, relativity theory and quantum theory, "both imply the need to look on the world as an undivided whole, in which all parts of the universe, including the observer and his instruments, merge and unite in one total body."[20]

The cycles of our bodies and minds are linked to the cycles of the earth, the moon, and the sun. The atoms of our bodies were forged in the heart of stars. In the words of astronomer Sir James Jeans, "In the deeper reality beyond space and time we may all be members of one body."[32] Albert Einstein made the point as beautifully and poetically as only a genius could:

> A human being is part of the whole called by us universe, a part limited in time and space. He experiences himself, his thoughts and feelings as something separated from the rest, a kind of optical delusion of his consciousness. This delusion is a kind of prison for us, restricting us to our personal desires and to affection for a few

> persons nearest to us. Our task must be to free ourselves from this prison by widening our circle of compassion to embrace all living creatures and the whole of nature in its beauty.[61]

From the earth sciences comes James Lovelock's "Gaia hypothesis," which Joseph Campbell called one of the great myths of our time. Lovelock's hypothesis, simply stated, is that the earth is a living organism, a single interconnected ecosystem. All its plants, rocks, animals, and atmosphere, suggests Lovelock, constitute a single living entity, which he named Gaia after the Greek earth goddess.[112, 113]

If it seems bizarre that the earth, with its thin ribbon of life sitting atop a 7000-mile-wide sphere of dead rock, could be considered a single living organism, consider the case of a giant tree. Such a tree consists almost entirely of dead matter. Only a thin skin of living tissue surrounds the mass of dead material that constitutes the vast majority of the trunk and branches. This living skin is also surrounded by a protective layer of dead bark on the outside.

The Gaia hypothesis points to the interconnection and interdependence of all life. A change in one area or species can have many widespread and unforeseeable consequences. To give but one example from the many provided by Lovelock, consider the effects on the Panama Canal of the American public's hankering for hamburgers. Much of the meat that goes into American hamburgers comes from cattle raised on Central and South American lands where whole forests were felled to make room for grazing. The loss of these forests has numerous and disastrous effects, including the loss of rare and even unknown species of plants and animals; the loss of atmospheric moisture and clouds that evaporate from forest trees; and consequent changes in climate, destruction of the ecosystem, and reduced fertility of the soil.

The destruction of these forests also affects the Panama Canal, which is kept filled with water by abundant rainfall. But the

rain and the forest are interdependent; as the forest is destroyed, rainfall declines, and it may soon be too sparse to sustain the canal.

The Gaia hypothesis remains controversial and is far from universally accepted. But whether it is finally accepted as fact or only as metaphor, it serves as a valuable reminder of the interconnection of life and of the dangers of tampering with nature's awesome harmony.

From philosophy and the life sciences comes the movement of "deep ecology." Like many other environmental movements, this one emphasizes the importance of ecological harmony and preserving our environment. However, it is motivated by more than the idea that a harmonious environment would be good for our health. It is also powered by a deeper philosophical perspective that appreciates how inextricably we are linked to and integrated with our environment and all life.[35]

A similar shift seems to be occurring in our perception and appreciation of one another. There seems to be a slowly growing recognition of the shared humanity and common human destiny that underlie racial, cultural, and ideological differences. As the editor of the journal *Foreign Affairs* wrote:

> Something beyond nationalism is slowly taking root in the world . . . the signs of a developing sense of common human destiny are present. . . . World affairs will have a very dim future if this international sentiment fails to show a steady increase from now on.

As Jerome Frank put it, "the psychological problem is how to make all people aware that whether they like it or not, the earth is becoming a single community."[49]

It seems, then, that fields as diverse as physics, biology, earth sciences, and ecology, together with social movements like feminism and animal rights, are converging on a world view, aligned in several ways with that of shamanism, that emphasizes the interconnection and independence of all life and even of our entire planet.

If taken seriously, experienced, and lived, these perspectives would change our perception of ourselves, all living beings, and our earth. We would see all people as sharing a common self and human destiny and being part of a single, gigantic, planetary organism. We would see all animals and all life as interconnected and interdependent and the earth itself as alive. Where before we saw separation, alienation, and chaos we would now more likely see unity, interconnection, and harmony.

Such a shift in perception could have dramatic psychological, social, ecological, and planetary effects. At the psychological level it might help to answer one of the deepest human longings, namely "the search for unity which is one of the strongest motivating forces for human beings."[85] According to psychiatrist Erich Fromm, the basic human problem is "how to overcome separateness, how to achieve union, how to transcend one's individual life and find at-one-ment."[53]

At the social, ecological, and planetary level this shift in perception might counter the beliefs and attitudes that have allowed us to so grossly mistreat our earth and each other. It could encourage us to see and treat ourselves, people, animals, and our entire planet as our sacred living selves or Self.

THE PERENNIAL PHILOSOPHY

Of course, such a world view is hardly new. As we have seen, the shamanic world view is closely aligned with it. Shamanism goes further, of course, to add a vertical or transcendental dimension or domain, the domain of souls and spirits.

A similar view is found at the heart of the world's great religions. This is the "perennial philosophy," the common core of wisdom and practice at the mystical heart of the world's great religions and perhaps first partly glimpsed by early shamans. It is, to quote Ken Wilber,

> a view held by a great majority of the truly gifted theologians, philosophers, sages, and even scientists at various times. Known in general as the "perennial philosophy" (a name coined by Leibniz), it forms the esoteric core of Hinduism, Buddhism, Taoism, Sufism and Christian mysticism, as well as being embraced, in whole or part, by individual intellects ranging from Spinoza to Albert Einstein, Schopenhauer, Jung, William James to Plato. . . . Many of the truly brilliant scientists have always flirted with, or totally embraced, the perennial philosophy, as witness Einstein, Schrodinger, Eddington, David Bohm, Sir James Jeans, even Isaac Newton.[202]

The perennial philosophy suggests that the universe is not only interconnected, living, and sacred but also multilayered. That is, the physical universe is not the only domain; there are also domains of mind and spirit. These domains are thought to form a hierarchy or progression from matter to mind to spirit, from gross to subtle, from unconscious to conscious. This is the so-called Great Chain of Being that has, "in one form or another, been the dominant official philosophy of the larger part of civilized humankind throughout most of its history."[111]

The number of levels recognized in this chain varies according to the tradition. However, the general principle is that the universe is multileveled and that in addition to the physical domain that preoccupies our senses there are also nonmaterial domains. These are the domains of pure consciousness, Mind, or of spirits (shamanism); Spirit (Christianity); purusha (yoga); and *sat-chit-ananda* (Vendanta's being-consciousness-bliss). According to the perennial philosophy, this realm of Spirit, for which the most meaningful contemporary term is probably consciousness, is ontologically primary and creates, or at the very least controls, the material realm. Moreover, the perennial philosophy says that our true nature is spirit or consciousness: we are, it says, fundamentally creatures and creations of this realm rather than being primarily physical entities.

We suffer, says the perennial philosophy, from a case of mis-

taken identity in which we dream ourselves to be only bodies, or, as Alan Watts put it, merely "skin encapsulated egos." Our consciousness is distorted, constricted, and deluded so that we live in what the East calls ignorance, *avidya, maya,* or illusion. In the West this has been called a shared dream, a consensus trance, or a collective psychosis.[180] We do not recognize this as a trance because we all share in it and because we all live, says the perennial philosophy, in the biggest cult of all: *culture.*

Within our collective trance we act blindly and destructively, as might be expected of anyone whose awareness is distorted and constricted. Our behavior is said to be driven by greed and fear in ways destructive to ourselves, our fellow beings, and our planet. For the perennial philosophy, then, our global crises can be traced to our shared insanity.

But the perennial philosophers suggest that there are a few who have awakened from this trance, have recognized their true nature, and have then returned to point the way for the rest of us. These are the spiritual heroes, the Master Game players, the great saints and sages, those who escape from and then voluntarily return to Plato's cave. These are the people who have created and refreshed the perennial philosophy. The essence of their message has been "wake up!": wake up to your true nature, to the fact that you are not separate from anyone or anything, to the fact that, as the Confucians say, "heaven, earth and the ten thousand things form one body"; awaken to the recognition that, as one Zen master put it, "you are more than this puny body or limited mind. Stated negatively, it is the realization that the universe is not external to you. Positively, it is experiencing the universe as yourself."[100]

The person who awakens to this recognition is said to realize that "the I, one's real, most intimate self, pervades the universe and all other beings. That the mountains and the sea, and the stars are a part of one's body and that one's soul is in touch with the souls of all creatures."[72] Nor are such descriptions the exclusive province of mystics. They have been echoed by philosophers, psychologists, and

physicists.[201] "Out of my experience . . . one final conclusion dogmatically emerges," said the great American philosopher William James. "There is a continuum of cosmic consciousness against which our individuality builds but accidental forces, and into which our several minds plunge as into a mother sea."[125]

The practical implication of this realization and perspective is that since we are not separate from everyone or everything, we should treat them, quite literally, as our self. Hence we have the biblical injunction to "love thy neighbor as thy self," to which Gandhi added, "and every living being is thy neighbor." Likewise in the words of the Buddha:

See yourself in others
Then whom can you hurt?
What harm can you do?[28]

So the holistic world view emerging from diverse areas of contemporary thought, which may be essential to our survival, is in some ways consistent with the millennia-old view of the perennial philosophy in general and with aspects of shamanism in particular. Both ancient and modern perspectives recognize and honor the interconnected, interdependent nature of life and the world. The perennial philosophy and shamanism add an explicit transcendental view and ethic that not only seek to honor and preserve life but also to awaken it. Whether or not one subscribes to the perennial philosophy and its transcendental claims, the implications and guidelines for relating to our fellow creatures and our planet are the same: treat them as we would our self because they are our self.

We do not know whether this shift in perception, beliefs, and self-image will be large enough or soon enough to avert environmental or nuclear disaster. Clearly we are engaged in a race between consciousness and catastrophe, and the outcome is uncertain. However, remembering the words of Henry Ford that "those who

believe they can do something and those who believe they can't are both right," there seems no sane choice but to assume that we can re-vision our lives, our relations, and our world in time to preserve our planet and our species.

Our task, then, is to work to shift our perception from a focus on our differences to a focus on our similarities; from a dualistic emphasis on conflicting groups and cultures to a unitive appreciation of our shared humanity; from a fragmentary view that sees us apart from nature, and nature itself in parts, to a holistic vision that recognizes the unity and interconnection of all parts. Each person we meet, every situation, every interaction, presents us with a choice. We choose whether to see ourselves apart from others or whether to look past the otherness to the self we share; whether to see ourselves as separate and independent from others and the world or affecting and affected by all. It is not a minor choice. The way we choose to see ourselves and our relationship to the world may decide its fate and ours.

Few traditions are as explicitly nature- and ecology-oriented as shamanism. Both its world view and its techniques support this orientation. It views nature as a vast sacred mystery with which humankind is intimately linked and on which it is ultimately dependent. It offers simple techniques for accessing intuitive wisdom and experiences that foster this ecological perspective. In short, shamanism is aligned with the holistic views of both the ancient perennial philosophy and modern ecological sciences, and its practices may induce experiences supportive of these views. Shamanism, therefore, may be able to support these philosophies and sciences in the crucial task of fostering a perception of the world and ourselves that will help ensure the survival of both our planet and our species.

For a further discussion of the psychological roots of our contemporary global crises, see R. Walsh, *Staying Alive: The Psychology of Human Survival.*

CHAPTER 22

Shamanism Today and Tomorrow

Indigenous peoples have rich storehouses of information about nature, man and the balanced relationship of the two. From their beliefs about the spiritual world to their traditional knowledge of rain forests, healing and agriculture, these societies provide the opportunity for new interpretations about the world and our selves. Many of these populations face severe discrimination, denial of human rights, loss of cultural and religious freedoms, or in the worst cases, cultural or physical destruction. . . . If current trends in many parts of the world continue the cultural, social, and linguistic diversity of humankind will be radically and irrevocably diminished . . . immense undocumented repositories of ecological, biological and pharmacological knowledge will be lost, as well as immeasurable wealth of cultural, social, religious, and artistic expression.

UNITED STATES CONGRESS,
INTERNATIONAL CULTURAL SURVIVAL ACT OF 1988

Shamanism stands today at historic and paradoxical crossroads. It is endangered in many of its native homelands yet is becoming popular, even faddishly so, in the West.

What will be the future and fate of this ancient tradition? In its native homelands there seem to be four main possibilities. The first is that, among those increasingly rare peoples who remain relatively untouched by the industrialized world, shamanism may remain as a major religious, medical, and cultural resource. The

second possibility is that in newly industrialized countries it may manage to survive or even flourish alongside Western medicine and religion. In countries such as Korea and Nepal, for example, wily shamans have been observed to carefully cull their clientele, retaining those they feel are likely to be successes and referring more difficult illnesses to doctors.[138] Yet in other cultures shamanism may disappear completely.

A final possibility is that shamanism might revive in some places. If it is becoming popular in the West, could it also revive and become popular among native peoples whose forefathers were nourished by it? Could it perhaps help to heal the effects of cultural disintegration, the loss of meaning, values, and social cohesion, the alcoholism and psychopathology wrought by the loss of traditional ways of life?

There are several ways in which such revivals might occur. One is the emergence of new forms inspired by spontaneous shamanic experiences. Such experiences played a significant role in the nineteenth century in the major North American Indian religious revival, the Ghost Dance.[88]

Another possibility is the rediscovery of practices that either languished or were outlawed under times of cultural repression. A contemporary example is the reemergence among the Northwest American Salish Indians of the shamanically related winter spirit dance. Those who participate in the dance are less susceptible to the depression, alcoholism, and other problems that many of these Indians are experiencing as they wrestle to adapt to Western ways.[95] Whether shamanism can serve similar functions among other peoples remains to be seen.

A third possibility is the reintroduction of practices by people outside the culture. The American-based Foundation for Shamanic Studies has been doing this upon request, but it is probably too early to assess the impact.[77]

In the West it remains to be seen how much of the current lively interest in shamanism will endure. Some of the interest may

be merely faddish. However, some probably reflects more durable spiritual seeking, a search for early spiritual roots, an interest in the traditions of native peoples, and a desire for a tradition that honors the earth. Growing numbers of Westerners are now using shamanic techniques, especially shamanic journeys, both for their own benefit and for helping others. For the practitioners themselves the techniques may be used for learning and self-exploration, for religious and spiritual nourishment, and as a source of creativity. Shamanically inspired art and literature are beginning to appear. Shamanic techniques are also being used psychotherapeutically. Psychological and psychosomatic difficulties, stress disorders, addictions, and chronic physical pain have all been treated shamanically. It remains for future research to determine how effective these treatments are.

Research and Evaluation

Religious practices tend to change when they enter new cultures. Almost invariably they adapt to cultural requirements and combine to varying degrees with dominant traditions. The practices of shamanism will probably be no exception. The West has become a melting pot of the world's spiritual and healing practices. Consequently, shamanic practices may adapt to both Western technology and non-Western practices. Some practitioners are already claiming benefits from combining shamanic, yogic, and meditative techniques,[71] while the use of stereo cassettes and headsets for journeying to recorded drumming is already popular. It is a matter of debate, however, whether a Westerner who uses shamanic practices divorced from the social, cultural, and mythological setting in which they were originally embedded can usefully be called a shaman.

The surge of interest in shamanism and the importation of techniques to the West make expanded research possible. Much

research needs to be done, some of it very soon. The rapid expansion of First World cultures means that every effort should be made to study shamans in their native habitat as quickly as possible before the opportunity is lost.

At the present time psychological studies are almost nonexistent. We need psychological profiles of shamans in order to determine those characteristics that facilitate entry into this career, those that change with training, and those that mark accomplished practitioners. We also need direct observation of shamanic initiation crises by psychiatrically trained researchers.

It will be important to map the psychological, physiological, and biochemical changes that occur in shamans during their training, rituals, journeys, and psychedelic experiences. It would also be valuable to obtain similar data on their patients during healing rituals. This would provide clues as to how effective shamanic healing is, how it works, and whether patients, like shamans, enter altered states.

It could be especially valuable to study practitioners who have been trained both in shamanism and in a Western discipline such as anthropology or psychiatry. Charles Tart has pointed to the need for new strategies to research consciousness-altering traditions. He suggests that we need participant-experimenters, or yogi-scientists as he calls them, who are trained in both a consciousness-altering technique or tradition and in careful self-observation and analysis of their experiences. Perhaps we need shaman-scientists as well.

It may also be possible to use Western technology to enhance shamanic technology. For example, future research might be able to determine the best musical rhythms, tones, and frequencies for inducing shamanic experiences and thereby produce deeper, more powerful experiences for more people. Clearly there are numerous questions and possibilities.

Careful studies of shamanic healing are essential. If any shamanic techniques are to take their place alongside Western therapies, they must at some stage be subject to experimental test-

ing. The capacity for self-deception of both healer and patient is, as we have seen, enormous. The most useless or even harmful technique, if believed in by both doctor and patient, can seem nothing short of miraculous, at least for a time. Such is the power of the placebo effect. Therefore it is not enough that shamanic techniques, or any other therapeutic techniques for that matter, seem to work. The only way to be certain is to test them experimentally in carefully controlled studies.

Assessing the richness, complexities, and paradoxes of this tradition will be no small task. No one approach or perspective can fully encompass its many dimensions. Yet in this book our psychological explorations have provided insights and understandings that have escaped other approaches. Clearly much of what shamans do—the training they undergo, the techniques they use, the myths they live by, the fears they face, the crises they confront, the capacities they develop, the experiences they have, the states of consciousness they enter, the insights they gain, the visions they see, the cosmic travels they take, the treatments they employ—can now be understood psychologically.

Yet there is much that remains mysterious about this, the most ancient of humankind's religious, mystical, medical, and psychological traditions. The more we explore shamanism, the more it points to unrecognized aspects and potentials of the human body, mind, and spirit. For untold thousands of years the spirit of shamanism has helped, healed, and taught humankind, and it may have still more to offer us.

E P I L O G U E

Further Explorations

Those interested in exploring shamanism further can take two approaches: theoretical and experiential. The bibliography at the back of this book lists important publications. Many additional books and papers are now appearing, but careful discernment is important since the quality of publications in this field is highly variable.

For those desiring personal experience of the tradition, a large number of workshops and training programs are available. Considerable caution and discretion are essential, since the quality of such training varies widely. Two well-known and highly regarded training programs that are offered in many parts of the United States and abroad are those provided by Michael Harner and the faculty of his Foundation for Shamanic Studies, and those of Angeles Arrien. These trainers have many years of experience with the tradition, approach it with great respect, and maintain the highest ethical standards. In addition, both Harner and Arrien are trained as anthropologists and so are able to integrate Western intellectual and shamanic experiential approaches.

Angeles Arrien, 3221 Pierce #5, San Francisco, CA 94123; telephone: (415) 567-1414.

Foundation for Shamanic Studies, Box 670, Belden Station, Norwalk, CT 06852; telephone: (203) 454-2827.

Quotations

This list is for readers who would like to locate the quotations used in this book. For each quotation, the Bibliography reference number of the original article or book is given, followed by the page on which the quotation originally appeared.

Chapter 2
165, p. 269; 140, p. 408; 41, p. 4; 41, p. 5; 73, p. 25; 76, pp. 4–5; 41, p. 11

Chapter 3
34, p. 11; 34, p. 12; 34, p. 19; 34, p. 21; 201, p. 80; 118, p. 36; 34, p. 26; 185, pp. 140, 173

Chapter 4
147, pp. 116–118; 147, p. 54; 147, p. 56; 19, p. 419; 41, p. 35; 19, p. 420; 139, p. 164

Chapter 5
120, p. 121; 24, p. 214; 18, p. 23; 18, p. 88; 18, p. 91; 18, p. 92; 147, p. 114; 147, pp. 118–119; 189, p. 161; 52, p. 252; 146, pp. 82–84; 134, p. 99; 209, p. 398

Chapter 6
186, p. 250; 121, p. 83; 41, p. 420; 147, pp. 112–113; 147, p. 119; 209, p. 30; 147, p. 114; 44, p. 203; 68, p. 85; 68, p. 170; 69, p. 234

Chapter 7
98, p. 90; 130, p. 452; 116, p. 5; 131, p. 192; 130, p. 447; 3, p. 372; 185, p. 156; 200, p. 78; 165, p. 347; 129, p. 950; 36, p. 285; 169, pp. 22–23

Chapter 8
41, p. 27; 2, p. 46; 41, p. 29; 114, p. 155; 114, p. 157; 31, p. 80; 137, pp. 33, 34, 36; 66, pp. 10–11; 66, p. 11; 66, p. 15; 137, p. 35

Chapter 9
19, p. 429; 147, p. 147; 147, p. 133; 147, p. 122; 147, p. 132; 195, p. 43; 78, p. 24; 195, p. 49

Chapter 10
41, p. 259; 76, p. 4; 41, p. 21; 41, p. 266; 76, pp. 4–5; 41, p. 85; 205, p. 340; 133, p. 47; 41, pp. 87–88; 41, p. 89; 69, p. 121; 168, p. 228; 158, p. 56; 129, p. 950; 203,

p. 14; 172, p. 134; 172, p. 127; 172, p. i; 203, p. 34; 148, pp. 385, 390, 388; 80, p. 1; 183, p. 393; 102, p. 223; 97, pp. 182–183; 1, p. 98

Chapter 11
41, p. 5; 41, p. 182; 73, p. 27; 73, p. 32; 147, pp. 123–127; 147, p. 129; 99, pp. 11, 15; 10, p. 301; 75, p. 452; 96, p. 65

Chapter 12
21, p. 11; 197, p. 17; 18, p. 23; 180, p. 80; 41, p. 80; 78, pp. 16–17; 177, p. 353; 174, pp. 520, 523; 173, p. 523; 174, p. 529; 68, p. 264; 186, p. 58

Chapter 13
147, pp. 141–142; 147, pp. 128–129

Chapter 14
50, pp. 49–50; 153, p. 133; 171, p. 262; 89, p. 4; 89, p. 5; 182, p. 65; 157, pp. 17–18

Chapter 15
92, p. 787; 50, p. 72; 12, p. 175; 19, p. 436; 19, p. 429; 154, p. 138; 199, p. 340; 68, pp. 270, 272; 68, p. 270

Chapter 16
84, p. 84; 19, p. 419; 42, p. 70; 73, p. 139; 117, p. 28; 117, p. xii; 73, p. 139

Chapter 17
39, p. 223; 99, p. 23

Chapter 18
142, p. 15; 40, p. 78

Chapter 19
87, p. 42; 86, p. 28

Chapter 20
41, p. 508; 39, p. 223; 99, p. 236; 93, p. 51; 159, p. 67; 94, p. 424; 42, pp. 70–71; 146, p. 83

Chapter 21
54, p. x; 76, p. 16; 20, p. 11; 32, p. 395; 61, p. 126; 85, p. 240; 202, pp. 3, 4; 111, p. 26; 100, p. 143; 72, p. 14; 125, p. 324

Bibliography

1. Achterberg, J. (1985). *Imagery and Healing: Shamanism and Modern Medicine.* Boston: New Science Library.
2. Ackerknecht, E. (1943). Psychopathology, primitive medicine, and primitive culture. *Bulletin of the History of Medicine* 14, 30–67.
3. Alexander, F. and Selesnich, S. (1966). *The History of Psychiatry.* New York: New American Library.
4. American Psychiatric Association. (1987). *Diagnostic and Statistical Manual of Mental Disorders,* 3d ed. revised. Washington, D.C.
5. Andrews, L. (1987). *To Thy Own Self Be True.* New York: Anchor/Doubleday.
6. *A Course in Miracles* (1975). Tiburon, Calif.: Foundation for Inner Peace.
7. Arrien, A. (1987). Personal communication.
8. ———. (1989). Personal communication.
9. Bachrach, A. (1985). Learning theory. In H. Kaplan and B. Sadock (Eds.). *Comprehensive Textbook of Psychiatry,* Vol. 1, 4th ed. (184–98). Baltimore: Williams and Wilkins.
10. Baldrian, F. (1987). Taoism: An overview. In M. Eliade (Ed.). *The Encyclopedia of Religion,* Vol. 14 (288–306). New York: Macmillan.
11. Bandura, A. (1986). *Social Foundations of Thought and Action.* Englewood Cliffs, N.J.: Prentice-Hall.
12. Barker, D. (1980). Psi information and culture. In B. Shapiro and L. Coly (Eds.). *Communication and Parapsychology.* New York: Parapsychology Foundation.
13. Barry, J. (1968). General and comparative study of the psychokinetic effect on a fungus culture. *Journal of Parapsychology* 32, 237–43.
14. Benson, H. (1980). The placebo effect. *Harvard Medical School Health Letter,* August, 3–4.
15. Bible. Revised Standard Version. 2 Kings 3:15.
16. ———. Revised Standard Version. Numbers 12:6.
17. ———. New English Bible. John 12:23–24.
18. Blacker, C. (1986). *The Catalpa Bow: A Study of Shamanistic Practices in Japan.* Boston: Allen & Unwin.
19. Bogoras, W. (1909). In F. Boas (Ed.). *The Chukchee.* Leiden, Netherlands: E. J. Brill.
20. Bohm, D. (1980). *Wholeness and the Implicate Order.* London: Routledge and Kegan Paul.
21. Bourguignon, E. (Ed.). (1973). *Religion, Altered States of Consciousness, and Social Change.* Columbus, Ohio: Ohio State University.

22. Boyer, B., Klopfer, B., Brawer, F., and Kawai, H. (1964). Comparisons of the shamans and pseudoshamans of the Apaches of the Mescalero Indian reservation: A Rorschach study. *Journal of Projective Techniques and Assessment* 28, 173–80.
23. Brown, D. (1986). The stages of meditation in cross cultural perspective. In K. Wilber, J. Engler, and D. Brown (Eds.). *Transformations of Consciousness: Conventional and Contemplative Perspectives on Development* (219–84). Boston: New Science Library/Shambhala.
24. Brown, D., and Engler, J. (1986). The stages of mindfulness meditation: A validation study. Part II. Discussion. In K. Wilber, J. Engler, and D. Brown (Eds.). *Transformations of Consciousness: Conventional and Contemplative Perspectives on Development* (191–218). Boston: New Science Library/Shambhala.
25. Brown, D., Forte, M., and Dysart, M. (1984). Differences in visual sensitivity among mindfulness meditators and non-meditators. *Perceptual and Motor Skills* 58, 727–33.
26. ______. (1984). Visual sensitivity and mindfulness meditation. *Perceptual and Motor Skills* 58, 775–84.
27. Buddhagosa. (1975). *The Path of Purity* (P. M. Tin, Trans.). London: Pali Text Society. (Original work published 1923.)
28. Byrom, T. (Trans.). (1976). *The Dhammapada: The Sayings of the Buddha.* New York: Vintage.
29. Campbell, J. (1968). *The Hero with a Thousand Faces,* 2d ed. New York: World.
30. ______. (1986). *The Inner Reaches of Outer Space: Metaphor as Myth and as Religion.* New York: Alfred van der Marck Editions.
31. Casteneda, C. (1969). *The Teachings of Don Juan: A Yaqui Way of Knowledge.* New York: Ballantine.
32. Commins, S., and Linscott, R. (Eds.). (1969). *Man and the Universe, the Philosophers of Science.* New York: Washington Square Press.
33. Dabrowski, K. (1964). *Positive Disintegration.* Boston: Little Brown.
34. De Ropp, R. S. (1968). *The Master Game.* New York: Delta.
35. Devall, B., and Sessions, B. (1985). *Deep Ecology: Living as if Nature Mattered.* Layton, Utah: Gibbs M. Smith.
36. Devereaux, G. (1961). *Mohave Ethnopsychiatry and Suicide.* Washington, D.C.: U.S. Government Printing Office.
37. Dobkin de Rios, M. (1972). *Visionary Vine.* San Francisco: Chandler Publishing Co.
38. Dodds, E. (1972). *The Greeks and the Irrational.* Berkeley, Calif.: University of California Press.
39. Doore, G. (Ed.). (1988). *Shaman's Path.* Boston: Shambhala.
40. Eliade, M. (1958). *Yoga: Immortality and Freedom,* 1st ed. Princeton, N.J.: Princeton University Press.
41. ______. (1964). *Shamanism: Archaic Techniques of Ecstasy.* Princeton, N.J.: Princeton University Press.
42. Elkin, A. (1977). *Aboriginal Men of High Degree.* New York: St. Martin's Press.

43. Ellenberger, H. (1970). *The Discovery of the Unconscious.* New York: Basic Books.
44. Fabrega, H., and Silver, D. (1970). Some social and psychological properties of Zinacanteco shamans. *Behavioral Science* 15, 471–86.
45. Ferrucci, P. (1982). *What We May Be.* Los Angeles: Tarcher.
46. Feuerstein, G. (1989). *Yoga: The Technology of Ecstasy.* Los Angeles: Tarcher.
47. Fielding, W. (1983). An interim report of a prospective, randomized, controlled study of adjuvant chemotherapy in operable gastric cancer. *World Journal of Surgery* 7, 390–99.
48. Flach, F. (1988). *Resilience.* New York: Ballantine.
49. Frank, J. (1982). *Sanity and Survival in the Nuclear Age: Psychological Aspects of War and Peace.* New York: Random House.
50. ———. (1985). Therapeutic components shared by all psychotherapies. In M. Mahoney and A. Freeman (Eds.). *Cognition and Psychotherapy* (49–79). New York: Plenum.
51. Free, John. (1985). *The Dawn Horse Testament.* San Rafael, Calif.: The Dawn Horse Press.
52. Freud, S. (1917). *A General Introduction to Psychoanalysis.* Garden City, N.Y.: Garden City Publishers.
53. Fromm, E. (1956). *The Art of Loving.* New York: Harper & Row.
54. Fulbright, W. (1982). Preface. In J. Frank, *Sanity and Survival in the Nuclear Age.* New York: Random House.
55. Furst, P. (1987). South American shamanism. In M. Eliade (Ed.). *The Encyclopedia of Religion,* Vol. 13. New York: Macmillan.
56. Gallegos, A. (1987). *The Personal Totem Pole: Animal Imagery, the Chakras and Psychotherapy.* Santa Fe, N.M.: Moon Bear Press.
57. Giesler, P. (1985). Differential micro-PK effects among Afro-Brazilian cultists: Three studies using trance significant symbols as targets. *Journal of Parapsychology* 49, 329–66.
58. ———. (1985). Parapsychological anthropology: II. A multimethod study of psi and psi-related processes in the Umbanda ritual trance consultation. *The Journal of the American Society for Psychical Research* 79, 113–66.
59. ———. (1986). GESP testing of shamanic cultists: Three studies of an evaluation of dramatic upsets during testing. *Journal of Parapsychology* 50, 123–53.
60. Goffman, E. (1959). *The Presentation of Self in Everyday Life.* Garden City, N.Y.: Doubleday Anchor Books.
61. Goldstein, J. (1983). *The Experience of Insight.* Boston: Shambhala Press.
62. Goleman, D. (1988). *The Meditative Mind.* Los Angeles: Tarcher.
63. Grad, B. (1967). The "laying on of hands": Implications for psychotherapy, gentling, and the placebo effect. *Journal of the American Society for Psychical Research* 61, 286–305.
64. Greeley, A. (1988). Mysticism goes mainstream. In E. Bragdon (Ed.). *A Sourcebook for Helping People in Spiritual Emergency* (228–36). Los Altos, Calif.: Lightening Up Press.

65. Grinspoon, L., and Bakalar, J. (1983). *Psychedelics Reflections.* New York: Human Sciences Press.
66. Grof, C., and Grof, S. (1986). Spiritual emergency: the understanding and treatment of transpersonal crises. *ReVision* 8(2), 7–20.
67. ______. (1990). *The Stormy Search for the Self: A Guide to Personal Growth through Transformational Crisis.* Los Angeles: Tarcher.
68. Grof, S. (1980). *LSD Psychotherapy.* Pomona, Calif.: Hunter House.
69. ______. (1988). *The Adventure of Self-Discovery.* Albany, N.Y.: SUNY.
70. Grof, S., and Grof, C. (Eds.). (1989). *Spiritual Emergency: When Personal Transformation Becomes a Crisis.* Los Angeles: Tarcher.
71. Halifax, J. (1989). Earth, sky and psyche: A shamanic convergence. *Common Boundary* 7(5), 14–20.
72. Harman, W. (1979). An evolving society to fit an evolving consciousness. *Integral View* 1, 14.
73. Harner, M. (1982). *The Way of the Shaman.* New York: Bantam.
74. ______. (1984). *The Jivaro.* Berkeley, Calif.: University of California Press.
75. ______. (1985). Comments. *Current Anthropology* 26, 452.
76. ______. (1987). The ancient wisdom in shamanic cultures. In S. Nicholson (Ed.). *Shamanism* (3–16). Wheaton, Ill.: Quest.
77. ______. (1988). Helping reawaken shamanism among the Sami (Laplanders) of Northernmost Europe. *The Foundation for Shamanic Studies Newsletter* 1(3), 1–2.
78. ______. (Ed.). (1973). *Hallucinogens and Shamanism.* New York: Oxford University Press.
79. Hastings, A. (1990). *Tongues of Men and Angels.* New York: Holt, Rinehart & Winston.
80. Hilgard, E. (1986). *Divided Consciousness: Multiple Controls in Human Thought and Action,* 2d ed. Somerset, N.J.: John Wiley & Sons.
81. Hoffman, E. (1981). *The Way of Splendor: Jewish Mysticism and Modern Psychology.* Boston: Shambhala.
82. Hopkins, J. (1984). *The Tantric Distinction: An Introduction to Tibetan Buddhism.* London: Wisdom.
83. Hoppal, M. (Ed). (1984). *Shamanism in Eurasia.* Gothingen: Herodot.
84. ______. (1987). Shamanism: An archaic and/or recent belief system. In S. Nicholson (Ed.). *Shamanism* (76–100). Wheaton, Ill.: Quest.
85. Horney, K. (1950). *Neurosis and Human Growth.* New York: Norton.
86. Hultkrantz, A. (1973). A definition of shamanism. *Temenos* 9, 25–37.
87. ______. (1978). Ecological and phenomenological aspects of shamanism. In V. Dioszegi and M. Hoppal (Eds.). *Shamanism in Siberia* (27–58). Budapest: Akadamiai Kiado.
88. ______. (1987). Ghost dance. In M. Eliade (Ed.). *The Encyclopedia of Religion,* Vol. 5 (544–547). New York: Macmillan.
89. Hurley, T. (1985). Placebo: The hidden asset in healing. *Investigations* 2(1).
90. Institute of Noetic Sciences (1989). *Noetic Science Bulletin* 4(1).

91. Jahn, R., and Dunne, B. (1987). *Margins of Reality: The Role of Consciousness in the Physical World.* New York: Harcourt Brace Jovanovich.
92. James, W. (1977). In J. McDermott (Ed.). *The Writings of William James.* Chicago: University of Chicago Press.
93. ______. (1899). *Talks to Teachers on Psychology and to Students on Some of Life's Ideals.* New York: Dover.
94. ______. (1961). *Psychology: Briefer Course.* New York: Harper Touchstone.
95. Jilek, W. (1974). *Salish Indian Mental Health and Culture Change: Psychohygienic and Therapeutic Aspects of the Guardian Spirit Ceremonial.* Toronto: Holt, Rinehart & Winston of Canada.
96. Jowett, B. (Trans.). (1937). *The Dialogues of Plato.* New York: Random House.
97. Jung, C. (1961). *Memories, Dreams, Reflections* (R. Winston and C. Winston, Trans.). New York: Vintage Books.
98. Kakar, S. (1982). *Shamans, Mystics and Doctors: A Psychological Inquiry into India and Its Healing Traditions.* New York: Knopf.
99. Kalweit, H. (1988). *Dreamtime and Inner Space.* Boston: Shambhala.
100. Kapleau, P. (1965). *The Three Pillars of Zen.* Boston: Beacon Press.
101. Kleinman, A., and Sung, L. (1979). Why do indigenous practitioners successfully heal? *Social Science and Medicine* 13B, 7–26.
102. Klimo, J. (1987). *Channeling.* Los Angeles: Tarcher.
103. Klopfer, B. (1957). Psychological variables in human cancer. *Journal of Projective Techniques* 21, 337–39.
104. Krieger, D. (1975). Therapeutic touch: The imprimatur of nursing. *American Journal of Nursing* 75, 784–87.
105. Krippner, S. (1987). Dreams and shamanism. In S. Nicholson (Ed.). *Shamanism* (125–32), Wheaton, Ill.: Quest.
106. LaBerge, S. (1985). *Lucid Dreaming.* Los Angeles: Tarcher.
107. Laing, R. (1972). Metanoia: Some experiences at Kingsley Hall, London. In H. Ruitenbeck (Ed.). *Going Crazy* (11–21). New York: Bantam.
108. Leighton, A., and Hughes, J. (1961). Cultures as causative of mental disorder. In *Causes of Mental Disorder: Review of Epidemiological Knowledge.* New York: Milbank Memorial Fund.
109. Levi-Strauss, C. (1972). *Structural Anthropology* (C. Jacobson and B. Schoepf, Trans.). Middlesex, England: Penguin Books.
110. Loeb, E. (1929). Shaman and seer. *American Anthropologist* 41, 60–84.
111. Lovejoy, A. (1936). *The Great Chain of Being.* Cambridge, Mass.: Harvard University Press.
112. Lovelock, J. (1979). *Gaia: A New Look at Life on Earth.* New York: Oxford University Press.
113. ______. (1988). *The Ages of Gaia.* New York: W. Norton.
114. Lukoff, D. (1985). The diagnosis of mystical experiences with psychotic features. *Journal of Transpersonal Psychology* 17, 155–82.
115. Malkin, S. (1989). Confessions of a former channel. *New Realities* 10(1), 25–29.
116. Maslow, A. (1968). *Toward a Psychology of Being.* Princeton, N.J.: Van Nostrand.

117. ______. (1970). *Religions, Values and Peak Experiences.* New York: Viking.

118. ______. (1971). *The Farther Reaches of Human Nature.* New York: Viking.

119. McGashan, T., and Carpenter, W. (1981). Does attitude toward psychosis relate to outcome? *American Journal of Psychiatry* 138, 797–801.

120. Merton, T. (1969). *The Way of Chuang Tzu.* New York: New Directions.

121. Metzner, R. (1986). *Opening to Inner Light.* Los Angeles: Tarcher.

122. Monroe, R. (1971). *Journeys Out of the Body.* New York: Doubleday.

123. Moody, R. (1975). *Life After Life.* Atlanta: Mockingbird Books.

124. ______. (1988). *The Light Beyond.* New York: Bantam.

125. Murphy, G., and Ballou, R. (Eds.). (1960). *William James on Psychical Research.* New York: Viking.

126. Murphy, M., and Donovan, S. (1989). *The Physical and Psychological Effects of Meditation.* San Rafael, Calif.: Esalen Institute.

127. Neher, A. (1961). Auditory driving observed with scalp electrodes in normal subjects. *Electroencephalography and Clinical Neurophysiology* 13(3), 449–51.

128. ______. (1962). A physiological explanation of unusual behavior in ceremonies involving drums. *Human Biology* 34, 151–60.

129. Nemiah, J. (1985). Dissociative disorders (hysterical neurosis, dissociative type). In H. Kaplan and B. Sadock (Eds.). *Comprehensive Textbook of Psychiatry,* 4th ed., Vol. 1 (942–57). Baltimore: Williams & Wilkins.

130. Noll, R. (1983). Shamanism and schizophrenia: A state specific approach to the "schizophrenia metaphor" of shamanic states. *American Ethnologist* 10, 443–59.

131. ______. (1984). Reply to Lex. *American Ethnologist* 11, 192.

132. ______. (1985). Mental imagery cultivation as a cultural phenomenon. *Current Anthropology* 26, 443–51.

133. ______. (1987). The presence of spirits in magic and madness. In S. Nicholson (Ed.). *Shamanism* (47–61). Wheaton, Ill.: Quest.

134. Ostermann, H. (1952). *The Alaskan Eskimos, as described in the posthumous notes of Dr. Knud Rasmussen* (Report of the Fifth Thule Expedition, 1921–24, Vol. X, No. 3). Copenhagen: Nordisk Forlag.

135. Peck, M. S. (1983). *People of the Lie: The Hope for Healing Human Evil.* New York: Simon & Schuster.

136. Pelleteir, K., and Garfield, C. (1976). *Consciousness: East and West.* New York: Harper & Row.

137. Perry, J. (1986). Spiritual emergency and renewal. *ReVision* 8(2), 33–40.

138. Peters, L. (1981). An experiential study of Nepalese shamanism. *Journal of Transpersonal Psychology* 13, 1–26.

139. ______. (1987). The Tamang shamanism of Nepal. In S. Nicholson (Ed.). *Shamanism* (161–80). Wheaton, Ill.: Quest.

140. Peters, L., and Price-Williams, D. (1980). Towards an experiential analysis of shamanism. *American Ethnologist* 7, 397–418.

141. ______. (1983). A phenomenological view of trance. *Transcultural Psychiatric Research Review* 20, 5–39.

142. Prabhavananda, S., and Isherwood, C. (1953). *How to Know God: The Yoga Aphorisms of Patanjali.* Hollywood, Calif.: Vedanta.
143. Prem Dass. (1988). Shamanism among the Huichol Indians. Talk given at Esalen Institute, Big Sur, Calif.
144. Presidential Commission on World Hunger. (1979). *Preliminary Report of the Presidential Commission on World Hunger.* Washington, D.C.: U.S. Government Printing Office.
145. Ramana Maharshi. (1955). *Who Am I?* 8th ed. (T. Venkataran, Trans.) India.
146. Rasmussen, K. (1927). *Across Arctic America.* New York: G. P. Putnam.
147. ______. (1929). *Intellectual Culture of the Iglulik Eskimos.* Copenhagen: Gyldendalske Boghandel, Nordisk Forlag.
148. Reed, G. (1989). The psychology of channeling. *The Skeptical Inquirer* 13, 385–90.
149. Reichel-Dolmataoff, G. (1987). *Shamanism and Art of the Eastern Tukanoan Indians.* Leiden, Netherlands: E. Brill.
150. Ring, K. (1980). *Life at Death.* New York: Coward, McCann & Geoghegan.
151. ______. (1984). *Heading Toward Omega: In Search of the Meaning of the Near Death Experience.* New York: William Morrow.
152. ______. (1986). Near-death experiences: Implications for human evolution and planetary transformation. *ReVision* 8(2), 75–86.
153. Rogers, S. (1982). *The Shaman.* Springfield, Ill.: C. C. Thomas.
154. Rogo, D. (1987). Shamanism, ESP, and the paranormal. In S. Nicholson (Ed.). *Shamanism* (133–44). Wheaton, Ill.: Quest.
155. Rothberg, D. (1986). Philosophical foundations of transpersonal psychology: An introduction to some basic issues. *Journal of Transpersonal Psychology* 18, 1–34.
156. Saklani, A. (1988). Preliminary tests for psi-ability in shamans of Garhwal Himalaya. *Journal of the Society for Psychical Research* 55, 60–70.
157. Sandner, D. (1979). *Navaho Symbols of Healing.* New York: Harcourt Brace Jovanovich.
158. Schultz, T. (Ed.). (1989). *The Fringes of Reason.* New York: Harmony.
159. Schumacher, E. F. (1977). *A Guide for the Perplexed.* New York: Harper & Row.
160. Segal, R. (1987). *Joseph Campbell: An Introduction.* New York: Garland Publishing.
161. Sengstan (Third Zen Patriarch). (1975). *Verses on the Faith Mind* (R. Clarke, Trans.). Sharon Springs, N.Y.: Zen Center.
162. Shapiro, A. (1959). The placebo effect in the history of medical treatment: Implications for psychiatry. *American Journal of Psychiatry* 116, 298–304.
163. Shapiro, D. (1980). *Meditation: Self Regulation Strategy and Altered State of Consciousness.* New York: Aldine.
164. Shapiro, D., and Walsh, R. (Eds.). (1984). *Meditation: Classic and Contemporary Perspectives.* New York: Aldine.
165. Shirokogoroff, S. (1935). *Psychomental Complex of the Tungus.* London: Kegan Paul, Trench, Trubnor.

166. Shweder, R. (1972). Aspects of cognition in Zinacanteco shamans: Experimental results. In W. Lessa and E. Vogt (Eds.). *Reader in Comparative Religion: An Anthropological Approach,* 3d ed. (407–412). New York: Harper & Row.
167. Siegel, R., and Hirschman, A. (1984). Hashish near-death experiences. *Anabiosis* 4, 69–86.
168. Siikala, A. (1978). *The Rite Technique of the Siberian Shaman.* Helsinki: Suomalainen Tiedeakatemia.
169. Silverman, J. (1967). Shamanism and acute schizophrenia. *American Anthropologist* 69, 21–31.
170. Singer, P., and Ankenbrandt, K. (1982). Comment. *Current Anthropology* 23, 52–58.
171. Skultans, V. (1986). On mental imagery and healing. *Current Anthropology* 27, 262.
172. Skutch, R. (1984). *Journey Without Distance.* Berkeley, Calif.: Celestial Arts.
173. Smith, H. (1958). *The Religions of Man.* New York: Harper & Row.
174. ______. (1964). Do drugs have religious import? *The Journal of Philosophy,* LXI, 517–530.
175. ______. (1976). *Forgotten Truth: The Primordial Tradition.* New York: Harper & Row.
176. Smith, M. (1972). Paranormal effects on enzyme activity through laying on of hands. *Human Dimensions* 1, 15–19.
177. Stafford, P. (1983). *Psychedelics Encyclopedia,* revised ed. Los Angeles: Tarcher.
178. Tart, C. (1977). *Psi: Scientific Studies of the Psychic Realm.* New York: Dutton.
179. ______. (1983). *States of Consciousness.* El Cerrito, Calif.: Psychological Processes.
180. ______. (1986). *Waking Up: Overcoming the Obstacles to Human Potential.* Boston: New Science Library/Shambhala.
181. ______. (1989). *Open Mind, Discriminating Mind.* New York: Harper & Row.
182. Thomas, L. (1980). *The Medusa and the Snail.* New York: Bantam Books.
183. Thomason, S. (1989). Entities in the linguistic mine field. *The Skeptical Inquirer* 13, 391–96.
184. Toynbee, A. (1934). *A Study of History.* New York & London: Oxford University Press.
185. ______. (1948). *Civilization on Trial.* New York: Oxford University Press.
186. Underhill, E. (1974). *Mysticism.* New York: New American Library.
187. Vaughan, F. (1979). *Awakening Intuition.* New York: Doubleday.
188. ______. (1986). *The Inward Arc: Healing and Wholeness in Psychotherapy and Spirituality.* Boston: New Science Library/Shambhala.
189. Walsh, R. (1977). Initial meditative experiences: Part I. *Journal of Transpersonal Psychology* 9, 151–192.
190. ______. (1982). Psychedelics and psychological well-being. *Journal of Humanistic Psychology* 22, 22–32.
191. ______. (1984). *Staying Alive: The Psychology of Human Survival.* Boston: Shambhala/New Science Library.

192. ______. (1989). Can Western philosophers understand Asian philosophies?: The challenge and opportunity of states of consciousness research. *Crosscurrents*. XXXIX, 281–299.
193. Walsh, R., and Shapiro, D. H. (Eds.). (1983). *Beyond Health and Normality: Explorations of Exceptional Psychological Well-Being*. New York: Van Nostrand Reinhold.
194. Walsh, R., and Vaughan, F. (Eds.). (1980). *Beyond Ego: Transpersonal Dimensions in Psychology*. Los Angeles: Tarcher.
195. Warner, R. (1980). Deception and self deception in shamanism and psychiatry. *International Journal of Social Psychiatry* 26, 41–52.
196. Wasson, G. (1978). *The Road to Eleusis: Unveiling the Secrets of the Mysteries*. New York: Harcourt Brace Jovanovich.
197. Weil, A. (1972). *The Natural Mind.* Boston: Houghton Mifflin.
198. ______. (1981). *The Marriage of the Sun and Moon*. New York: Macmillan.
199. Wescott, R. (1977). Paranthropology. In J. Long (Ed.). *Extrasensory Ecology*. Metuchen, N.J.: Scarecrow Press.
200. Wilber, K. (1980). *The Atman Project*. Wheaton, Ill.: Quest.
201. ______. (1981). *Up From Eden: A Transpersonal View of Human Evolution*. New York: Doubleday.
202. ______. (1983). *Eye to Eye: The Quest for the New Paradigm*. Garden City, N.Y.: Anchor/Doubleday.
203. ______. (1988). There is no new age: Baby boomers, narcissism and the 1960s. *Vajradhattu Sun.*
204. Wilber, K., Engler, J., and Brown, D. (Eds.). (1986). *Transformations of Consciousness: Conventional and Contemplative Perspectives on Development*. Boston: New Science Library/Shambhala.
205. Wilson, S., and Barber, T. (1982). The fantasy-prone personality. In A. Sheikh (Ed.). *Imagery: Current Theory, Research and Applications*. New York: Wiley.
206. Winkelman, M. (1982). Magic: A theoretical reassessment. *Current Anthropology* 23, 37–66.
207. ______. (1984). *A Crosscultural Study of Magico-religious Practitioners*. Ph.D. Dissertation. University of California, Irvine. Ann Arbor, Mich.: University Microfilms.
208. ______. (1989). A cross-cultural study of shamanistic healers. *Journal of Psychoactive Drugs* 21, 17–24.
209. Yalom, I. (1980). *Existential Psychotherapy*. New York: Basic Books.
210. Yap, P. (1951). Mental diseases peculiar to certain cultures: A survey of comparative psychiatry. *Journal of Mental Science* (April), 313–327.
211. Byrd, R. (1988). Positive therapeutic effects of intercessory prayer in a coronary care unit population. *Southern Medical Journal* 81, 826–829.
212. Orme-Johnson, D., Alexander, C., Davis, J., Chandler, H., and Larimore, W. (1988). International peace project in the Middle East: The effects of the Maharishi technology of the unified field. *Journal of Conflict Resolution* 32, 776–812.

Index

INDEX

ABOUT THE AUTHOR

ROGER WALSH, M.D., Ph.D. attended Queensland and Stanford Universities and is currently professor of psychiatry, philosophy, and anthropology at the University of California at Irvine. He has published more than one hundred scientific papers and ten books and his writings have received some twenty national and international awards.